"Beauty, long shunned from the pulpit, is given a renewed place of primacy in Michael Pasquarello's hopeful vision for preaching. Understood theologically, beauty is related to the mystery of grace and the glory of the Triune God, uniting all things in Christ. Like this fine book, the subject of beauty awakens a desire for the gospel and quickens a love of God."

—*Paul Scott Wilson*
Emmanuel College, University of Toronto

"Given contemporary angst about the ineffectiveness of the lowly sermon, *The Beauty of Preaching* is a timely reminder that a central function of proclamation is the adoration of God. Drawing on voices from the Christian tradition, particularly Augustine, Mike Pasquarello invites deep meditation on the idea of the sermon as doxology, a refreshing alternative to revisit in a context where words can function as weapons instead of plowshares, even from the pulpit."

—*Angela Dienhart Hancock*
Pittsburgh Theological Seminary

"Pasquarello, drawing deeply on the well of Scripture and our rich tradition, reminds us of the constancy of themes of beauty, delight, pleasure, and wonder in God's word and, in so doing, reminds us preachers of the hankering the church has for beauty in preaching that word."

—*James Howell*
author of The Beauty of the Word:
The Challenge and Wonder of Preaching

"Michael Pasquarello provides us with a strangely subversive account of preaching, sidestepping the usual preoccupation with method so as to focus on something less tangible yet no less real: theological beauty. Preaching, he contends, both inspires and is inspired by love for God, and love of God is inspired by delight in divine beauty. Reminding us to consider glory, joy, and the aesthetic dimensions of proclamation, he situates the sermon in the context of true worship and in so doing reorients us to a truly theological vision of this most important ministry."

— *Michael P. Knowles*
McMaster Divinity College

"Two things set this book apart: (1) wonder, praise, and gratitude for the Triune God who speaks himself to us in the humble Lord Jesus Christ; (2) joyful appreciation for the preachers, theologians, and Scripture scholars whose proclamation and teaching enrich our every word. Like his teacher Augustine, Pasquarello takes as his vocation the task of pointing to the wondrous beauty of our Creator and Redeemer. Let us recommit ourselves to this ever-new beauty that is the subject of all preaching worthy of the name."

— *Matthew Levering*
Mundelein Seminary

The BEAUTY *of* PREACHING

God's Glory in Christian Proclamation

Michael Pasquarello III

WILLIAM B. EERDMANS PUBLISHING COMPANY
GRAND RAPIDS, MICHIGAN

Wm. B. Eerdmans Publishing Co.
4035 Park East Court SE, Grand Rapids, Michigan 49546
www.eerdmans.com

26 25 24 23 22 21 20   1 2 3 4 5 6 7

ISBN 978-0-8028-2474-5

Library of Congress Cataloging-in-Publication Data

Names: Pasquarello, Michael, author.
Title: The beauty of preaching : God's glory in Christian proclamation /
    Michael Pasquarello III.
Description: Grand Rapids, Michigan : William B. Eerdmans Publish-
    ing Company, 2020. | Includes bibliographical references and index. |
    Summary: "A work of homiletical theology on the role of preaching in
    revealing God's beauty"—Provided by publisher.
Identifiers: LCCN 2020004854 | ISBN 9780802824745 (paperback)
Subjects: LCSH: Methodist preaching. | Doxology. | Aesthetics—
    Religious aspects—Christianity. | God (Christianity)—Beauty. |
    Bible—Homiletical use.
Classification: LCC BX8349.P74 P37 2020 | DDC 251—dc23
LC record available at https://lccn.loc.gov/2020004854

Unless otherwise noted, Scripture quotations are taken from the New Revised
Standard Version of the Bible.

This book is dedicated to my mother,
Angelina Pasquarello,
whose care has enabled me to see God's humble love
revealed in Christ,
which constitutes the beauty of preaching.

CONTENTS

Contents

FOREWORD

In seminary I wrote a paper for Paul Holmer, "Kierkegaard on Preachers Who Try to Be Poets," my riff on Kierkegaard's aphorism that "truth is not nimble on its feet." I took aim at preachers posing as poets and sermons that succumb to Kierkegaard's dreaded lure of the aesthetic, that is, preachers and sermons that were too pretty for their own good. The article that I eventually published from that paper got me my first job at Duke.

It's a shame that neither SK nor I had Mike Pasquarello to set us straight on the aesthetics of preaching. Mike has become one of our premier homiletical theologians. In his many books on preaching, Mike reiterates that preaching doesn't begin and end with us; preaching is about the triune God who meets us in the incarnate Word. In this book Mike reminds us that Jesus Christ is not only the way, the truth, and the life but is also beautiful.

Eschewing modernity's limp aestheticism, Mike, in this encouraging book, does his usual sweeping survey of theological literature to produce a loving, bold proclamation that Christian preaching's beauty is not a set of rhetorical devices whereby we sugarcoat and pretty-up a sermon to make it more palatable. No, Mike joins Augustine in joyfully preaching that beautiful is who God is, beauty is the truth about the God who delights in delighting us through faithful preaching. Mike calls Christ "evangelical beauty" who, through preaching, evokes our adoration and allures us toward his beautiful holiness for, as Augustine said, "we imitate whom we adore."

Good preaching is not primarily about therapy, delivery of information, advocacy of social programs, carping criticism, or the enunciation of practical principles for better living. Preaching is that event whereby we invite the beauty of Christ to shine upon his church. The preacher is the one ordained by God and the church to stand up on a regular basis and exclaim to Christ's church, "O taste and see that the LORD is good" (Ps. 34). What good news is this, living as we do in a time when all around there is ugliness. Mike shows how beauty is not simply a matter of homiletical style or delivery but a theological matter, a central aspect of communication by and with Father, Son, and Holy Spirit. In the beautiful life of the Trinity we see light, and that light helps to reform the ugly deformations we have allowed to distort who we were created to be. Our sin and its consequences are ugly; only God's beauty can heal us.

Mike's is an encouraging word for us preachers. Something about the inherent beauty of Jesus Christ required someone named Mark to become an artist and invent a literary form—a gospel—in order adequately to talk about Jesus. Every time we stand up to preach, we preachers have the opportunity to participate in that same harmony of content and form that characterized gospel preaching from the first. In an age in which preaching often is defaced by utilitarianism, instrumentalism, and one-two-three prosaic pragmatism, Mike reminds us that preaching is delightfully useless, pointless preparation for no more serious business than to glorify God so that we might know how to enjoy God forever.

I'm sure Mike the sanctificationist would want me to add that as we form our sermons, our sermons are forming us, making even the lives of us preachers into something beautiful for God. Holiness is a gracious by-product of our preacherly submission to our vocation to bring the truth of the gospel to speech. The beauty of sermons is not a product that we preachers learn how to produce; it's a gift of a relentlessly self-revealing God who is determined to have us.

In Alabama, I got to know a renowned outlier artist, Lonnie Holly, a master in "found art." Lonnie gathered up all sorts of junk off the streets and junkyards of Birmingham and created amazing sculpture. One of Lonnie's slogans was "God don't make nothin' ugly. Our junk don't look like junk to the eyes of God." Amen. Mike's book rescues contemporary preaching from the lure of oversimplification, quick-fix techniques, and essentially anthropological (rather than theological) preoccupations and helps us to, just for a while on a Sunday, look at ourselves and our world *sub specie aeternitatis*, thus to see the beauty of it all.

We live in an age that urges us to adjust to the ugliness of life, including the life of the church, as just "the way things are." Mike reminds us that because of who God is, truth, beauty, and goodness are the way things really are and are meant to be. In a time of much ugly speech, nasty conflict, and docile accommodation to ugliness, Mike gives us preachers a mission—to proclaim the strange, fragile beauty that's running rampant in a world redeemed by God in Christ, to keep speaking beautiful words about a beautiful Savior until that blessed eternity when all shall be (in the hymn of Wesley the poet) graciously subsumed in wonder, love, and praise.

I never said that preaching is the easiest of vocations. None of us preachers asked for this assignment. It's hard to find the right words for the God who has spoken so eloquently to us in Christ. Powerful, unattractive forces mitigate against the faithful preaching of the gospel. Mike Pasquarello has reminded me what a beautiful vocation a beautiful God has given us.

Will Willimon

PREFACE

This book invites preachers to behold the beauty of Christ, which is inherent to the gospel we proclaim. It does this by offering a "homiletical aesthetic" that returns preaching to the joy of knowing and making known God's glory to the world. This is the language of doxology, of living faith oriented to God's majesty by who God is and what God is doing on our behalf.[1] Beautiful preaching is dependent upon the work of the Holy Spirit, who transforms our thinking, feeling, and acting, including our capacity for speaking, in restoring us to our true vocation of knowing, loving, and enjoying God. If the end of human life is conformity to the image of Christ in communion with the Father through the Spirit, then all human actions—including preaching—may be true, good, and beautiful, we

---

1. Catherine Mowry LaCugna, *God for Us: The Trinity and Christian Life* (San Francisco: HarperSanFrancisco, 1991), 16; I have found Geoffrey Wainwright's presentation of doxology to be a compelling invitation to look at preaching from a whole new angle of vision: the praise of God. This is because doxology is our very reason for being human, and the praise of God gathers up our thinking, speaking, feeling, and acting into God's glorification of himself in Jesus Christ and the Holy Spirit. "I see Christian worship, doctrine, and life as conjoined in a common 'upwards' and 'forwards' direction towards God and the achievement of his purpose, which includes human salvation. They intend God's praise. His glory is that he is already present and within to enable our transformation into his likeness, which means participation in himself and his kingdom." Geoffrey Wainwright, *Doxology: The Praise of God in Worship, Doctrine, and Life* (Oxford: Oxford University Press, 1980), 9.

may say "fitting," when directed to the triune God, who is praised and adored for his own sake—rather than a means to achieving other ends and goals.[2]

We preachers need a keen sense and appreciation of Christ's beauty to not only know love but to enjoy the triune God, who is the source and end of all our preaching. We need this to embrace our vocation of bearing witness to divine and human beauty in an age of ugly. Without delight in beauty the true and the good are easily subject to instrumental and functional use. When this happens, knowing the truth of Christ becomes programmatic and moralistic, desire for Christ's goodness becomes utilitarian and self-absorbed, and Christ's divine worth and value are diminished by human necessity and efficiency.[3] The otherness of God, people, and things is easily reduced to resources at our disposal rather than being an invitation to wonder, love, and praise that calls forth our delight as a matter of sharing in Christ's justice, rendering gladly the service due both God and our neighbor, especially those to whom we preach.

I am convinced that beauty matters for preaching because God matters for preaching. The Spirit's beautifying work illumines the "eyes" of faith in single-minded devotion to Christ, who is himself both the beautiful form of God's self-giving love *and* the form of human beauty restored by the Spirit from the ugliness of sin. Beauty, then, is a profoundly theological, spiritual, and moral matter for the church as a people called to confess, praise, and proclaim the glory of God, the Holy Trinity. Jason Byassee's comments on Augustine's theology of the Trinity point to the beauty of God's holiness, which is our delight as preachers. "The Son is the form, the image, the splendor of the Father, who delights in the Son who is his image. He

2. Here I recommend the excellent theological exposition of divine and human beauty in Jonathan King, *The Beauty of the Lord: Theology as Aesthetics* (Bellingham, WA: Lexham Press, 2018).

3. Edward T. Oakes, SJ, "The Apologetics of Beauty," in *The Beauty of God: Theology and the Arts*, ed. Daniel J. Treier, Mark Husbands, and Roger Lundin (Downers Grove, IL: IVP Academic, 2007), 214–15.

gives to the Son not only his delight but also his delighting, which mutual delight simply is the Holy Spirit."[4]

The paradox of Christian faith is that fixing our minds on the incarnate beauty of God made known in Christ—instead of our-selves—provides the "fitting" environment, a culture of praise, for cultivating the necessary intellectual, imaginative, and emotional capacities for speaking as human creatures destined to share God's glory. Saint Paul encourages us to continually return to the truth, beauty, and goodness that are able to guard our hearts and minds in the peace of God made by Christ through his life, death, and resurrection.

> Finally, beloved, whatever is true, whatever is honorable, what-ever is just, whatever is pure, whatever is pleasing, whatever is commendable, if there is any excellence and if there is anything worthy of praise, think about these things. (Phil. 4:8)[5]

I want to show that Christian preaching is a graced activity by which we participate in the humble receptivity and generous self-giving of Christ, whose beauty adorns the gospel. With the Spirit's guidance, perceiving the truth of Christ's self-emptying love fashions our lives into a beautiful way of being, thinking, and speaking with one another as a new creation.[6] Such preaching is not dependent upon our wisdom and power. It is dependent upon God's Word and Spirit, who create the conditions for proclaiming the beauty of divine love as the wisdom and power of our being, the end of all our yearnings, needs, and desires, and the abundant freshness from

---

4. Jason Byassee, *Praise Seeking Understanding: Reading the Psalms with Augustine* (Grand Rapids: Eerdmans, 2007), 142.

5. Unless otherwise noted, all Scripture quotations come from the New Revised Standard Version.

6. Mark McIntosh, "Faith, Reason, and the Mind of Christ," in *Reason and the Reasons of Faith*, ed. Paul J. Griffiths and Reinhard Hütter (London: T&T Clark, 2005), 139.

which worship, discipleship, evangelism, and mission spring. My aim, then, is to show that theological and aesthetic considerations in preaching are inseparable, as has been the case for the majority of church history.

I have attempted to explore these important matters in a fresh way by attending to the beauty of Christ, which we bear in proclaiming the "gospel of God's glory." This reunites the purpose of preaching with its content and form "to discern, articulate, and commend visions of flourishing life in light of God's self-revelation in Jesus Christ."[7] My hope is that demonstrating a *theologically informed and spiritually inspired homiletical aesthetic* will encourage beautiful preaching as intelligent and adoring praise to the triune God, who reveals his glory through the humility and weakness of the "Word made flesh."

As the ministry of the Word of God enfleshed in Jesus, preaching begins and ends in need and receptivity and is expressed in gratitude and praise. Paradoxically, the glory of preaching is found in its humility, struggle, and incompleteness, just as the love and delight shared by the Father and the Son are the measure of its beauty. As the living Word who proclaims himself in being proclaimed, Christ is both the content and form of the gospel to which the Spirit draws and conforms the church. The beauty of preaching is the radiance of God's glory that shines, sometimes brightly and at other times

---

7. Here I am drawing from Miroslav Volf and Matthew Croasmun, *For the Life of the World: Theology That Makes a Difference* (Grand Rapids: Brazos, 2019), 11. I have taken their definition of the purpose of theology and applied it to preaching. I have done this because I believe their assessment of contemporary theology is fitting for contemporary preaching: "Christian theology [preaching] has lost its way because it has neglected its purpose" (11). At the same time, I continue to believe preaching is a theological activity because of its unique subject, God's self-revelation in Jesus Christ. I have attempted to show this in Michael Pasquarello III, *Christian Preaching: A Trinitarian Theology of Proclamation* (Grand Rapids: Baker Academic, 2007; reprint, Eugene, OR: Wipf & Stock, 2011) and *Dietrich: Bonhoeffer and a Theology of the Preaching Life* (Waco, TX: Baylor University Press, 2017).

dimly, in the almighty powerfulness of Christ as the way of humble self-giving love brought to speech.

This will entail cultivating a capacity to be still and to behold the "strange beauty" that shines brightly from the depths of darkness and ugliness of Christ's suffering and death on a cross. This is a "fragile beauty" that is seen with eyes of faith judged, purified, and renewed by the gift of the Spirit's love. In a sermon from Psalm 99 (100), Augustine acknowledges the inexpressibility of God before stating this important truth: "He spoke, and we came to be, but we have no power to utter him. The Word in whom we were spoken is his Son, and to enable us weaklings to utter him in some degree, the Word became weak."[8]

At the heart of this book is the conviction that our true good and happiness as human creatures are found in knowing, loving, and enjoying the triune God disclosed in the humble beauty of Christ; and that offering ourselves in proclaiming "Christ, and him crucified" springs from and leads back to doxology—the praise of God's glory. Beautiful preaching is not what we produce or control but rather is an effect of and response to a prior grace; the gift of delight in the divine being and goodness communicated by the Father in the Son through the Spirit's radiant love. Jean Corbon states this truth in a lovely manner. "The Father 'gives away' his Word and his Breath, and all things are called into being. Everything is his gift and a manifestation of his glory. Nothing is rightly called sacred or profane; everything is a pure outpouring of his holiness. Our God does not simply do this or do that, like the First Cause whom the philosophers speak of as God; rather he gives himself in everything that is, and whatever is is because he gives himself. He speaks, and the being is; he loves, and it is good; he gives himself, and it is beautiful."[9] Our life and work as

---

8. Augustine, "Exposition of Psalm 99 (100)," in *Expositions of the Psalms*, vol. 5 (Pss. 99–120), vol. III/19 in the *Works of Saint Augustine: A Translation for the 21st Century* (Hyde Park, NY: New City Press, 2003), 18.

9. Jean Corbon, OP, *The Wellspring of Worship*, trans. Matthew J. O'Connell (San Franscisco: Ignatius, 1988), 32.

preachers must be rooted in prayer, in attentive receptivity to God's self-sharing by which the Spirit illumines our minds to contemplate, delight in, and long for the beauty of Christ's holiness as the fruit and effect of our preaching. Moreover, as an offering of thankful praise, our language and life are transposed by the Spirit's love and made fitting for showing forth the glory radiating from God's identity and work in Christ. And if by the Spirit's love our life and words are graced with the beauty of Christ's suffering and death on behalf of the world, then the "attractiveness" of our preaching does not rest primarily on decorating, dressing up, and making sermons "pretty." I am convinced that the beauty of preaching is found in its blessed uselessness. By this I mean preaching with no purpose other than delighting in the truth of God, who communicates his goodness through the presence of the risen Lord whose glory is the eternal weight we have been created to bear. The work of Don Saliers is immensely helpful in this regard. He writes, "Doxa, of course, has the wonderful ambiguity of referring both to human belief and to something intrinsic to God: *doxa* as the divine glory. *Ortho-doxa* is the practice of right ascription of honor and praise and glory to God, the One whom all ascription is due. Orthodoxy is learning the long, hard, joyous way to ascribe unto God the *doxa* due God's name."[10] Saliers's identification of *doxa* as the "intrinsic" character of God, the glory shared in the blessed communion of the triune God, before all time and in all time, points to the splendid affirmation of the prologue to John's Gospel: "The Word became flesh, and dwelt among us."

We are graced to "see" God's glory in beholding the being, life, and ministry of Christ by the illumination of the Spirit. God's desire is that the whole creation praise his glory, that human creatures enjoy the glorious freedom of sons and daughters of God. This "strange glory" shows its astonishing beauty in a way of generous self-giving that is revealed fully in the incarnate, crucified, and risen

10. Don E. Saliers, *Worship as Theology: Foretaste of Glory Divine* (Nashville: Abingdon, 1994), 40.

Lord. Moreover, this glory is manifested in both Word and sacrament; Christ taking human form in the church for the sake of the world "today."[11]

As Saliers notes, this "theology of glory" generates a "theology of the cross." He continues, "But the theology of the cross is not a contradiction to the theology of glory when our worship is attuned to the whole Word of God, and to the whole story of Jesus Christ."[12] Attunement in gladness and gratitude to the revealed glory, or doxa, of God shapes the practice of worship as a particular way of thinking, perceiving, acting, and speaking. He shows why gratitude is essential for the life and work of a preacher.

> The person without gratitude rooted and grounded in God's self-giving sees the world differently from those who catch a glimpse of seeing the world anew in light of God's first gift (creation) and in light of God's ultimate gift (redemption). The deepening capacity for gratitude and thankfulness of the heart in the community leads to a greater sense of the truth of how things are. We should not be surprised that God has so arranged matters so that if we learn gratitude grounded in God's self-giving and the *doxa* of God shown in Christ, we will see more.[13]

Worship as a way of life draws us into the joy of knowing and loving God as whole persons. As Irenaeus states, "The glory of God is a human being fully alive." God's glory is manifested in the art of being human. Saliers continues, "We also say it is the humanly embodied arts that Christ prompts when we receive some sight and some sense of glory. Christian liturgy [which includes preaching] ought always and everywhere to be our response to that glorious self-giving of God in, with, and through our humanity in Christ."[14] The

11. Saliers, *Worship as Theology*, 41–42.
12. Saliers, *Worship as Theology*, 43.
13. Saliers, *Worship as Theology*, 47.
14. Saliers, *Worship as Theology*, 45.

attractiveness of God's astonishing love summons us into a way of being that is perceived in the whole of Scripture that finds its fullness in the communion of Christ and the church.

I want to show that responding to the beauty of God's glory is the heart of preaching as human speech, as an expression of doxological gratitude.[15] God's will is expressive and delightful, a "joyous action" that is deeply relational, and situated within the Trinitarian life in relating to reality other than God. As human creatures, we are not merely passive objects, but in the gift of our creaturely being we express God's glory. In its worship, the church presents itself before God in attentive receptivity to Christ, who gives himself through the work of the Spirit. Worship, then, is an act of loving trust and intimate loyalty that announces God's glory through acts of reading, speaking, hearing, singing, praying, communing, and rejoicing in God's Word that forms the life of the church in the world.[16]

Christian preaching is an offering of thanks and praise for God's glory in human form: beautiful expressions of the Word that spring from receptivity to God's self-giving, a sharing in the vulnerabil-

---

15. David H. Kelsey, *Eccentric Existence: A Theological Anthropology*, 2 vols. (Louisville: Westminster John Knox, 2009), 1:340–45. "Doxology is the appropriate response to God's glory in Godself, or more exactly, the appropriate response to the hospitable generosity of the triune God's glory in se. Further, on that basis, doxology is an appropriate response to the (derivative) glory—that is, the hospitable generosity—of God's creative relating to all that is not God. It is not praise for anything God has done, does, or will do for us in the events of our lives, not praise for God's providential governance of creation. Rather, it is praise for creation's ultimate context" (344). Here Kelsey's reflections are similar to that of Rowan Williams on Rom. 15: that the church announces God's glory to the nations so that the nations will share in the delight of glorifying God as God, which is even more important than praising God for being graciously disposed toward them. *On Christian Theology* (Oxford: Blackwell, 2000), 255–56. To give God glory in this manner is an "eccentric existence."

16. Kelsey, *Eccentric Existence*, 1:311, 313–14; see also the insightful work of James E. Beitler, which argues for recovering the persuasive nature of the church's worship, speech, and life, the "rhetorics" of Christian witness. James E. Beitler III, *Seasoned Speech: Rhetoric in the Life of the Church* (Downers Grove, IL: IVP Academic, 2019).

ity of Christ.[17] By "following after" Scripture's witness to Christ, such vulnerable receptivity, which is prayer, opens us to the "strange, fragile" glory displayed in the "ugly" beauty of the cross. "Christian liturgy is the ongoing prayer, act, and word flowing from the cross and empty tomb. We also say it is the humanly embodied arts that Christ prompts when we receive some sight and some sense of grace and glory."[18]

Saliers notes how this "involves the art of self-presentation, and hence the character of faithfulness counts as part of the action." The Word of God spoken, heard, prayed, sung, and celebrated in human words is demonstrated in the lives of those who do these things. The "art" of worship is thus "attuned" to the gift of beauty intrinsic to the truth and goodness of Christian faith. "The *doxa* of God (and the glory God wishes to confirm and renew in us) comes to human means of expression, not so much in 'works of art,' but in the artistic expressions of liturgical assembly. . . . Thus, the art of true liturgy is congruent with the self-giving of God in our humanity at full stretch."[19]

In our preaching the gospel is brought to speech by "following after" the pattern of the incarnation—dispersed through the whole narrative of Scripture, from creation, to new creation, to the consummation of all things. David Kelsey's comments are helpful for seeing the interrelation of Scripture, preaching, and giving glory to God as "doxological gratitude."

> The existential interests that govern the study of the Bible as Holy Scripture clearly focus primarily on God, and neither on the communities of Christian faith themselves nor on the individuals whose existential interests govern their study of the texts. . . . When studied as Holy Scripture, these texts are properly studied in a manner that generates preaching that has as its proper subject

17. Saliers, *Worship as Theology*, 196.
18. Saliers, *Worship as Theology*, 45.
19. Saliers, *Worship as Theology*, 196, 198.

God for us. . . . They tell, allude to, or assume about what God is doing with, to, and within and through other subjects, physical and non-physical worlds, ordinary people and royalty, sinners and prophets, animals and angels and evil spirits.[20]

Saliers argues that aesthetic experience, beauty for beauty's sake (here we may include dressed-up, "pretty preaching"), is not the primary aim of worship. Rather, the end of worship is the glorification of God and the sanctification of all things human. The art of worship is expressed in forms of preaching that are always "at the service of the holy," or "holy preaching."[21] Such expressions of beauty cannot be judged solely on artistic grounds but are perceived in light of "the beauty of divine holiness, regarded eschatologically, what God intends in the fullness of time." The gathering up of all things in Christ for the praise of God's glory is the measure of homiletical wholeness, coherence, integrity, and clarity—which grants preaching its beauty. Saliers's comments are fitting for describing the transformative power of placing ourselves in the presence of God's beauty revealed in Christ. "To gather in the name of Jesus to praise God and to hear with delight and awe what God speaks and does in our midst is to come to the place where duty and delight embrace. If we should discover in such a place God's way with us, then it will be in

20. Kelsey, *Eccentric Existence*, 1:140–41. Kelsey describes the necessary dispositions and capacities or virtues for reading and speaking in this manner: good judgment, imagination, trained perception that is a practical "knowing how" exercised in particular times, places, and circumstances in order for a practice such as preaching to be enacted. To these he adds faith, hope, and love; the disposition to rejoice in God's ways; giving thanks to God; fidelity to God; and commitment to fellow members of the Christian community, including trust, respect, care, gratitude, desiring reconciliation, sharing in the work of ministry with others; and disciplined study with committed members of the Christian community (142–43). I would identify such capacities as constituting the "art" of preaching.

21. See here "Holy Preaching: Ethical Interpretation and the Practical Imagination," in Ellen F. Davis, *Preaching the Luminous Word: Biblical Sermons and Homiletical Essays*, with Austin McIver Dennis, foreword by Stanley Hauerwas (Grand Rapids: Eerdmans, 2016), 89–105.

wonder and praise. *Would this not send us to live with a deeper delight and gladness than if we only celebrate ourselves as we already are?*"[22]

I believe a reinvigorated vision of homiletical beauty is capable of renewing our desire for preaching shaped by intelligent love in eloquent expressions of wisdom that build up the church in its public work, or "liturgy"—the praise of God's glory in the whole of life. The cosmic scope of God's glory and the universal relevance of Christ, the image and icon of the invisible God, generate a homiletical discourse that is irreducible to either privatized or politicized autonomous expressions of faith that delight in other than the evangelical beauty of Christ as Lord of all that is.

Recovering the astonishing vision of the triune God whose glory is expressed in relating to all that is through Christ and the Spirit will require a rehabilitation of the vocation of preacher as one who seeks to render the intelligibility and attractiveness of God and God's way with the world. Kelsey's comments on the beauty of God's glory are worthy of our consideration as preachers. "God's own glory is God's arresting splendor. It is the splendor of that which is ultimately important and commands utmost attention. God's splendor is arresting in virtue of God's gravitas. . . . God is ultimately important in attractive fashion. As that which is ultimately important, God is splendidly beautiful. God's splendor is the dazzling brilliance of God's beauty."[23]

I have approached this study through exemplars of a homiletical art by which the Spirit awakens listeners to the joy of offering praise to God, who speaks the Word of Life that finds its fullness in the risen, crucified Jesus.[24] My purpose in writing is not to make a case

---

22. Don E. Saliers, *Worship Come to Its Senses* (Nashville: Abingdon, 1996), 42 (emphasis added).

23. Kelsey, *Eccentric Existence*, 1:313.

24. Those I have drawn from do not exhaust the possibilities. Other iterations of this book might look to the work of exemplars such as Irenaeus, Ambrose, Gregory of Nyssa, Aquinas, Bonaventure, Hildegard, Erasmus, Calvin, Andrewes, Donne, Newman, Edwards, Barth, Bonhoeffer, and King, to name a few. See the

for our return to previous and better times in Christian tradition. This would neither be possible nor desirable. Nor am I suggesting that we should merely replicate what our predecessors in the faith said and did, even though much of what they said and did was salutary. My primary interest in the figures I have selected for this book is that they possess a particular wisdom that is urgently needed in our time: a theologically informed intellectual, affective, and spiritual sensibility to the truth, beauty, and goodness of the triune God, who alone is worthy of our praise.

Chapter 1 begins by discussing a remarkable claim made by the prophet Isaiah:

> How beautiful upon the mountains
>   are the feet of the messenger who announces peace,
> who brings good news,
>   who announces salvation,
>   who says to Zion, "Your God reigns." (Isa. 52:7)

I have long been interested in knowing what makes the feet of preachers who proclaim the gospel to be seen as "beautiful." I follow Isaiah's lead to Romans 10, where Paul echoes the prophetic word in his discussion of the Word that God has spoken in Christ and continues to speak through beautiful preaching of the gospel. The message "your God reigns" also points us to the joyful announcement of God's kingdom by Jesus at the beginning of Mark's Gospel, which the Lord enacts through his life, suffering, death, and resurrection. I then look to the story of a poor widow who gave all she had in the temple offering, thus serving in Mark's narrative as a sign and "word" that beautifully proclaim Christ's humility and weakness as both the arrival and answer to God's reign.

Chapter 2 remembers the story of an unnamed woman in Mark 14

---

magisterial survey of theological aesthetics in Hans Urs von Balthasar, *The Glory of the Lord: A Theological Aesthetics*, 7 vols. (San Francisco: Ignatius, 1981–1989).

who anointed Jesus with expensive perfume as an act of loving devotion and preparation for his death. This occurred in the home of a leper named Simon, where Jesus had gone to visit. Speaking in response to the protest of his disciples about the woman's wasteful act, Jesus said what the woman had done was a *"beautiful thing."* I read the story of the unnamed woman as a type of God's generous, costly love, extravagantly poured out in Jesus on behalf of the world. It is fitting to consider the significance of her selfless act of love in a book about the beauty of preaching, since Jesus told his disciples that "wherever the gospel is proclaimed in the whole world, what she has done will be told in remembrance of her." Remembering the unnamed woman's act of costly love for Jesus in the home of a leper offers wisdom that may yet assist preachers in discerning how to preach beautifully as an act of devotion to God.

Chapter 3 turns to Augustine, focusing on the story of his conversion as narrated by his *Confessions.* One of the aspects I find pertinent for preachers in Augustine's story is that, prior to his conversion, he was in love with natural beauty, with the pleasures and enjoyment provided by his inordinate desire for using people and things. This included his love for words and the praise his eloquent use of words elicited from people during an impressive career as a teacher of rhetoric in Rome and a renowned public speaker. It is significant that Augustine's conversion took place in and through his disordered loves for created beauty. Despite his professional success and rise to the honor and "glory" of Rome's elite, he longed to know Beauty, whom he addressed as "so ancient, and so new." After much searching for happiness, Augustine's affections were transformed; his attention was captured by Beauty, the living God, through the humble love of the "Word made flesh" in the weakness and lowliness of Jesus. Augustine was converted from a love for the praise of people to a love for the praise of God. The story of his conversion offers much to consider regarding a preacher's moral and spiritual formation, a preacher's temptations, a preacher's love for the Word, and praise as the most fitting language of Christian preaching.

> Chapter 4 looks at Augustine the preacher, whose Trinitarian theology of beauty was the basis of his life and work as a preacher. This chapter engages with the theological and pastoral wisdom displayed by Augustine as a preacher and example for other preachers. The heart of the matter for Augustine is that preaching is oriented by and directed toward the end for which we have been created; to know, love, and enjoy the triune God made known in Christ, whose beauty is the form of the church's life. I engage with Augustine's reflections on the challenges and difficulties of being a preacher, and his way of perceiving the beauty of preaching in light of God's self-disclosure in Christ. I interpret Augustine's sermons as a persuasive invitation to delight in the beauty of Christ, God's incarnate Word whose glory shines brightly from the whole of Scripture. I see the scope of his preaching as fitting for the abundant goodness of God, and also for the depth of our human weakness and neediness before God. The beauty of his sermons shines brightly from the truth of their subject: God's glory and salvation, the goodness of creation and the redemption of humanity in Christ, the church as the visible sign and hope of the renewal of all things.

> Chapter 5 presents my reflections on the simple beauty of John Wesley's preaching. Wesley's sermons, and the hymns of his brother Charles, show the intimate connection between God's holiness and love, which constitutes the beauty of Christian believing, living, preaching, singing, praying, and celebrating in the Spirit. I discuss Wesley's ministry, which was characterized by an embrace of people from all walks of life, social and economic circumstances, and spiritual and moral conditions. This ministry was driven by a desire that the gospel of God's holiness in Jesus Christ be made available to even those who found themselves outside the bounds of the church for any number of reasons, especially the poor, the prisoners, the sick, the orphaned, and the widowed. I discuss how the simple beauty of Wesley's preaching is intimately related to his perception of Christ's humble love with and for the poor.

Wesley serves as a good exemplar of holy preaching and holy

living, which he perceived in the beauty of Christ's Sermon on the Mount. He was firmly rooted in the wisdom of Christian tradition, and he grasped the life of faith, hope, and love as hard but grand beyond telling. He labored to educate and equip preachers for proclaiming Christ in plain, passionate speech to communicate the joy of knowing and loving God. His pedagogy is instructive for the education of preachers today, in that he expected his Methodist preachers to have a good grasp of human nature as created in the image of God, as well as the virtues, spiritual fruits, and means of grace that lead to real human happiness and goodness in Christ. This involved rigorous training within an ecclesial environment constituted by doctrine, devotion, and discipline to dispose a preacher's thoughts, words, and affections toward sound judgment, wise discernment, and good taste in the ministry of the Word that erred to the side of neither moralism nor antinomianism.

Chapter 6 discusses the beauty of preaching in the ministry of Martin Luther. I have selected Luther because his work is not typically associated with theological beauty. Balthasar, for example, dismisses Luther as contributing nothing to a theological aesthetic. In this chapter I draw from the recent work of Mark Mattes, *Martin Luther's Theology of Beauty: A Reappraisal.* Mattes's excellent study encouraged me to include a chapter on Luther as the leading Protestant Reformer and an important preacher in the whole of Christian tradition. This chapter shows that Luther does indeed offer much wisdom for discerning the beauty of the Word as the form of God's justifying grace in Christ, who takes upon himself the ugliness of sin and gives to sinners the beauty of his righteousness. Although Luther was strongly opposed to a "theology of glory" that was based on the sin of human pride and self-sufficiency, he was a strong advocate for a theology of glory that makes known the humility and love of Christ as the incarnate, crucified, and risen Lord. I do this by engaging with selected readings of Psalms and the Magnificat to show Luther's theological, aesthetic, and spiritual sensibilities to divine and human beauty reconciled in Christ.

As theology expressed in doxological form, the language of praise, preaching draws its being and life from delighting in the goodness of God's mighty acts of creation, incarnation, and new creation. A eucharistic prayer, an act of thankful praise, follows the narrative of Scripture: God's glory in creation, in the exodus and election of Israel, in the incarnation of Christ, and in the work of reconciliation and redemption. My hope is that our sermons may too become beautiful expressions of prayer and praise spoken in the name of the Father, and of the Son, and of the Holy Spirit.

We give thanks to you, O God, for the goodness and love which you have made known to us in creation; in the calling of Israel to be your people; in your Word spoken through the prophets; and above all in the Word made flesh, Jesus, your Son. For in these last days you sent him to be incarnate from the Virgin Mary, to be the Savior and Redeemer of the world. In him, you have brought us out of error into truth, out of sin into righteousness, out of death into life.[25]

---

25. Eucharist Prayer B, in *The Book of Common Prayer and Administration of the Sacraments and Other Rites and Ceremonies of the Church: Together with the Psalter or Psalms of David, according to the use of the Episcopal Church* (1979), 368.

ACKNOWLEDGMENTS

The idea for this book was initially stirred when I was introduced to Augustine's *Confessions* and was drawn to a particular prayer of confession that is also an offering of praise to God, "Late have I loved you, Beauty, so ancient and so new." My interest in Augustine was sparked, which led me to read his *De doctrina Christiana* (*Teaching Christianity*), arguably the most influential handbook for preachers in Christian tradition. What grabbed my attention is how Augustine, with his love enflamed for God, assimilated the art of rhetoric, or persuasive speech, into a Trinitarian vision of truth, beauty, and goodness, proposing that preaching the Word made known in Christ and Scripture should aim to instruct, *delight*, and persuade.

I was intrigued by Augustine's emphasis on delight in preaching, that in Christ we are not only blessed to know and love God, but to enjoy God's ravishing beauty. I was accustomed to hearing sermons that aimed to instruct and persuade, to teach and move, to explain and motivate. I saw this reflected in my own preaching, but was unclear as to just how delight factored in. When I talked with other preachers about this, the conversation inevitably led to a discussion about what made the sermon "work," to what was the "hook" in the sermon, to what was used to entertain and evoke listeners' attention and response. This kind of talk would leave me wondering if who we are and what we do is more important than who the triune God is and what the Word does in the Spirit as the attractive, delightful, compelling, and moving quality and power of preaching. I found myself caught between a commitment to taking God seriously and a commitment to taking listeners seriously. I struggled with this tension between my theological and pastoral responsibilities, between what appeared to be a choice of either preaching that is homiletically abstract or preaching that is theologically shallow. This question set in motion many years of reading, thinking, and practice as a preacher, and eventually, as a teacher of preachers.

The works cited in this book have informed years of theological and pastoral reflection on how best to understand the "beauty" of preaching in light of the identity and activity of the triune God. They have shown me in many ways that recovering the grandeur, wholeness, and integrity of preaching in our time requires addressing the loss of beauty, and delight in beauty—as a quality of being—in relation to God's truth and goodness incarnate in Christ. With time I began to understand better how this loss has contributed to a homiletical "aestheticism" that downgrades beauty to something external, as mere appearance, decoration, or "prettiness," without theological and spiritual considerations. I observed how this method of "adding on" to enhance the effectiveness or relevance of a sermon would often remain distinct from the message of the gospel that is its own efficacy: God's self-communication in the beautiful form of Christ through the power of the Spirit's abundant love.

I want to express my deep gratitude to the editorial staff of William B. Eerdmans for the assistance, patience, and generosity that have made it possible to complete this project with its many unexpected but necessary delays. Being able to write for a publisher that values theological work, even in the so-called practical disciplines, is a wonderful gift. In my writing I have benefited at every turn from the work of scholars whose knowledge of theological aesthetics far exceeds mine. I am, of course, responsible for my interpretations of their work. I also want to express my appreciation for the critical eye of an external reader whose comments made my work of editing and revising much clearer. In addition, I am indebted to the contributions of others who have devoted many years to the study of Augustine's life, ministry, and theology. I am thankful for the late David Steinmetz of Duke Divnity School, who introduced me to the enduring wisdom and value of Augustine's work. I also want to thank my doctoral mentor, Peter Iver Kaufman, who in his work on the significance of Augustine's episcopal leadership has reminded me of the critical role of Augustine's sermons in leading the church. I am continually reminded of Augustine's conviction that, as preachers, we have nothing that we have not received as a gift and expression of God's self-giving love. I am also grateful to numerous friends, as well as fellow members of the Academy of Homiletics and the North American Academy of Liturgy for their helpful responses to conference presentations from this material. I have been encouraged by students in my preaching classes at Asbury Theological Seminary and Fuller Theological Seminary who have "caught" something of the hopeful vision of a homiletical aesthetic I have tried to set forth as a response of thankful praise for God's "incarnate beauty." I also want to thank Bishop William Willimon for writing the foreword to this book. In his peculiar way, Will is a good exemplar of the beauty of preaching I have written about. He also taught me that preaching like him does not necessarily mean sounding like him (I am from Pennsylvania; Will is from South Carolina). Yet I am thankful for his encouragement to pursue a way of preaching that is fitting for our calling to serve Christ by serving the church. I can't think of anything more beautiful. My greatest debt, however, is to Patti, my constant partner and friend through my preoccupation with the writing process. I am thankful for our life and look forward to the next chapter we will write together. By God's grace, it will be a "beautiful thing."

RECLAIMING BEAUTY

Thinking about the beauty of preaching locates us within a tradition of doxology, praising and giving glory to God that bear fruit in "generous orthodoxy." Rowan Williams, former archbishop of Canterbury, has written of the "charismatic memory" of the church. By this he means the historical memory activated by the Holy Spirit in the body of Christ as a form of grace. Williams sees this memory at work in worshiping communities where the Bible, as the primary record of God's self-communication, is read not just as a relic of the past but as a work bearing the present communication of God.

Williams notes that the habit of charismatic memory and inherited speech tells us how and why the two false certainties that characterize much modern thinking—the certainty of the present and the certainty of the past—are false for a people called to worship God and serve God's mission through history and time that have been sanctified by God's incarnate presence.[1] His comments on the gift of Christian speech are helpful:

> We speak because we are called, invited and authorized to speak, we speak what we have been given, out of our new "belonging," and this is a "dependent" kind of utterance, a responsive speech.

---

1. Rowan Williams, *Why Study the Past? The Quest for the Historical Church* (Grand Rapids: Eerdmans, 2005), 93.

But it is not a dictated or determined utterance: revelation is address, not so much to a will called upon to submit as to an imagination called upon to "open itself.". . . The integrity [and beauty]
of theological utterance [including preaching] . . . does not fall
into line with an authoritative communication, but in the reality
of its rootedness, its belonging in the new world constituted in
the revelatory event or process . . . God "speaks" in the response
as the primary utterance: there is a dimension of "givenness,"
generative power, and the discovered new world in the work of
the imagination opening itself.[2]

A Spirited Beauty

The amazing newness of the gospel story is rendered beautifully by
the paradigmatic performance of Spirit-inspired preaching in the
book of Acts: Peter's breathtaking proclamation during the obser-
vance of Pentecost, an annual festival during which Israel remembered and gave thanks for God's faithfulness.

Pentecost was a time of worship, a liturgical event, the "work
of the people" that paradoxically was a day of rest and renewal for
offering gratitude and praise to God.

At the heart of Pentecost was the joyful acknowledgment of
God's generous provision in the ordinary cycles of planting, tending,
waiting, and harvesting. Moreover, Pentecost also marked the remembrance of the events at Sinai, of God's giving of the law to Israel
in fire and loud thunder. Peter's announcement of Christ as Lord is
situated within the story of a pilgrim people gathered to remember
the future of God's faithfulness in a mighty outpouring of God's
Spirit as the end time arriving "today."[3]

2. Rowan Williams, *On Christian Theology* (Oxford: Blackwell, 2000), 146–47.
3. Bryan Stone, *Evangelism after Christendom: The Theology and Practice of
Christian Witness* (Grand Rapids: Brazos, 2007), 100–103; see Stone's recent work,
especially the final chapter, "Evangelism and Beauty," in Stone, *Evangelism after*

Pentecost marks the origins of Christian preaching as speech generated by God's action rather than human action. Peter is receptive and responsive to the Spirit, his sermon an act of worship proclaiming God's mighty action in the past and unveiling God's astonishing activity in Christ's presence. Peter reaches back to the Scriptures of Israel, particularly the poetic speech of the prophet Joel, to declare the delightfully disruptive beauty of God's Spirit poured out in abundance on all flesh. Michael Welker describes Peter's preaching well: "The 'frank' proclamation—an open and public proclamation, unafraid and borne by joyful confidence—of God's 'deeds of power' is just as much the result of the pouring out of God's Spirit as is a new community of diverse persons and groups of people."[4]

Peter exercises a practical wisdom similar to that of the prophets. His attentiveness to the Spirit *and* Israel's Scripture reframes the experience of his listeners within the narrative of the gospel, the story of Jesus Christ. Peter does not merely lecture or talk about Christ as Lord. Peter boldly testifies to the mighty acts of God, who has generated a remarkable new state of affairs for both Israel and the nations through the life, death, and resurrection of Jesus of Nazareth. There

---

Pluralism: The Ethics of Christian Witness (Grand Rapids: Baker Academic, 2018), 117–34. The account of preaching provided in this work moves in a similar manner to Stone's fitting description of "aesthetic evangelism" as Christian witness that joins art, embodiment, and imagination.

4. Michael Welker, *God the Spirit*, trans. John F. Hoffmeyer (Minneapolis: Fortress, 1994), 230. Willie Jennings's comments are worth repeating here. "If this is the first Christian sermon, then we must take note of several of its moments. First, it exists only within the Holy Spirit. It begins only after the Spirit has come. It is a second word after the words of praise have been given by God. Before the Spirit came, Peter had little to say. His words will now and forever be only commentary on what the Spirit is doing, and God has done for us in Jesus. Second, he does not stand alone. As he stands, the other disciples stand. As he stands and speaks, Israel's prophets are echoing in his words. It is a life-draining deception to ever believe that one preaches alone. Of course, one voice speaks in the preaching, yet at every moment, at any given moment when a speaker speaks, many preachers past and present are speaking. The preacher is always a company of preachers." Willie James Jennings, *Acts* (Louisville: Westminster John Knox, 2017), 34.

is a timeliness about this proclamation. The grand narrative of Israel's Lord and his faithfulness through the life and ministry of Jesus is of such cosmic scope that it generates a multitude of languages for "gospeling" the mighty works of God to the nations.[5]

A reading of Acts 2 conveys the sense of such homiletical beauty. God is already here; God is for, with, in, and among us, addressing and calling us to a change of mind and heart in joyful response to the way things are now that Jesus, as Israel's Messiah, has been raised from the dead and has poured out the Spirit on "all flesh." This is both God's conclusive revelation of himself and beautiful expression of his design for the world: the creation of a new heavens and a new earth. Peter describes the appropriate response to the announcement of this new state of affairs as blessed freedom of allowing oneself to be taken up by the Spirit into the beauty of living in the world ruled by the risen crucified Lord over all created rulers, authorities, and powers.[6]

The proclamation of good news evokes the gift of repentance as an intellectual, affective, and volitional turning, a conversion of our whole selves in relation to God and others in the Spirit's joy. While this re-turning is not the cause of salvation, it is a consequence of God's saving beauty enjoyed in communion with neighbors from all nations, peoples, and cultures. What this looks like for the life of the church in the world shines brightly through the whole narrative of Acts. The astonishing announcement that God rules heaven and earth through the crucified, risen Jesus takes beautiful form as the Word advances in the Spirit's power and through the joyful obedience of faith manifested by the church in common witness to Christ.[7]

---

5. William H. Willimon, *Acts: A Biblical Commentary for Teaching and Preaching* (Atlanta: John Knox, 1988), 28–33.

6. See here C. Kavin Rowe, *World Upside Down: Reading Acts in the Graeco-Roman Age* (Oxford: Oxford University Press, 2009), 91–138.

7. Stone notes, "The church, far from being one more social organization within civil society . . . is instead the eschatological sign, the living demonstration that the end of time has come. Its very existence is a witness to the resurrection

Peter's preaching springs from and enacts the good news announced by Jesus in Luke 4 at a synagogue in Nazareth. The proclamation of good news by Jesus announced an astonishing "reversal of norms and values" in which the empowerment of the Spirit joined with the prophetic word of Isaiah 61.[8] "Peter's speech at Pentecost thus functions for the narrative of Acts much the way in which Jesus' inaugural speech at Nazareth functions in the Gospel narrative." In both instances, proclaiming good news in the power of the Spirit is programmatic for a narrative of prophetic speech and its enactment by a people whose life manifests God's rule in intensely personal and social ways.[9] "When the Spirit is received and given room in the church, the world will be created anew—toward its perfection."[10]

I hope this makes clear how contemporary strategies of topical teaching, motivational speaking, and social or political analysis are substitutes for the gospel and a departure from Peter's astonishing announcement of Jesus, the crucified and exalted Lord who addresses the church in the Spirit's power "today." Peter spoke in a manner that echoes the narrative of the prophets and Jesus, and his joyful announcement of Christ as Lord must be seen as the effect of nothing less than his being taken up and filled by the joy of God's Spirit. Fr. Danielou writes of the missionary zeal that desires to see God known and loved: "A saint is always someone who has a sense of God's

---

of Jesus, and this means that believers are now to live together before the world *as if* the end has come." Stone, *Evangelism after Christendom*, 104.

8. Russell Mitman writes, "The approach of the . . . interpreter is that of a servant who allows the texts of Holy Scripture to take over so that, through the working of the Holy Spirit, these encounters with the texts may become communal experiences of the presence of God in Christ. . . . What constitutes the community and community's conservation is the one Word, Jesus Christ, becoming enfleshed in the body of Christ through the conversation with the Scriptures that occurs in the worship event." F. Russell Mitman, *Worship in the Shape of Scripture* (Cleveland: Pilgrim, 2001), 26.

9. Luke Timothy Johnson, *Prophetic Jesus, Prophetic Church: The Challenge of Luke-Acts to Contemporary Christians* (Grand Rapids: Eerdmans, 2011), 87–89.

10. Gerhard Lohfink, *Jesus of Nazareth: What He Wanted, Who He Was*, trans. Linda M. Maloney (Collegeville, MN: Liturgical Press, 2012), 306.

grandeur, who has found joy in God, and who, filled with his love, desires to communicate it and share it, just as one would desire to speak of whatever fills one's heart. If we do not speak enough about God, it is because our hearts are not sufficiently filled with him. A heart filled with God speaks of God without effort, whereas it often takes effort for us because our hearts are not sufficiently enflamed."[11]

Much popular preaching today appears to be devoted to topics, ideas, principles, positions, and programs in the name of being relevant. However, if the primary emphasis of preaching is what we need to know and do, the timeliness of God's "saving beauty"—descending upon us in the Spirit here and now—recedes into the distant past and remains enclosed within an ancient text.[12] The underlying assumption is that being Christian entails the acquisition of knowledge that, given right application, self-awareness, and sufficient motivation, leads to effective and influential action in the "real world."

This approach, however, shows little interest in the attractiveness of the gospel by which the Spirit awakens the church to delight in the astonishing initiative of God, who speaks and acts through the announcement and advent of Christ the risen Lord "today." God takes the initiative; God fulfills God's promises; God creates faith; God commands; God empowers obedient response. "Faith always includes

---

11. Jean Daniélou, *Prayer: The Mission of the Church*, trans. David Louis Schindler Jr. (Grand Rapids: Eerdmans, 1996), 97.

12. "Preaching tells us who God is and what he does: it is about God. . . . Preaching that is about us is not gospel preaching: in fact, it is not preaching at all. That would be bad news, not good news." Eugene Peterson, *The Jesus Way: A Conversation on the Ways That Jesus Is the Way* (Grand Rapids: Eerdmans, 2007), 163–64; see here the extended argument in James K. A. Smith, *Desiring the Kingdom: Worship, Worldview, and Cultural Formation*, Cultural Liturgies 1 (Grand Rapids: Baker Academic, 2009). "The telos [or end] to which our love is aimed is not a list of ideas or propositions or doctrines; it is not a list of abstract, disembodied concepts or values. Rather, the reason a vision of the good life moves us is because it is a more affective, sensible, even aesthetic picture of what the good life looks like. A vision of the good life captures our hearts and imaginations not by providing a set of rules or ideals, but by painting a picture of what it looks like for us to flourish and live well" (53).

knowledge; it includes recognition. It responds to the other, surrenders itself to the other, and adopts the other's view of reality."[13] It is faith in the crucified, risen Lord that illumines the "eyes of our hearts" to delight in the "strange beauty" of the gospel that summons us to rejoice in giving God glory "today." There is a paradox at work in preaching, that we find our true selves and "voices" by losing ourselves in wonder before the beauty of Christ. As Eugene Peterson notes, "Truth removed from Beauty becomes abstract and bloodless. Goodness divorced from Beauty becomes loveless and graceless."[14]

The wisdom of the Christian past encourages us to see the art of preaching—its loves, dispositions, perceptions, intuitions, habits, and sensibilities—in terms of the church's calling of giving glory to God in the whole of life. What if we were to understand our identity as preachers by remembering the originating story of Israel, Jesus, and the creation of the church at Pentecost? What if we were to see ourselves as God's pilgrim people rather than as students, consumers, or partisan political advocates? What if preaching begins with confessing that, as Christian people, we walk by faith and not by sight, with acknowledging that all we are, have, do, and say is the superabundantly generous gift and delightful expression of the extravagant love of God in Christ, whose amazed witnesses we are? What if we were to understand our calling as bringing listeners into contact with the beauty inherent in the Trinitarian faith that finds its center in Christ? What if, as preachers, we were to humbly acknowledge that "the most important things in human life, such as affection, love, fidelity, and devotion, are based on a different kind of knowledge"?[15]

While the work of preaching includes acquiring knowledge, technique, and skill, faithful proclamation of the gospel also requires the formation of wisdom, rightly ordered knowledge and affection for God, and an awakened aesthetic sensibility that delights in the truth

---

13. Lohfink, *Jesus of Nazareth*, 21.

14. Eugene H. Peterson, *Practice Resurrection: A Conversation on Growing Up in Christ* (Grand Rapids: Eerdmans, 2010), 8.

15. Lohfink, *Jesus of Nazareth*, 22.

and goodness of God's beauty. Here Lesslie Newbigin's theological assessment of the church's being and action is apt and provides a beautiful depiction of the Spirit's fruit and effect in preaching.

> [These effects] are the radiance of a supernatural reality. That reality is, first of all, the reality of God, the superabundant richness of the being of the Triune God, in whom love is forever given and forever enjoyed in an ever-new exchange. . . . It is said of this superabundant glory that it has been given to believers in order that they may be recognizable as a community where the love of God is actually tested and known. . . . This is what makes the church a place of joy, of praise, of surprises, and of laughter—a place where there is a foretaste of the endless surprises of heaven.[16]

Peter's sermon in Acts 2 was not a teaching that must be applied to make life better, to make a difference, or to have an impact in the "real world." Peter's bold, daring, and provocative preaching narrates the astonishingly uncontrollable irruption of the "real world"—the radiant glory of a new creation generated by the Spirit's witness to the presence of the risen Lord, who fills up and extends the prophetic tradition of Israel's Scripture to the nations.[17]

In Peter's remarkable preaching, the promised end of all things has burst upon his hearers. God's radiant beauty shines brightly from the depths of a shared way of living poured out in abundance by the Spirit of the crucified, risen Christ.[18] This is the beauty of

16. Lesslie Newbigin, *Foolishness to the Greeks: The Gospel and Western Culture* (Grand Rapids: Eerdmans, 1986), 149.

17. "In some sense, powerful prophetic preaching will always call us to wake up and turn around. It will never simply or easily comfort us with easy platitudes or cheap moralisms or feel-good projects and activities. It will announce a whole new world and challenge us to let go of our old ways and world and enter, repenting, into the new creation set in motion in Jesus Christ." Anthony B. Robinson and Robert W. Wall, *Called to Be Church: The Book of Acts for a New Day* (Grand Rapids: Eerdmans, 2006), 66.

18. Ford and Hardy see three dynamics that converge at Pentecost: the over-

preaching that is inseparable from the praise of God. The recovery of preaching as an act of worship may yet serve to "entice and enchant us not only to desire but also to fall in love with God the Trinity, and thereby love our neighbors."[19] As Mark McIntosh notes, because the church is a life of grace, it may itself be a "divine speaking" or "word of God" within the world. The church is a sign of the possibility of a new creation appearing in the midst of the old creation, a provisional yet visible sharing that even now anticipates the hope of attaining our true end in the joy and delight of the Trinity.[20] Luke testifies to the beauty of the church created by the Spirit of Christ: "All who believed were together and had all things in common; they would sell their possessions and goods and distribute the proceeds to all, as any had need. Day by day, as they spent much time together in the temple, they broke bread at home and ate their food with glad and generous hearts, praising God and having the goodwill of all the people" (Acts 2:44–47a).

flow of praise to God; the offering of everything as the overflow of love in a community that shares in the Holy Spirit; and the overflow in mission to the world. Thus, "the Church becomes what it is meant to be: a prophetic community whose vocation is to witness to the love of God in Jesus Christ." David F. Ford and Daniel W. Hardy, *Living in Praise: Worshiping and Knowing God* (Grand Rapids: Baker Academic, 2005), 185. See also the discussion in Matthew L. Skinner, *Intrusive God, Disruptive Gospel: Encountering the Divine in the Book of Acts* (Grand Rapids: Brazos, 2015), 9–22.

19. Bryan D. Spinks, *The Worship Mall: Contemporary Responses to Contemporary Culture* (New York: Church Publishing, 2010), 216.

20. Here I have benefited from the insight of Mark A. McIntosh, *Divine Teaching: An Introduction to Christian Theology* (Oxford: Blackwell, 2008), 187. See also Jennings's helpful comments: "What is at stake here was not the giving up of all possessions but the giving up of each one, one by one as the Spirit gives direction, and as the ministry of Jesus may demand. Thus anything they had that might be used to bring people into sight and sound of the incarnate life, anything they had that might be used to draw people to life together and life itself and away from death and end the reign of poverty, hunger, and despair—such things were subject to being given up to God. The giving is for the sole purpose of announcing the reign of the Father's love through the Son in the bonds of communion together with the Spirit." Jennings, *Acts*, 40–41.

An Eschatological Beauty

Contemporary preaching, or speaking "with the times," is typically determined by attending to immediately pressing personal, cultural, and political concerns and is therefore valued for its relevance. However, preaching that makes itself relevant on the terms of a culture that increasingly does not know God, or assumes, in practice, the "death of God" and the negation of worship, will quickly become preaching that has lost its capacity to speak of God's truth, beauty, and goodness. This is not primarily a matter of finding the right cause, method, or personal aesthetic, but one of "orthodoxy," that is, "right praise or glory," which provides the measure of preaching for a people whose calling is the blessed delight of praising and knowing God in this life and the life to come.

Augustine's *City of God* has been a source of encouragement and hope in my desire to preach in a "timely" manner. By this I mean preaching that is "fitting" for the church during this current "time of the world" in which we find ourselves living "between the times" of Christ's first and final advents. The *City of God* is a beautiful narration of the Christian story of the church as a pilgrim people called to the way of Christ's humble love as the truth of our life in communion with God. As a community of "resident aliens," the church is drawn by the Spirit to the living Word who shepherds it along the way of faith, hope, and love toward the joy of eternal happiness with all the saints and angels in the heavenly city.[21] Augustine was arguably the most salutary exemplar of such narrative reading of Scripture during the early centuries of the church.[22] He began with the scriptural word, with the particular story the Bible has to tell in which are

21. Augustine, *The City of God*, ed. David Knowles, trans. Henry Bettenson (New York: Pelican, 1972). See here the excellent discussion in Carol Harrison, *Beauty and Revelation in the Thought of Saint Augustine* (Oxford: Clarendon, 1992), 239–69.

22. Hans W. Frei, *The Eclipse of Biblical Narrative: A Study in Eighteenth and Nineteenth Century Hermeneutics* (New Haven: Yale University Press, 1974), 1.

found both individual and communal stories of God's people and their destiny. "His book shadows the books of the Bible."[23]

While his ministry was theological and pastoral in nature, it possessed a striking doxological quality and eschatological orientation. His thinking, writing, and preaching were animated by desire for giving glory to God as the true source and end of all that is.[24] Interpreting the life of the church within the narrative of Scripture, Augustine described an Easter sermon in the following manner: "The appointed lessons from holy Scripture were read. . . . I simply said a few words appropriate to the occasion and the joy and happiness of the event; for I thought it better to give them a chance to hear, or rather to ponder in their hearts, what might be called the *eloquence of God in a work of divine power.*"[25]

Reading the "time of the world" through the lens of Scripture, Augustine interpreted history as an open-ended narrative of two cities adhering to opposing ways of life; one devoted to the love of God, the other to love of the self.[26] He viewed the church in history as a mixed body that struggles internally with the power of sin and externally with the powers that rule the earthly city. The life of the church is marked by an incompleteness and longing for the gift of eschatological peace, rest, and joy in the city of God.[27] Robert Wilken

23. Gerard J. P. O'Daly, *Augustine's City of God: A Reader's Guide* (Oxford: Oxford University Press, 1999), 160.

24. O'Daly, *Augustine's City of God*, 2.

25. Augustine, *City of God* 22.9 (emphasis added).

26. For the "time of the world" as signifying creation and history, I am indebted to Charles Mathewes, *A Theology of Public Life* (Cambridge: Cambridge University Press, 2007).

27. Robert L. Wilken, "Augustine's City of God Today," in *The Two Cities of God: The Church's Responsibility for the Earthly City*, ed. Carl E. Braaten and Robert W. Jenson (Grand Rapids: Eerdmans, 1997), 35; Francis Mannion offers this insightful observation: "A restoration of the doxological and the eschatological would allow the neglected element of beauty to find a new theological and practical importance in the liturgy of the West." M. Francis Mannion, *Masterworks of God: Essays in Liturgical Theory and Practice* (Chicago and Mundelein, IL: Hillenbrand Books, 2004), 152.

comments, "Christians . . . belonged to a community whose end lay outside of history, and whose company was even larger than the church. Its history extended back into the history of Israel, and it included men and women who had lived in former times, the saints who had gone before; and it awaited others who were not yet born (or already born) who would one day become its citizens. . . . The church is that part of the city of God which is on pilgrimage. . . . The church lives in the company of a much larger community."[28]

As the city on pilgrimage through time, the church needs preachers whose business is to know and make known the particular wisdom and way of life that finds its true happiness in worshiping and serving God—the Father, Son, and Holy Spirit. As Peter Brown comments, "So the *City of God*, far from being a book about flight from the world, is a book whose recurrent theme is 'our business within this common mortal life'; it is a book about being otherworldly in the world."[29]

Augustine points us to a fundamental conviction that enlivens the church and its ministries, including preaching: without true worship of God, there can be no human fulfillment, happiness, or genuine life in community. He notes that the just live by faith in God, but justice is only found where God is rightly worshiped.[30] "A society incapable of giving God his due fails to give its citizens their due—as human beings made for the quest and enjoyment of God."[31] Preaching serves this end in directing human loves and desires to delight in the good that is God, since all human actions find their fullness and completion in giving glory to God. Such preaching is guided by a vision of the new Jerusalem, the peace for which the city on pilgrimage yearns. This is

28. Wilken, "Augustine's City of God Today," 35. See also the discussion in Nicholas M. Healy, *Church, World, and the Christian Life: Practical-Prophetic Life* (Cambridge: Cambridge University Press, 2000), 54–56.

29. Peter Brown, *Augustine of Hippo: A Biography* (Berkeley: University of California Press, 2000), 324.

30. Augustine, *City of God* 1.1.

31. Rowan Williams, *On Augustine* (London: Bloomsbury, 2016), 112.

an inherently social reality, a fellowship of people united in the praise of God and the enjoyment of one another in God. "The church is not an instrument to achieve other ends than fellowship with God."[32]

Living in the light of this final end in the knowledge and enjoyment of God is the beautiful gift the church is for the world, offering itself as a social fact *and* eschatological witness to Christ's justice and virtue in unrivaled love for God and our neighbors in God.[33] Augustine writes, "Justice is found where God . . . rules an obedient city according to his grace . . . so that just as the individual righteous man lives on the basis of faith which is active in love, so the association, or people, of righteous men lives on the same basis of faith, active in love, the love with which a man loves God as God ought to be loved, and loves his neighbor as himself. But where this justice does not exist, there is certainly no 'association of men united by a common sense of right and by a community of interest.'"[34] Here we may see how Augustine's wisdom has resonated deeply with preachers across the centuries. He was writing as a pastor of the church to provide a truthful and compelling contrast to the arrogant pride of the Roman Empire, its sense of superiority and self-aggrandizing ways grounded in self-love rather than love for God. He saw this as a certain kind of "piety," an expression of worship and devotion to Rome, its pantheon of gods, and its natural families. It was also a patriotism, fusing the religious and the political, a civil religion driven by a fear of death and a related desire to preserve Rome's lasting significance, honor, and "glory."[35] Brown

32. Robert Wilken, *The Spirit of Early Christian Thought: Seeking the Face of God* (New Haven: Yale University Press, 2003), 210; Mathewes, *A Theology of Public Life*, writes, "The meaning of history itself is determined in Christ, and Christ has come, but his first coming only inaugurated the end times, only began the definitive determination of history; so we await the second coming, the parousia, as the ultimate revelation and thus determination of the meaning and significance of history, of our lives, and God's purposes" (308).

33. See the discussion of the *City of God* in Wilken, *The Spirit of Early Christian Thought*, 186–211.

34. Augustine, *City of God* 19.23.

35. Augustine, *City of God* 5.19. See here Robert Dodaro, *Christ and the Just*

summarizes Augustine's aims well: "Throughout the *City of God*, it is to this basic denial of dependence, and so of gratitude, that Augustine will point, in politics, in thought, in religion."[36]

Augustine viewed the glory of Rome as a particular passion and love that was idolatrous and corrupt. This was not the love of God but was the power of self-love seeking status, admiration, and praise as means of evading human vulnerability and death. On the one hand, this had produced a certain degree of public goods, benefits, and stability for the citizens of the empire. On the other hand, it was a way of life driven by pursuing dominion and self-sufficiency rather than devotion to God and true virtue.[37] Augustine's "ideological critique" of Rome is instructive for preachers called to make known the glory of God in Christ: that delight in and lust for honor and glory on our own terms, rather than love and desire for true justice as embodied by Christ, are in effect a displacement of God. Rome's glory in its chosen virtues and strengths is an example of such displacement; they serve as mere imitations of true virtue by the perversion of human love.[38]

> Now according to the witness of historians, the ancient Romans—those of the earliest epoch—no doubt worshipped false gods, like the other races (except only the Hebrew people) and sacrificed victims not to God, but to demons; nevertheless they "were greedy for praise, generous with their money, and aimed at vast renown and honorable riches." They were passionately devoted to glory; it was for this that they desired to live, for this they did not hesitate to die. This unbounded passion for glory,

---

Society in the Thought of Augustine (Cambridge: Cambridge University Press, 2004), 50–53.

36. Brown, *Augustine of Hippo*, 326.

37. Dodaro, *Christ and the Just Society*, 6–26; Mathewes, *A Theology of Public Life*, 214–40; Mathewes, *The Republic of Grace: Augustinian Thoughts for Dark Times* (Grand Rapids: Eerdmans, 2010), 80–81.

38. See here Mathewes's discussion of Augustine's critique of Rome. *A Theology of Public Life*, 230–36.

above all else, checked their other appetites. They felt it would be shameful for their country to be enslaved, but glorious for her to have dominion and empire; and so they set their hearts first on making her free, then on making her sovereign.[39]

Blinded by its own self-deception, Rome had failed to see beyond an inordinate desire for power and preeminence that represented a "social stagnation as a pathology in wonder."[40] Rome's citizens believed in the heroic exercise of human will and reason to attain the justice and virtue that was necessary for attaining human happiness. Augustine saw such heroism as a form of false worship preventing Rome's people from attaining true justice. It had prevented them from knowing and loving themselves and their neighbors in God, and most important, it prevented them from delighting in the splendor of God, in God's wisdom and goodness.[41] Augustine's assessment of the "uselessness" of Rome's gods is helpful for considering the theological integrity of preaching that engages the sin of idolatry, or false worship, in summoning hearers to embrace a doxological way of life in praising the true and living God. "[I] have given a sufficient refutation of those who suppose that many false gods are to be venerated and worshiped for advantages in this mortal life, and the benefits to temporal things. They would accord them the ceremonies and the humble devotion which the Greeks call '*latreia*,' a worship due only the one true God. Christian truth proves those 'gods' to be useless images or unclean spirits and malignant demons, creatures at any rate, and not the Creator."[42]

Christian people find true happiness in remembering the story of

---

39. Augustine, *City of God* 5.12.

40. John Cavadini, "The Anatomy of Wonder: An Augustinian Taxonomy," *Augustinian Studies* 42, no. 2 (2011): 162.

41. Rowan Williams writes, "The *De civitate* is not at all a work of political theory in the usual sense, but sketches for a theological anthropology and a corporate spirituality. The political and the spiritual are not separate concerns." Williams, *On Augustine*, 111.

42. Augustine, *City of God* 6, pref.

God's love and admiring the beauty of God's works rather than boasting of achievements aligned with the false glories valued by the earthly city. Piety, the worship of God, is the source of true virtue and justice that constitute the contributions of Christians to the earthly city. "It is the conviction of all those who are truly religious, that no one can have true virtue without true piety, that is without the true worship of the true God; and that the virtue which is employed in the service of human glory is not true virtue: still, those who are not citizens of the Eternal City—which the holy Scriptures call the City of God—are of more service to the earthly city when they possess even that sort of virtue than if they are without it."[43] The significance and worth of Christian lives, which is their "glory," is dependent upon neither self-sufficiency nor self-preservation but is a gift received through preaching that inspires the church's delight in walking by faith in the way of Christ. In a meditation on Christ from Matthew 11:28–30, Augustine describes an ennobling Christian way of being and living, depicting the church as both an example of Christ's humility and a sacrament of the humble love that fills the city of God.

> So brothers [and sisters], don't let pride swell in you, let it shrivel instead and rot. Be disgusted by it, throw it out. Christ is looking for a humble Christian. Christ in heaven, Christ with us, Christ in hell—not to be kept there, but to release others from there. That's the kind of leader we have. He is seated at the right hand of the Father, but he is gathering us up together from the earth; one in this way, one in that; by favoring this one, chastising that one, giving this one joy and that one trouble, may he gather us up, otherwise we are lost; may he gather us together where we can't get lost, into that land of the living where all deserts are acknowledged and justice is rewarded.[44]

43. Augustine, *City of God* 6.19.
44. Augustine, *Essential Sermons*, in *The Works of Saint Augustine: A Translation for the 21st Century* (Hyde Park, NY: New City Press, 2007), 106.

This is a happiness that shares in God's abundant joy. Although the church is not identical to the city of God in its historical and institutional form, Augustine saw it as an imperfect and yet real sign or symbol of the city, a holy people who long for true happiness in God. "But even the righteous man himself will not love the life he wishes until he reaches that state where he is wholly exempt from death, deception and distress, and has the assurance that he will forever be exempt. That is what our nature craves, and it will never be fully and finally happy unless it attains what it craves."[45]

Although our earthly pilgrimage is marked by weakness and incompleteness, we may find such happiness and hope in Scripture, which points us to God as the source and goal of all that is. By opening ourselves to receive the gifts of faith and love in our "use" of Scripture, we are enabled to resist despairing of God's goodness during our present time of exile.[46] Augustine understood this struggle as a profoundly pastoral matter. "Augustine was not a system builder in anything like the modern or epic sense. His work is occasional, responding to the pastoral problems facing the church of his day. . . . His ecclesiology in the *City of God* takes the form of an open-ended narrative of the history of the two cities 'in their interwoven, perplexed and only eschatologically separable reality.'"[47]

The gift of faith that comes by hearing the word of Christ sustains the life of a pilgrim people, who, by acknowledging the human limitations of finitude, sin, and death, confess their need for God's compassion.[48] In offering its praise to God, the church receives the grace of Christ by which it is formed and its life is ordered as a community of Christian speech, memory, and hope. "Only people

45. Augustine, *City of God* 14.25.
46. Augustine, *City of God* 19.19.
47. Healy, *Church, World, and the Christian Life*, 56.
48. On the epistemic humility and the "pilgrimage of testimony," see Rodney Clapp, *Border Crossings: Christian Trespasses on Popular Culture and Public Affairs* (Grand Rapids: Brazos, 2000), 19–32.

schooled in the religious life can tell the difference between serving the one God faithfully and bowing down to idols."[49]

It may be that our strongest challenge as preachers is overcoming the church's pervasive forgetfulness of God's glory, goodness, and works. This requires a life of prayer; of giving ourselves in humble receptivity to Christ, who generously gives himself to us as the way and goal of faith. By the beauty of his holy love, perceived in the ugliness of suffering and death on a cross, the Spirit enlightens our intellect and strengthens our will, effecting the healing of our ignorance and weakness.[50] Augustine offers a striking image of Christ, fully human and fully divine, who is the subject, object, and delight of our preaching. "As man he is our Mediator; as man he is our way. For there is hope to attain a journey's end when there is a path which stretches between the traveler and his goal. . . . As it is, there is one road, and one only, well secured against all possibility of going astray; and this road is provided by one who is himself both God and man. As God, he is the goal; as man, he is the way."[51]

Christ has spoken as Mediator: in former times through the prophets, through his ministry and words, and through the apostles. Christ continues to speak through preachers whose true delight is in making known the glory of God. And If we are to be found "fitting" for this task, we will be hearers of the Word before we are its speakers. Augustine calls us to remember that "he also instituted the Scriptures, those which we call canonical. These are the writings of outstanding authority in which we put our trust concerning those things we need to know for our good, and yet are incapable of discovering by ourselves."[52]

49. Wilken, *The Spirit of Early Christian Thought*, 209–10.

50. Augustine, *City of God* 11.2.

51. Augustine, *City of God* 11.2.

52. Augustine, *City of God* 11.3. Wilken writes, "Augustine's thinking, like that of other Christians in antiquity, began with the facts of revelation, God's disclosure in Christ as narrated in the Scriptures. . . . Historical knowledge requires witnesses, and witness invites faith, or confidence in the word of the one who bears witness. . . . Authority in Augustine's view does not impose or coerce, it

An Invitation to Beauty

I have written this book for preachers and students of preaching from both mainline and evangelical churches, traditions I have been privileged to serve for many years as a pastor and teacher of preaching. I am convinced that reclaiming the beauty of preaching is necessary for the healing of our ecclesial divisions and theological fragmentation, and for resisting the "ugly" talk comprising the ideological "background noise" of American culture that has infected the church.

While this cacophony of conflicting voices, angry invective, and idle chatter contributes little to the good work of preaching, it works effectively to dull our affections and sensibilities to the astonishing beauty of the gospel: that God was in Christ reconciling the world to himself. As an act of faith, preaching demands more of us than promoting our chosen tribal affiliations and identities to denounce what and whom *we are against.* The vocation of preaching is measured, elevated, and compelled by the gospel itself, by the truth, goodness, and beauty of the Lord, who calls and commissions the church to confess, praise, and proclaim his glory to the nations. "The language of praise is the primary language of Christian faith. . . . We are most fully human when we praise God, since this is the purpose for which were made."[53]

In addition to a politicized church, there is privatized faith, which reduces our vision of God, church, and world to the self-interested problems, purposes, concerns, and desires of the individual "self." This has been aptly described as "moral therapeutic Deism," which manifests itself in a diversity of forms, styles, and expressions of self-righteousness, self-justification, and self-regard.[54] There is preaching

---

enlightens. Its appeal is to the understanding, not to the will." Wilken, *The Spirit of Early Christian Thought*, 170–74.

53. Catherine Mowry LaCugna, *God for Us: The Trinity and Christian Life* (San Francisco: HarperSanFrancisco, 1991), 342, 357.

54. On "moralistic therapeutic Deism," see Christian Smith and Melinda

that promotes self-improvement. There is preaching that promotes social change. There is preaching that seeks to attract people to attend and get more involved in the church. And there is preaching that seeks to motivate people to get out of the church and be more involved in the world. In any case, the stunning reality of the triune God's eternal purpose of gathering up all things in Christ for the praise of his glory is easily forgotten, neglected, or dismissed.

As preachers we are called to submit our language to be judged by Christ's wisdom and purified by the Spirit's love. I am not convinced that the familiar categories of liberal/conservative or progressive/traditional possess sufficient theological "weight" to address our current challenges and opportunities as preachers. Sustaining the identity and mission of the church requires language that is "fitting" for Christian people who have been united with Christ by the Spirit in baptism; as a holy people called and raised up to share a common worship and life in the Spirit, which is indifferent to all prior honor, value, worth, and ways of identifying human "glory."

I have found it helpful to think of preachers and congregations as either those who believe they are the primary speakers and actors in the world or those who believe God is the primary speaker and actor in the world. These two convictions need not be seen as antithetical to each other, since they have been reconciled in Christ, fully divine and fully human, the incarnate Word, who is himself the source, means, and goal of our speech and action. As speech that is derivative of the identity and activity of God revealed fully in Christ, preaching cannot be reduced to communication determined by pragmatic and utilitarian considerations. Nor can the gospel be reduced to voicing our personal or social ethical positions and views. The preaching of the gospel nurtures the virtue of "religion" (not to be confused with "organized religion"), which entails reverent fear, prudent respect, and loving recognition that finds happiness in loving God, others, and the

Lundquist Denton, *Soul Searching: The Religious and Spiritual Lives of American Teenagers* (Oxford: Oxford University Press, 2005).

creation in God, a holistic sensibility that many are seeking under the guise of "spirituality" but apart from the faith and life of the church.

As women and men who occupy a calling and office of the church—that we speak because we have first been spoken—we are not free to determine how we think and speak without reference to and appreciation for what and how preaching has been done in the past. If we leave the past behind, presumably for its intellectual, moral, and practical deficiencies, we will find ourselves wandering aimlessly in the present and searching for the future. An important part of the maturing process in preaching is learning humility before God, out of love for God, the Lord of past, present, and future, and to do so as members of the "communion of saints." As Erasmus of Rotterdam noted in the sixteenth century, a time that was marked by far-reaching changes, "To restore great things is sometimes not only harder but a nobler task than to have introduced them."[55]

Many who call into question the validity of preaching often show little acquaintance with, or interest in, a living tradition that has been sustained by the Spirit and originates with God's speaking creation into being; is amplified through the calling of Israel and the faith formed by its Scriptures; finds its central focus in the history of the incarnate Word; has been received by the church through the centuries and handed down to the present; and will continue until the consummation of all things in the reign of God. In addition to criticizing the Christian past for its sins and shortcomings (while often neglecting our own need for confession, repentance, forgiveness, conversion, and reconciliation as members of the body of Christ), we may also benefit from appreciating the consistency of Christian tradition, the faithfulness of God, and the great "cloud of witnesses" who in particular times and places have demonstrated exemplary, although partial and incomplete, fidelity to the gospel. John Webster's clarifying

---

55. *The Correspondence of Erasmus: Letters 298 to 445, 1514 to 1516*, vol. 3 of *The Collected Works of Erasmus*, trans. James M. Estes et al., ed. Douglas F. S. Thomson (Toronto: University of Toronto Press, 1976), 221–22.

comments are helpful. *"Tradition is the apostolic life of the church.* . . . The apostolic form of the life of the church is what it is because of the presence and activity of Jesus Christ, the one who ever afresh makes himself present and manifest in the event of the Spirit's coming. . . . Tradition is 'eschatological': its center is the presence and activity of another, in the event of the coming of Jesus Christ, and its primary activity is the Spirit-produced activity of faith."[56] I am keenly aware that seminarians, pastors, as well as listeners and interested skeptical onlookers have many doubts concerning the future of preaching. They have witnessed the abuse of pastoral authority and preaching that sought personal popularity and professional success. They have seen malpractice committed in preaching to acquire economic, social, and political power. They have observed, participated in, and even suffered from the "ugliness" of preaching that exchanges the love of God for love of ourselves, the praise of God's glory for the glory of praise.

A consequence of this homiletical "ugliness" is that preachers and listeners alike have become disillusioned or even despairing of the goodness of God made known in Christ and the church as his body. Many are increasingly disenchanted with the church's received vision of humanity created in the divine image and completed in Christ. Encouraged by pervasive cynicism, nihilism, or utopian idealism, many have turned against or left behind what they perceive as hopelessly inept, corrupt, and irrelevant forms of "organized religion."

An increasing number of books seek to address these problems, offering critical perspectives and constructive proposals for change across the whole range of theological and homiletical views. However, a pressing question remains as to whether our visions of preaching are sufficient to attract both current and future generations of preachers to the joy of proclaiming the beauty inherent to the gospel of Jesus Christ. Pope Francis states the matter clearly in his apostolic exhortation *The Joy of the Gospel*: "A renewal of preaching can offer

56. John Webster, *The Culture of Theology*, ed. Ivor J. Davidson and Alden C. McCray (Grand Rapids: Baker Academic, 2019), 90–92.

believers, as well as the luke-warm and the non-practicing, new joy in the faith and fruitfulness in the work of evangelization. The heart of its message will always be the same: the God who revealed his immense love in the crucified and risen Christ. God constantly renews his faithful ones, whatever their age: 'They shall mount up with wings like eagles, they shall run and not be weary; they shall walk and not be faint' (Isa. 40:31)."[57]

I hope to encourage preachers and congregations who in our current time of church decline, divisions, denominational defensiveness, and self-preservation seek to worship the triune God and continue to delight in knowing Christ and making him known to the world.

Such preachers and communities may indeed go unnoticed in a church culture that glories in the powerful, the impressive, the trendy, and the fashionable. On the other hand, they may be living signs of a yet-to-be-completed beauty taking form in the world as the "whole Christ"—the Head and his body—by the Spirit's abundant outpouring of God's love, which is the source of our being and life. Such communities, so ordered by the worship and service of God, make known the attractiveness of Christ by the fruit of the Spirit's sanctifying grace. This is the church's missionary proclamation of the gospel, which is God's appeal to be reconciled in Christ, whose beauty is nourished in us by the Spirit's love, fruit, and gifts.[58] In the Epistle to the Ephesians, Saint Paul writes these words of hope in the beauty of Christ's inexhaustible love, which exceeds all human understanding of God, ourselves, and the world:

> For this reason I bow my knees before the Father, from whom every family in heaven and on earth takes its name. I pray that, according to the riches of his glory, he may grant that you may be

---

57. Pope Francis, *The Joy of the Gospel (Evangelii Gaudium): Apostolic Exhortation* (Vatican City: Libreria Editrice Vaticana, 2013), 6.

58. Here I am following the discussion in Veli-Matti Kärkkäinen, *Christ and Reconciliation*, A Constructive Christian Theology for the Pluralistic World, vol. 1 (Grand Rapids: Eerdmans, 2013), 368–72.

strengthened in your inner being with power through his Spirit, and that Christ may dwell in your hearts through faith, as you are being rooted and grounded in love. I pray that you may have the power to comprehend, with all the saints, what is the breadth and length and height and depth, and to know the love of Christ that surpasses knowledge, so that you may be filled with all the fullness of God. (Eph. 3:14–19)

Lastly, I have written for preachers who have grown weary from pressures to conform themselves to the expectations of a culture that delights in arrogance, ignorance, celebrity, and entertainment; for those who feel they must justify themselves according to standards of ministry that require for their success a spirit of pride or fear rather than humble, courageous faith inspired by the love the Spirit pours into our hearts with lavish abundance. I have in mind pastors who are discouraged and even repelled by the ugliness of ministry framed primarily as a mode of faithless, market-driven competition and soulless ecclesial survival; by pastoral methodologies that disfigure the beauty of the gospel, diminish desire for the Word, and detract from delight in God and God's will.

The Beauty of Preaching is an invitation to "see" afresh the heart of the church's vocation of preaching: to know, love, and enjoy God in all we think, say, do, desire, and suffer. My hope is that this book will be read as a welcomed breath of fresh air, inspiring renewed appreciation for and deeper delight in the "disarming beauty" of the living God, who is with us in our preaching of the crucified Christ, the risen Lord of all that is.[59]

---

59. On God's "disarming beauty," see Julian Carron, *Disarming Beauty: Essays on Faith, Truth, and Freedom* (Notre Dame: University of Notre Dame Press, 2017).

– one –

SAVING BEAUTY

Although it is true that listeners respond to sermons in a variety of ways, it would be odd for a preacher to hear it said, "Your feet were beautiful today!" However, there is a remarkable passage in Isaiah that invites us to see anew the astonishing beauty of proclaiming the good news of God.

> How beautiful upon the mountains
>   are the feet of the messenger who announces peace,
> who brings good news,
>   who announces salvation,
>   who says to Zion, "Your God reigns." (Isa. 52:7)

The saving beauty of the gospel awakens the church to behold God as the primary actor in the world, and thus the primary speaker in preaching. The aim is to glorify God by proclaiming what God has done with the fitting response expressed supremely in lives of thanks and praise.[1]

The beauty of preaching is most fittingly expressed as doxological speech, the offering of a preacher's whole self in adoring praise to the God of Israel embodied in Jesus Christ, the Creator and Redeemer of

---

1. David F. Ford and Daniel W. Hardy, *Living in Praise: Worshiping and Knowing God* (Grand Rapids: Baker Academic, 2005), 19.

all that is.[2] Walter Brueggemann describes Isaiah's prophetic message as "a core model for the preaching task."[3] There is real "homiletical beauty" in the timeliness of messengers who selflessly announce the good news to Israel. The news of God's saving work in the world is indeed so wondrous that its messengers run and skip with joy in delivering this remarkable message, "Your God reigns." This dramatic announcement is a delightful sound to a people waiting and yearning for God to act, hoping in Yahweh, who is indeed more trustworthy than all other powers and gods. The roots of this proclamation are found in the poetic discourse of Isaiah.

2. Walter Brueggemann offers the following testimony. "Such praise is indeed our duty and our delight, the ultimate vocation of the human community, indeed of all creation. Yes, all of life is aimed toward God and finally exists for the sake of God. Praise articulates and embodies our capacity to yield, submit, and abandon ourselves in trust and gratitude to the One whose we are. Praise is not only a human requirement and a human need, it is also a human delight. We have a resilient hunger to move beyond self, to return our energy and worth to the One from whom it has been granted. In our return to that One, we find our deepest joy. That is what it means to 'glorify God and enjoy God forever.'" Walter Brueggemann, *Israel's Praise: Doxology against Idolatry and Ideology* (Philadelphia: Fortress, 1988), 160. Although Brueggemann is describing the worship of Israel and the church, I find this to be a very helpful way of thinking about the nature and purpose of preaching.

3. My indebtedness to Brueggemann's work will be obvious in the first part of this chapter. His commitment to preaching is well known, particularly his thinking on the significance of Isa. 52 for Israel's faith and prophetic tradition. For this chapter I have drawn from Brueggemann, *Israel's Praise*; Brueggemann, *Cadences of Home: Preaching among Exiles* (Louisville: Westminster John Knox, 1997); and Brueggemann, *The Practice of Prophetic Imagination: Preaching an Emancipating Word* (Minneapolis: Fortress, 2012). Three claims made by Brueggemann are especially pertinent for my work. (1) Doxology speaks both in praise of God and against idolatry and ideology. (2) Truly "evangelical" preaching is a poetic alternative that speaks hopes and possibilities aiming toward a new people, new community, and new creation that is the astonishing work of God. (3) Proclamation imagines the world as though Yahweh—the creator of the world, the deliverer of Israel, the Father of our Lord Jesus Christ whom Christians name as Father, Son, and Holy Spirit—were a real character and an effective agent in the world.

> Get you up to a high mountain,
>   O Zion, herald of good tidings;
> lift up your voice with strength,
>   O Jerusalem, herald of good tidings, . . .
> say to the cities of Judah,
>   "Here is your God!" (Isa. 40:9)

Brueggemann describes this as "invitational poetry" that conveys an alternative perception of reality. Saving beauty is not found in history, doctrine, politics, morality, or culture, but rather in the surprising new reality Zion and Jerusalem have been commissioned to announce, suffer, and enact before God and the nations.[4] A great reversal is unfolded as the surprising newness generated by Yahweh's self-communication is unveiled: "Therefore my people shall know my name; therefore in that day they shall know it is I who speak; here am I" (Isa. 52:6). The announcement is in the indicative and echoes Isaiah 40:9, "Here is your God":

> for in plain sight they see
>   the return of the LORD to Zion . . .
> and all the ends of the earth shall see
>   the salvation of our God. (Isa. 52:8–10)

God's saving beauty is made visible by the image of messengers running exuberantly to deliver "glad tidings"—Yahweh has decisively defeated all opposing and resistant powers. Significantly, it is the messenger's feet that are described as beautiful, in that "they glide with buoyancy."[5] It can be observed from a distance that the news

---

4. Abraham Heschel notes, "It is prophecy tempered with human tears, mixed with joy that heals all scars, clearing a way for understanding the future in spite of the present. No words have ever gone further in offering comfort when a sick world cries." Abraham J. Heschel, *The Prophets: An Introduction*, vol. 1 (New York: Harper & Row, 1962), 145.

5. Brueggemann, *Israel's Praise*, 48, cf. 45–53.

is truly good, with the messenger's bearing and comportment a delight to behold.[6] "Praise is always overflowing where we have got to in thought and action, as it risks greater and greater receptivity and response, and so it becomes the catalyst of prophetic knowledge of God and his will."[7]

The proclamation of the gospel points to a strange, elusive beauty that draws the world into the joy of God that is life itself. As an "external" word that originates with God—rather than the preacher—the gospel not only informs and motivates but also transforms perceptions, desires, speech, actions, and understanding. God's saving beauty, moreover, generates a style appropriate for communicating God's identity and activity that is the language of praise.[8] "How beautiful are the feet of him who brings peace, who brings good tidings of God, who publishes salvation, who says to Zion, 'Your God reigns.'" However, to think of prophetic preaching as beautiful may sound strange. Eugene Peterson comments, "Beauty is commonly trivialized in our culture, whether secular or ecclesial. It is reduced to decoration, equated with the insipidities of 'pretty' or 'nice.' But beauty is not an 'add on,' not an extra, nor a frill. Beauty is not what we indulge ourselves in after we have taken care of the serious business of making a living, or getting saved, or winning the lottery. It

---

6. Heschel comments, "In answer to the prophet's fervent invocation (51:9) the Lord is about to bare His arm or His might before the eyes of all the nations." Heschel, *The Prophets*, 149.

7. Ford and Hardy, *Living in Praise*, 13.

8. Here I am following Ford and Hardy, *Living in Praise*. Rather than beginning with problems, questions, political issues, social evils, and the corruption of what is good, all of which are given more than their share of attention, Ford and Hardy propose beginning with God. "The greatest blow that can be struck against them is to pay more attention to the God of joy. God is the supremely interesting reality, far more exciting than anything else, and from involvement with God comes the perspective in which the ultimate pointlessness, misery, and boring emptiness of evil are clear" (176). Brueggemann writes, "The fact that the formula 'Yahweh rules' is news, a message, creates a decisive, dramatic recognition. . . . The reality of Yahweh's new future is effected in this moment when the news is asserted." *Israel's Praise*, 35–36, passim.

is evidence and witness to the inherent wholeness and goodness of who God is and the way God works."[9]

Saving beauty, moreover, is intimately related to the condescension of God.[10] Peterson connects the strange beauty of the gospel to the servant song of Isaiah 53. It is "a root out of dry ground, no beauty, despised and rejected, we esteemed him as broken, smitten by God, oppressed, cut off out of the land of the living, his grave with the wicked."[11]

Paradoxically, it is the divinity of God, God's powerfulness and majesty, that shines from complete powerlessness, the revelation of the one good and beautiful truth of God. According to the prophecy of Isaiah, this "strange" beauty is perceived by those who have eyes to see and ears to hear. God's saving beauty, then, is neither pretty nor impressive. It is not sentimental and superficial, a useful tool for decorating and embellishing a preacher's message. Nor can it be equated with a preacher's personal aesthetic, brand, or style. Peterson concludes, "The prophet is schooling us in a theological aesthetic that is in contrast to virtually everything in both Babylon and North America."[12]

Isaiah's poetic speech invites preachers to reimagine the world as no longer bound by settled, established "facts" on the ground. Against the claims of false gods, God's abundant goodness is proclaimed to a people gripped by hopelessness and despair, or alternatively, driven by

9. Eugene H. Peterson, *The Jesus Way: A Conversation on the Ways That Jesus Is the Way* (Grand Rapids: Eerdmans, 2007), 181.

10. Brueggemann states this clearly. "All who share the dramatic moment of announcement and celebration are energized to live in this new world with these fresh possibilities. This is indeed the work of evangelism, of telling, of world making, of life offered imaginatively under the rule of and in response to this One who, in the moment of invasion, does indeed make all things new. . . . The pivotal point in Israel's liturgical life is the continued reassertion of the astonishing claim that the gods are defeated, Yahweh rules, and therefore the world can act out its true character of God's creation." *Israel's Praise*, 38.

11. Peterson, *The Jesus Way*, 181.

12. Peterson, *The Jesus Way*, 181–82.

desire for survival and success.[13] With simplicity and grace, the proclamation of good news articulates fresh possibilities for living in the joy of vulnerable receptivity to God's goodness and love "today."

We may be accustomed to thinking of prophetic preaching as social analysis and political critique, as passionate denunciations and calls for social justice typically not associated with praise.[14] However, to know, praise, and enjoy God is itself prophetic, since the central affirmation of Scripture can be summed up as "God is." As announced by the prophet Isaiah, God reigns, God will reign, and God is manifestly present in the life of the world.[15] Remembering the confession "God reigns" is significant for preachers, since God cannot be reduced to a useful concept, resource, or symbol to un-

13. Ellen Davis observes of the poetic speech of biblical prophecy, "Like good poets in every tradition, the prophetic poets of the Bible craft sharp images designed to make something visible to the mind's eye—most often viewed from a particular location in space and time, and yet imagined as part of the whole world, inhabited by the hearer as well as the poet. As poets, they must be committed to fidelity, to faithful representation of the world as it actually is, even as they make it possible for their hearers to imagine that God might be doing something radically new in their own time and place. The form of prophetic poetry thus matches its essential content; the poet's framing of words so that they ring true is itself an echo of God's own fidelity to the world." Ellen F. Davis, *Biblical Prophecy: Perspectives on Christian Theology, Discipleship, and Ministry* (Louisville: Westminster John Knox, 2014), 8.

14. Stanley Hauerwas writes, "It is the pastor's task to hold before the community the story that determines its existence and makes it possible, not for the pastor to be prophetic, but for the community to fulfill its calling as its own. The pastoral task is prophetic, insofar as the means that are peculiar to the church's ministry help to remind the community of the story that makes the community prophetic. There can be no more prophetic task than the preaching of the word and the serving of the Eucharist, for it is through them that the church is constituted as God's people in a world that does not know God." *Christian Existence Today: Essays on Church, World, and Living in Between* (Durham, NC: Labyrinth, 1988), 165.

15. Ford and Hardy, *Living in Praise*, 11, 173. "The prophet is typically one who is so taken up into worship and the vision that is given by God in it that he acts as a spokesman for God to the people and for the people to God" (53).

derwrite our personal and social agendas.[16] Recognizing God in the concrete circumstances of life is a strong affirmation and witness that lets "God be God" in the presence of competing news, gods, and forms of wisdom that contradict God's way with creation. As Ford and Hardy comment, "Prophecy is discerning this God and God's ways, and following through their practical consequences. It is an unavoidable part of Christian existence because it recognizes that the life of faith is a vocation with a mission, which requires risky discernment about the way into the future. Prophecy is essential because God is the sort of God who has a relationship with us that involves communication and shared responsibility for the future. Amazingly, God's life is shared with us, including God's freedom, creativity, and receptivity, and in every situation an alert attentiveness to God is the secret of appropriate response."[17]

The whole of Scripture invites us to behold a God of astonishing purposes and fresh surprises whose reign extends to the whole creation.[18] Remembering the narrative of God's past faithfulness summons the church to imagine a hope-filled future arriving in the Spirit's power "today."[19] This prophetic word inspires the community

16. Ford and Hardy conclude that in the West the "conventional wisdom" is that God is no longer the basis of life, so that human beings live as if they are self-sufficient and self-regulated. What I am proposing in following their logic is the delightful alternative of praising God. "If God is, then God is to be affirmed appropriately and appreciatively throughout the ecology of existence, and the truth, goodness, and beauty of God are only likely to have a chance of becoming clear in the process of doing this. Above all, the joy of God needs to be celebrated as the central and embracing reality of the universe and everything else seen in the light of this." Ford and Hardy, *Living in Praise*, 17.

17. Ford and Hardy, *Living in Praise*, 174.

18. Ford and Hardy, *Living in Praise*, 173.

19. Paul Minear writes, "[God's] kingdom is not merely one day among others, coming in sequence with others at their end. His is an eternal Day, which redeems evil time and makes it fruitful. Power over the new Day rests with God, not with [humankind]. This Day does not wait until various human specifications are met, because it is not a projection into the future of [humankind's] present desires. Rather, God hastens the Day by advancing his future into the

to confess its dependence and need in opening itself to the abundance of God's gifts. As Ford and Hardy remind us, "Prophecy that lives in praise can also give a vision of the proper shape of life in the Kingdom of God, and can offer inspiration, encouragement, and direction to realize it."[20]

Announcing God's saving beauty evokes responses of great joy. "To rejoice in this God [the God of joy] is a prophetic act which at once challenges the habitually worldly wisdom fed on suspicion, bad news, or cynical judgments." In the time in which we live, the joy of preaching will challenge a pervasive "practical atheism"—believing in God in theory but not in practice—since to confess faith in a God who is true, beautiful, and good is to be part of a community of praise that takes God and God's action seriously. "To lift up the God of joy shines the light of God's glory into some of the darkest and most corrupt places in modern life."[21]

The news is not that Israel's time to rule the nations has finally come, but rather that Israel's vocation of giving glory to God has been extended to embrace the nations.[22] A liturgical affirmation from Psalm 96 articulates the magnificent scope of this commission:

> Declare his glory among the nations,
>> his marvelous works among all the peoples. (Ps. 96:3)

An astonishing goodness and beauty summon the nations to join in the praise of Israel's God as Lord of all creation. "Say among the nations, 'The LORD is king!'" (Ps. 96:10). "Say to Zion, 'Your God is King.'" The evangelical proclamation of Yahweh's reign is to Israel—

---

present." Paul S. Minear, *The Kingdom and the Power: An Exposition of the New Testament Gospel* (Louisville: Westminster John Knox, 2004), 124.

20. Ford and Hardy, *Living in Praise*, 186–87.

21. Ford and Hardy, *Living in Praise*, 175–76.

22. Gerhard Lohfink, *Jesus of Nazareth: What He Wanted, Who He Was*, trans. Linda M. Maloney (Collegeville, MN: Liturgical Press, 2012), 46.

it is localized (Yahweh reigns) and to the nations—it is universal. (Yahweh is King.)[23]

Feet suffused with the beauty of holiness run with joyful abandon to announce the arrival of God's reign. To speak of feet as beautiful may sound odd, since they are typically seen as ugly and kept covered. However, as Paul Hanson comments, "Wrong! Human feet are not only beautiful but remarkable." Hanson alludes to the feet of messengers in the ancient world as "busy," and thus dusty, callused, cracked, and bleeding. It is of these feet that the prophet dares to exclaim, "How beautiful!" The beauty of messengers' feet, however, is not in their impressive appearance. The beauty is in the nature and purpose of the messengers' words, the joy of proclaiming a message that delights our hearts and stirs our desire to welcome and live gladly into the reality proclaimed. "Your God reigns!"[24]

Reading Israel's prophetic tradition in light of the gospel enables us to see Jesus as both the messenger and the message of God's joy. In fact and in deed, Jesus is the kingdom he proclaims. He *is* the kingdom in person, in that the content and form of God's reign of power and glory have become one in him.[25] Because the message and the messenger are one in Jesus, there is an essential integrity, harmony, and clarity in all he says, does, and suffers.[26] The proclamation of Isaiah 52:7 thus reaches a climax in the whole of his life and minis-

23. Brueggemann, *Israel's Praise*, 34–35. Smart comments, "Since the God of Israel alone is God, the establishment of his sovereignty cannot be limited to Israel in its claims or its benefits. The liberation of Israel leads to the liberation of a captive humanity. The herald of peace and blessing who skips across the mountains comes first to Zion with the message that the God of Israel has established his kingdom over all the earth. . . . The eyes of all the nations see the salvation of God." J. D. Smart, *History and Theology in Second Isaiah* (Philadelphia: Westminster, 1965), 190.

24. Paul D. Hanson, *Isaiah 40–66*, Interpretation: A Bible Commentary for Teaching and Preaching (Louisville: John Knox, 1995), 148–49.

25. Lohfink, *Jesus of Nazareth*, 170–75.

26. Richard Hays writes, "The announcement of God's powerful setting right of things is the keynote of Jesus' own apocalyptic message, which Mark describes as the . . . 'good news of God.' 'The time is fulfilled and the kingdom of God has come near' (Mk. 1:14b–15a). Mark is declaring that Israel's story has reached, in

try: "The time is fulfilled, and the kingdom of God has come near; repent, and believe in the good news" (Mark 1:15).[27] The prophetic announcement is realized:

> For in plain sight they see
>> the return of the LORD to Zion . . .
> and all the ends of the earth shall see
>> the salvation of our God. (Isa. 52:8, 10)

The reality of God's reign is given voice and visibility in Jesus, so that the good news becomes a reality among those who see, hear, and respond to him.[28]

The preaching of Jesus is remarkably concrete and timely rather than abstract and timeless. Mark's narration of his identity and action shows the saving beauty of God's beloved servant who *himself* is the good news of God. "That Jesus simply applied to himself a text that spoke of God's messenger of good news and the royal reign of God now manifesting itself assumes a breathtaking boldness."[29] By his manner of speaking, Jesus communicates the reality of God's reign in exact, precise, and pointed language. "There was not an ounce of fat in it."[30]

Jesus, its divinely ordained climax." Richard B. Hays, *Echoes of Scripture in the Gospels* (Waco, TX: Baylor University Press, 2016), 19, passim.

27. Hays comments, "Isaiah's poetic image of the return from exile as a 'new exodus' becomes a central organizing image for Mark's Gospel. Just as Isaiah employed the earlier exodus imagery to depict God's deliverance of Israel from the later Babylonian exile, so Mark draws on Exodus 23:20 and Isaiah 40:3, texts that evoke both of these past acts of God's deliverance of Israel, to introduce God's coming again in power through Jesus. The imagery is apocalyptic in character, emphasizing the inbreaking salvific power of God." Hays, *Echoes of Scripture in the Gospels*, 23.

28. Gerhard Lohfink, *Does God Need the Church? Toward a Theology of the People of God*, trans. Linda M. Maloney (Collegeville, MN: Liturgical Press, 1999), 153: "Jesus not only speaks words; his words are at work, they reveal reality, and therefore his proclamation is imbued with and accompanied by powerful action."

29. Lohfink, *Jesus of Nazareth*, 174.

30. Lohfink, *Jesus of Nazareth*, 101.

Neither proud nor self-promoting, his is a poetic way of speaking that kindles desire to let God be God and reorients everything around this priority. "The focus is on God's will, and other people, and there is a liberation from concern for the self."[31]

The God of Israel has spoken in all Jesus said, did, and suffered, the en-fleshing of the divine nature and action in "brilliance, beauty, and overflowing riches."[32] To behold God's glory in reading Mark's story of Jesus attunes a preacher's imagination and speech to the strange, fragile beauty of the gospel.[33] As Lohfink notes, "That we freely will what God wills is evidently possible only when we behold bodily the beauty of God's cause, so that we take joy in and even lust after what God wants to do in the world, and that this desire for God and God's cause is greater than all our human self-centeredness."[34]

Jesus proclaimed that God's time of gathering an "end time" people had come. His call to repentance is not the cause but rather the consequence of a salvation already accomplished by God.[35] "In the beginning, then, as throughout the whole of Scripture, is God's action

31. Ford and Hardy, *Living in Praise*, 107.

32. Lohfink, *Jesus of Nazareth*, 239.

33. Hays comments, "The identity of Jesus as the mysterious embodiment of Israel's God can never be separated from his identity as the crucified One. And therein lies a deeper layer of mystery: If Jesus is the embodiment of Israel's God, and if the body in whom these figural correspondences to Israel's Scripture are enacted ends up nailed to a cross, what does that tell us about the identity of God?" Hays, *Echoes of Scripture in the Gospels*, 104.

34. Lohfink, *Jesus of Nazareth*, 235.

35. Here Hays's caution warrants attention. "Mark is under no illusion that the kingdom of God proclaimed by Jesus has arrived in its fullness. Of all the Evangelists, Mark is the most reticent about claims of fulfillment and the most sensitive to the 'not yet' side of the eschatological dialectic. Surely that is one of the reasons for his remarkable decision not to narrate any resurrection appearances of Jesus; by ending his story with an announcement of the resurrection but without a narrated appearance of the risen Lord, Mark suggests that the community of his readers remains in the same posture of expectant waiting enjoined by the conclusion of the eschatological discourse in chapter 13, where Jesus' words to the disciples become a general admonition to all readers of the Gospel: 'And what I say to you I say to all: be awake!'" Hays, *Echoes of Scripture in the Gospels*, 23.

and not human action. God has taken the initiative, and God alone gives the reign of God. It is the business of the people of God to respond in faith, since God's action makes human action possible."[36] The beauty of the good news we are called to proclaim is that the transformation of the world is already under way as the prophetic word is spoken, heard, and enacted in particular times, places, and circumstances.[37]

A Useless Beauty

Rowan Williams comments on how the reality of God's reign announced by Jesus shows forth the "sheer, unimaginable differentness of God" that requires and transforms our speaking of God. This entails a "self-emptying" of predictability and all that we normally mean by sovereignty and greatness.[38] Naming God does not function as a symbol for what is highest, strongest, impressive, attractive, and holiest in ourselves. As Isaiah 53 announces, "He has not looks to attract our eyes." Williams articulates the challenge of the gospel: "to re-imagine what it is for God to speak to us as God—not as a version of whatever makes us feel secure, or appears more attractive than other kinds of security."[39]

The God proclaimed by Jesus does not fit into preconceived categories, since God's difference "cannot be reduced to underwriting our goals and agendas, no matter how spectacular they may be." Williams's comments invite preachers to read Mark's story of Jesus in a manner that directs attention to the strangeness of its central claim: "God has acted to remake the world from within, from within a life that is ended by desertion and failure and appalling suffering." We

---

36. Lohfink, *Jesus of Nazareth*, 30–31.

37. Lohfink, *Jesus of Nazareth*, 33.

38. Rowan Williams, *Christ on Trial: How the Gospel Unsettles Our Judgement* (Grand Rapids: Eerdmans, 2000), 9.

39. Williams, *Christ on Trial*, 11.

are thus summoned to "see" and name something of the "obstinate uselessness of witness to God's truth."[40]

Proclaiming the "uselessness" of God's truth, moreover, radiates a beauty that remains hidden to the pursuit of power, prestige, advantage, and success. The strange beauty of the gospel draws us to perceive God's glory, which is always "before us and within us here and now, a reality that will be scandalous and painful." This is the "timeliness" of the gospel that draws the church to embrace what may be the "hardest thing in the world . . . to be where you are." Following Mark's story of the gospel directs our attention to the "obstinate uselessness" of witnesses to who Jesus is: that we encounter in him God's glory on the "rough ground" of life.[41]

The saving beauty of God's reign, which is the subject of our preaching, shines brightly from the obscure image of a poor widow in Mark 12.[42] Lohfink comments, "There is probably no text in the gospel tradition that shows this more vividly than Mark 12:41-44." The story of the widow takes place in the temple, a stunningly impressive religious complex at the center of Israel's life. In an outer hall, the court of women, there was a place where visitors could leave sums of money for the maintenance of the sanctuary and its daily

40. Williams, *Christ on Trial*, 16–17.

41. Williams, *Christ on Trial*, 21–22. Here Paul Minear's comments are apt. "God's kingdom is inseparable from his glory and power. Where one is, there are the others also. That is why God's adversary seeks to implant in human hearts a false image of glory and a false conception of power. In so far as human institutions contribute to these illusions that become ramparts of the kingdom of blindness. In so far as earthly authorities witness to the true glory and power, they become signposts of God's kingdom. . . . Because God's glory is manifested in the person of Jesus, that glory is not a grandiose display of earthly grandeur, a fusion of all the stupendous colors of the honorific spectrum by which [humankind] adulate[s] their superiors. God does not bask in pomp and ceremony, but quietly proceeds to fill all creation with his invisible glory. His is a glory that requires sharing; the more it is shared with the Church and [others], the more it abounds." Minear, *Kingdom and the Power*, 224–25.

42. For this section I am following the discussion in Lohfink, *Jesus of Nazareth*, 219–21.

sacrifices. Those who gave were privileged to announce the amount of their gifts in public displays that directed attention to the giver's wealth and status as a particular kind of "glory."

Jesus sits down in a place opposite the treasury and observes the crowds of people who have come to give their money. Many put in large sums that are called out and named for particular purposes, a kind of calculated giving that basically served to honor the giver's name. It is a busy scene, with people coming from near and far, including the old and young, the rich and the poor. In addition to the size and importance of the gifts, this mixture of class and status can be discerned from the way people dress and their manner of speaking.[43]

A woman enters the sanctuary. Her dress makes it clear she is poor and a widow. She has lost much and lives in misery. She not only possesses very little, but she must also live without the protection of a man in an existence of vulnerable humility. When the woman silently drops two copper coins into the treasury, no one pays her the least bit of attention. It is the rich who out of their abundance give large, impressive sums of money. The woman, on the other hand, gives what amounts to a full day's supply of food, which is the very necessity of her life. The poor widow gives everything she has, she gives her whole living, and thus she gives her whole self.[44]

Jesus sees the widow and recognizes the significance of her act. Calling the disciples together, he interprets her gift in light of the temple's purpose of giving glory to God. His recognition of the poor widow is an epiphany of God's glory, in that her undivided devotion was a sign or "word" of God's undivided love for his people. Moreover, Jesus's pleasure with the widow's act makes sense only if worshiping and giving to God are not based on prior merit, status, or achievement, and if devotion to God is not a matter of promoting ourselves to impress others. The poor widow's gift, however, was too

43. Lohfink, *Jesus of Nazareth*, 219.
44. Lohfink, *Jesus of Nazareth*, 220.

small and unimpressive to attract attention from the temple crowd. It was useless and thus free from the necessity of impressing either God or others to enhance her status, reputation, and "glory." According to Jesus, the others "have contributed out of their abundance; but she out of her poverty has put in everything she had, all she had to live on" (Mark 12:44).

The widow's sacrificial giving makes theological sense only within the narrative of Mark's Gospel, which, echoing Isaiah 52, announces that the reign of God has come near in Jesus. Now is the time to return to God. Now is the time to receive the fullness of God, who has turned to human beings totally and without reservation. Now is the time to share the gift of divine abundance with the world in the community created by Jesus. "Because the reign of God is already breaking in and the new creation of Israel has already begun, the business of the Temple cannot go on in the way that is now customary."[45]

Preaching that makes known the glory of God's reign attracts "those who are able to experience God's overflowing self-gift, so that they in turn give everything they have: their whole heart, their whole existence."[46] Giving her last two copper coins, the poor widow points to the way of God's generous love for the world. Moreover, her sacrificial love is an exemplary witness to the word spoken by Jesus in Mark 12: "You shall love the Lord your God with all your heart, and with all your soul, . . . and with all your strength."[47] The poor widow gave everything she had, holding nothing back, and therefore manifests what it is to live wholly and undivided before God.[48]

Mark's account also looks forward, in that the wholeness of the widow's giving anticipates the wholeness of Jesus's self-giving unto death.[49] We may here see the poor widow's gift as a type and participation in the paradox of the rich poverty of Christ, who, "though he

45. Lohfink, *Does God Need the Church?*, 188.
46. Lohfink, *Jesus of Nazareth*, 220.
47. Lohfink, *Jesus of Nazareth*, 220.
48. Lohfink, *Jesus of Nazareth*, 99.
49. Lohfink, *Does God Need the Church?*, 279.

was rich, yet for [our] sakes he became poor, so that by his poverty [we] might become rich" (2 Cor. 8:9).[50]

Here it is appropriate to ask if the widow should have held back something for herself. Should she have given more thought to where she would find her next meal? Are such practical considerations unimportant? Does not God allow a certain amount of calculation for the sake of self-preservation? And what if the story of the woman is merely symbolic, standing for something either behind or beyond itself? Is there not a principle, topic, ideal, or value we can extract from the "wrapping" of Mark's language, a biblical "truth" we can explain, illustrate, and apply? Does not the poor widow's sacrificial giving provide just the right touch for motivating listeners to give more generously in support of the church or a social cause? And does not the act of the poor widow provide a moral lesson that appeals to a sense of Christian duty, church commitments, and responsibility for the world?

The gospel points us elsewhere. Proclaiming the fullness of God's work in Christ summons listeners to perceive the beauty of Jesus's self-emptying to death on a cross. The poor widow's gift was a sign of the Father's giving away, of God's freely giving up his beloved Son for the life of the world. She offered all she was and had to God, but without seeking to justify herself before God. Secure in God's abundant goodness and love, she did not seek status or significance in the eyes of others. Paradoxically, her wholehearted giving in poverty, loss, and need shines with a particular richness, brilliance, and "glory" displayed by the followers of Jesus who share in his vulnerable receptivity to God. The fragile beauty that shines brightly from the depth of the poor widow's being and life gives joy to others who care for her and share their gifts with her.[51]

The joy of communion with God and others in God constitutes the beauty of the church that is built up by hearing the gospel of

50. Hans Urs von Balthasar, *The Glory of the Lord: A Theological Aesthetics*, vol. 7, *Theology: The New Covenant*, ed. John Riches, trans. Brian McNeil, CRV (San Francisco: Ignatius, 1989), 132, 429.

51. Lohfink, *Jesus of Nazareth*, 221.

Jesus Christ. "God's glory and God's liberating action meet with delighted surrender to God and each other."[52] The gospel does not merely call us to do more or give more, to work harder or more strategically, to either improve ourselves or solve the problems of the world. The beauty of preaching is made known in giving glory to God that reflects the freedom and self-giving love of Jesus. Preachers, too, give glory to God by freely surrendering themselves and their words to announcing God's wholly undivided turning toward humanity without distinctions.[53]

Mark's narrative of the gospel is a story of discipleship "in which denial of self, taking up one's cross, following Jesus, losing one's life and never being ashamed of Jesus and his words are inseparable from a right relation to the glory of God. . . . The way to acknowledge God is that of the cross, and the very concept of God's glory is thus transformed."[54] Lohfink sums up this transformation beautifully.

> When Mark speaks of the widow's sacrifice he is not only looking back to the Great Commandment quote just before. He is also looking forward to Jesus' death. This is the last story in Mark's Gospel before the passion narrative begins. For him the "whole-

---

52. Ford and Hardy, *Living in Praise*, 97.

53. Minear writes, "Obviously the gospel of Jesus is not a ready-made answer to the problem of world order such as the world seeks. Jesus did not die simply in order to be a tool by which the world can save itself. Christianity does not announce itself as a vehicle for saving a particular civilization from collapse. It begins by proclaiming a fiery judgment to which all [humankind] and nations are subject. The good news of the cross announces its revelation of the wrath of God on the body of sin and death. The mind and the institutions of society must justify themselves before the truth of God, and not vice versa. God's strategy does not first require drastic revisions in social organization of power in order to yield the desired security; it first of all creates [sons and daughters] with new hearts and casts from heaven the principalities and powers. It brings the Kingdom of God near to [humankind] so that eternal life may be received now, at the very point where world peace seems most distant and where all utopias seem impossible." Minear, *Kingdom and the Power*, 243.

54. Ford and Hardy, *Living in Praise*, 42–43.

ness" of the widow already reflects the "wholeness" of Jesus' death. The widow, with her offering, wanted to aid in providing for the Temple, the place of God's presence, the glory that was appropriate for it. Jesus gave his life so that the people of God, the place of God's presence in the world, might shine forth in its eschatological glory.[55]

Like the poor widow who placed all she had in the temple treasury, the beauty of preaching, as an offering of praise to God, will be perceived by many as unimpressive and ineffective. Some may dismiss it as irrelevant, unattractive, even "ugly" when assessed by standards other than the glory of God manifested in the humility, suffering, and death of Jesus.

On the other hand, preachers whose desire is to speak in a manner that makes known the glory of a crucified Lord will find themselves in good company with the poor widow. Their preaching will spring from a self-giving receptivity and self-emptying fullness in God's presence. At the same time, to preach with such penitent awareness of the temptation to justify oneself by superior knowledge and skill will be perceived by some as weakness, failure, and foolishness.[56] The story of the poor widow assures us that God sees, honors, and delights in Jesus, the suffering and resurrected Messiah. And God thus also sees preachers who proclaim the surprising new reality of God's reign arriving in him.

The wealthy patrons who offered their gifts in the temple were committed to a religious system that promoted and endorsed a particular kind of "glory." Jesus, however, saw in the poor widow a "strange glory" that was attentive to God and God's way with the world. Surrounded by the majestic splendor of the temple, the widow's poor image would have been perceived as a distorted form of beauty and therefore aesthetically repulsive. However, when our minds are illumined by following the way of discipleship proclaimed by Jesus, the

55. Lohfink, *Does God Need the Church?*, 279.
56. Rowan Williams, *On Christian Theology* (Oxford: Blackwell, 2000), 233–34.

strange beauty of the gospel effects a conversion of our imaginations, affections, and desires.[57] "One might call it the aesthetics of ugliness, or repulsion. But it is simultaneously a different form of beauty. It is the terrible beauty of the cross. The beauty of God is often revealed under circumstances that we would find offensive: the ugliness of the cross is the strange beauty par excellence. The paradox of this ugly beauty of the cross is that it evokes hope: in ugliness and suffering, beauty shines through and new possibilities are born."[58]

The story of the poor widow calls preachers to perceive the strange, fragile beauty of God's reign among the poor, the weak, the vulnerable, the dispossessed, the limited and incomplete—*including preachers and preaching*.[59] Although her undivided devotion to God was unnoticed, it mirrored the glory of God. She was a "living sermon"—making known God's glory to an unresponsive, unreceptive people. By honoring the poor widow, Jesus recognized her undivided love as the character of re-turning to God and God's reign, which is the way of repentance and discipleship.

The beauty of the gospel manifests a goodness so compelling that we are drawn to acknowledge that our lives and words are not our own. "The lives formed through worship must be at once beautiful and good reflecting the beauty and goodness of the One alone who is perfectly beautiful and good."[60] In Christ, God's goodness is be-

---

57. Lohfink, *Jesus of Nazareth*, 235.

58. Charles L. Campbell and Johan H. Cilliers, *Preaching Fools: The Gospel as a Rhetoric of Folly* (Waco, TX: Baylor University Press, 2012), 6.

59. Hays comments, "So, if we seek to read Scripture through Mark's eyes, what will we find? We will find ourselves drawn into the contemplation of a paradoxical revelation that shatters our categories and exceeds our understanding. We will learn to stand before the mystery in silence, to acknowledge the limitation of our understanding, and to wonder. The 'meaning' of Mark's portrayal of the identity of Jesus cannot be rightly stated in flat propositional language; instead, it can be disclosed only gradually in the form of narrative, through hints and illusions that project the story of Jesus onto the background of Israel's story." Hays, *Echoes of Scripture in the Gospels*, 103.

60. Stanley Hauerwas, *Performing the Faith: Bonhoeffer and the Practice of Nonviolence* (Grand Rapids: Brazos, 2004), 163.

held as the beauty that saves us from the ugliness of sin for a life of rejoicing in the glory of God.[61] "There is a rightful place for God's glory, and human glory as an extension of God's glory which displays God's goodness as communicated to others for their ultimate good, and for the praise of God's glory."[62]

"Your God reigns" is the good news of God who became human in Jesus Christ. The whole church is united in declaring this news when it prays, "thy kingdom come, thy will be done, on earth as it is in heaven." The messianic mission and message of Jesus cannot be separated, since his words and actions are mutually illuminating and revealing. As God's messenger of joy and message of joy, he makes known God's reign in all he says, does, and suffers. "Anyone who proclaims a joyful event is himself the bringer of joy, and is honored accordingly."[63] The whole of Jesus's life and ministry recalls the astonishing narrative of Israel's liberation from Egypt with fresh power, as a new exodus to the freedom and joy created by the announcement of God's Lordship.[64] "How beautiful upon the mountains are the feet of the messengers who proclaim peace, preach good news, announce salvation, who say to Zion, 'Your God is King!'"[65]

---

61. Bryan Stone writes, "The gospel the church offers the world is always public because it is, to put it bluntly, a body. The gospel is not a set of beliefs or doctrines that first need to be decoded and then reencoded so as to be intelligible in this or that context. The gospel is Christ himself; and Christ has a body. But bodies are public precisely because they are present. This is why it is so important that the church, which is Christ's body, be made holy in bodily ways through the worship, habits, and service it has been given by God, for as the body of Christ it is a public sign of God's glory, not its own." Bryan Stone, *Evangelism after Christendom: The Theology and Practice of Christian Witness* (Grand Rapids: Brazos, 2007), 211.

62. Rebecca Konyndyk DeYoung, *Vainglory: The Forgotten Vice* (Grand Rapids: Eerdmans, 2014), 19.

63. Jürgen Moltmann, *The Way of Jesus Christ: Christology in Messianic Dimensions*, trans. Margaret Kohl (Minneapolis: Fortress, 1990), 95.

64. Moltmann, *The Way of Jesus Christ*, 95–96.

65. "The Kingdom of glory is identical with new creation in the Lordship of God, whose efficacy already resides in this history of injustice and death, and is

The Joy of Preaching

The glory of God, God's reign of righteousness, is the joy of God without end, which is the great joy of preaching. In the preaching of Saint Paul, the gospel of God's glory and the righteousness of God's rule are intimately united in the person and work of Christ. To confess Christ as Lord is to be made alive to the new "life in God" that is God's righteousness and glory. This may also be seen as an aesthetic category; "when glory is coupled with affection and love, we can talk about grace and beauty . . . the redeeming power of God's beauty." Such "evangelical beauty" will be perceived as strange, even fearful, in that to look upon the face of God, to perceive the form of God's glory, is to receive the grace in which God's glory comes to us in the person of Christ.⁶⁶

Proclaiming the gospel shows the glory of God, who communicates his righteousness in the faithfulness of Christ, the risen Lord who generates the response of faithfulness in all who hear, believe, and "become" his gospel.⁶⁷ "We become obedient to those beautiful forms that shape our lives."⁶⁸ For example, Paul's interpretive path in Romans includes a fresh reading of Deuteronomy 30 to provide a scriptural basis for proclaiming the gospel. The preaching of Moses to Israel in Deuteronomy 30 is taken up by Paul for declaring the word of God to the nations. "The word is near you, on your lips and in your heart" (Rom. 10:8). Paul interprets this announcement to mean the word of what God has done in Jesus Christ: "If you confess with your lips that 'Jesus is Lord' and believe in your heart that 'God raised him from the dead' you will be saved. For one believes

---

accordingly to be understood as the newly creating, life-giving activity of God." Moltmann, *The Way of Jesus Christ*, 98.

66. Moltmann, *The Way of Jesus Christ*, 195.

67. A. Katherine Grieb, *The Story of Romans: A Narrative Defense of God's Righteousness* (Louisville: Westminster John Knox, 2002), xxi.

68. Stephen D. Long, *The Goodness of God: Theology, the Church, and Social Order* (Grand Rapids: Brazos, 2001), 165.

with the heart and is put right with God and one confesses with the mouth and is saved."[69]

In addition, Paul identifies the witness he and his coworkers share with the beauty of Isaiah's messengers, who hastened to announce God's liberating summons. The apostle's argument unfolds in a series of questions that lead to robust honor and appreciation of God's saving beauty in light of God's righteousness in Christ. "But how are they to call on one in whom they have not believed? And how are they to believe in one whom they have never heard? And how are they to hear without someone to preach him? And how are they to preach him unless they are sent? As it stands written, 'How beautiful are the feet of those who preach good news!'"[70]

Katherine Grieb comments on the abundant generosity of God revealed in this passage, a generosity made painfully visible in the image of God's outstretched arms. "The shame and vulnerability that Paul and his co-workers have experienced in Israel's rejection of the gospel is intrinsically related to the much deeper shame and vulnerability that Paul hears through the voices of Moses and Isaiah. God has every reason to walk away and not look back. Every reason but one: That is, God's covenant love that will not give up on Israel no matter what." Paradoxically, the beauty of proclaiming the gospel is woven into this very shame and vulnerability.[71]

Paul perceived the strange beauty of the gospel through his reading of Israel's Scripture in which the righteousness of God is disclosed. The poetic drama of the gospel does not negate or cancel God's calling and faithfulness to Israel. In addition, Paul's interpretation of Deuteronomy 30:12–14 depicts many who were seeking high and low for Christ but had actually turned their gaze toward the commandments of the law. He counters with the following: "Christ has already come down from heaven, already been raised up from

69. Grieb, *The Story of Romans*, 100.
70. Grieb, *The Story of Romans*, 102.
71. Grieb, *The Story of Romans*, 105.

the dead. In other words, God has already done the work in Christ's incarnation and resurrection and needs no help." We preachers must also discern the content and form of the word that was near to Israel in the law, the word that is identical with the word that comes near in the form of Christ's dying and rising. "Thus, Paul's interpretation presupposes what it argues and argues what it presupposes; that the real meaning of Deuteronomy 30 is disclosed not in law-keeping but in Christian preaching."[72]

The narrative of Isaiah, Mark, and Romans points us toward a "way" of preaching shaped by reading the word of Israel's Scripture in light of the life, death, and resurrection of Christ. We are called to offer our words in praise to the God of the gospel who raises up a people whose existence makes sense only if given by the God of Israel embodied in Jesus Christ. "The Christian narrative stands in contrast to explanation and understanding just to the extent that Christians offer descriptions that are unintelligible if our very existence does not come as a gift."[73]

This way of reading will be attentive to the relation between God, Scripture, the narrative of the gospel, and the concrete circumstances of our preaching to communities of hearers.[74] As Hauerwas comments, "Faithfully enacting the Christian story, then, is effectively to 'out narrate' the world by situating the world's 'givens' within a more determinative, peaceable, and hence more encompassing nar-

---

72. Hays, *Echoes of Scripture in the Letters of Paul* (New Haven: Yale University Press, 1989), 81–82. Bryan Stone notes, "If the story of the apostles shows anything, it shows that the shift in their understanding of God's salvation history occasioned by the death and resurrection of Jesus and interpreted as the fulfillment of messianic prophecy and the triumph of God over the powers is not all a shift away from Jesus' focus on God's reign. . . . Rather, it involves an insistence that since it is in the person of Jesus that God's reign has come near, the world can never be the same, and a whole new way of living is necessary and possible." *Evangelism after Christendom*, 109.

73. Hauerwas, *Performing the Faith*, 145.

74. Hauerwas, *Performing the Faith*, 139–41.

rative."[75] We read Scripture as poetic speech that shapes the identity and action of the church in the love of God that extends to the whole creation.[76] "The point is not that Scripture must be made relevant . . . rather the meaning of Scripture will never be understood at all until it is read in communities that embody the obedience of faith."[77]

Proclaiming the gospel builds up the church toward a wholly undivided way of living before God in the weak, vulnerable power of a crucified Lord. "No reading of Scripture can be legitimate, then, if it fails to shape the readers into a community that embodies the love of God as shown forth in Christ. . . . Community in the likeness of Christ is cruciform; therefore right interpretation must be cruciform."[78] We discover the joy of preaching in proclaiming a living Word, by which the Spirit transforms the church into a visible form of the righteousness of God in Christ: "the story of our life."[79]

75. Hauerwas, *Performing the Faith*, 92.

76. Richard B. Hays, *The Conversion of the Imagination: Paul as Interpreter of Israel's Scripture* (Grand Rapids: Eerdmans, 2005), xv–xvi. Hays concludes that Paul's reading of Israel's Scripture is (1) pastoral, a community-forming activity; (2) poetic, rich in image and metaphor; (3) narrative, in light of Israel's story; (4) eschatological, mindful of God's judgment on all humankind and looking forward to God's final reconciliation of all things.

77. Hays, *Echoes of Scripture in the Letters of Paul*, 184.

78. Hays, *Echoes of Scripture in the Letters of Paul*, 185. Hays notes that the Spirit illumines hearts and minds to behold the beauty of disruptive grace as prefigured in Scripture, a perceiving of the astonishing transfiguration of Scripture by the grace displayed in the self-emptying of Christ.

79. See here the classic statement by H. Richard Niebuhr, *The Meaning of Revelation* (New York: Macmillan, 1960). Eugene Peterson states well the church's need for formation over information. "It is the very nature of language to form rather than inform. When language is personal, which it is at its best, it reveals; and revelation is always formative—we don't know more, we become more. Our best users of language, poets and lovers and children and saints, use words to make—make intimacies, make character, make beauty, make goodness, make truth." Eugene H. Peterson, *Eat This Book: A Conversation in the Art of Spiritual Reading* (Grand Rapids: Eerdmans, 2006), 24. See also the important work of Pierre Hadot, which draws from the practices of ancient philosophy and early Christianity to show the formative nature of reading as transformative of the

The end or purpose of Paul's narrative of the gospel is that Christians will live and speak in a manner that gives glory to God according to the divine plan (Rom. 15:8).[80] Here Paul's proclamation of God's gift in Christ provides good insight for discerning a missionary theology of preaching. God's gift of his Son, or Christ's self-gift, is the focal expression of divine grace that is generously extended to Israel and the gentiles, a calling that is all of God, of grace, irrespective of ethnicity, status, education, virtue, gender, ancestry, and social power. The preaching of this missionary gospel "clarifies and radicalizes the incongruity of the gift of Christ."[81]

Paul understood the single event of Christ as bringing into question and dissolving every preexistent classification of worth, since the *incongruous* grace of God is given without distinctions. The Christ-gift thus forms the basis for innovative groups of converts, uniting them in their common faith in Christ, so that ties to former norms and distinctions are loosened. "Such social identities continue to exist, but they are declared insignificant as markers of worth in a community beholden to Christ. . . . Novel communities are encouraged

---

intellect, imagination, affections, and will. Interpretation is a "spiritual exercise" that involves one's whole way of being in the art of living wisely and well. Pierre Hadot, *Philosophy as a Way of Life*, ed. Arnold I. Davidson, trans. Michael Chase (Oxford: Blackwell, 1995), 47–144.

80. Williams, *On Christian Theology*, 254–58. Grieb writes of the concluding section of Romans: "The nature of the instruction is the enkindling of hope, which points forward to the eschatological uniting of Jews and Gentiles. God's integrity . . . is thus also the grounds for Christian ethics, since the correspondences between the Jesus narrative and the Scriptures of Israel reveal God's trustworthiness and truthfulness. It is this God of steadfastness and encouragement who speaks of hope through the steadfastness and encouragement of the Scripture. Paul closes this section (Rom 15:1–6) of his conclusion with a prayer—that the God of hope will unite the community of Christians at Rome, powerful and powerless together, in conformity to the pattern of the Messiah and therefore as a sign of the coming eschatologically united community of Jews and Gentiles." Grieb, *The Story of Romans*, 131.

81. John M. G. Barclay, *Paul and the Gift* (Grand Rapids: Eerdmans, 2015), 567. Hereafter, page references from this work will be given in parentheses in the text.

to relativize their differences in culture, welcoming one another on the unconditioned terms by which each was welcomed in Christ (Rom. 14–15)" (567).

Barclay's summary of Paul's missionary preaching and community-forming work offers much insight for the consideration of preaching as "beautiful." The self-gift of Christ is received from God and returned to God, creating a life that is "fitting" for God and humanity, imparting new standards of worth and value in the practice of those who speak and listen.

> The goal of Paul's mission is the formation of communities whose distinct patterns of life bear witness to an event that has broken with normal criteria of worth. Paul expects baptism to create new life orientations, including forms of bodily habitus that express the reality of resurrection life in the midst of human mortality. The gift needs to be realized in unconventional practice or it ceases to have meaning as incongruous gift. It creates new modes of obedience to God, which arise from the gift as "return" to God, but without instrumental purpose in eliciting further divine gifts. The transformative power of grace thus creates a fit between believers and God, which will be evident at the eschaton. (569)

Paul's notion of the gift provides pastoral wisdom for a new social movement that has its roots in a missionary theology of grace. Grace can mean "the quality of charm or agreeableness," or "the attitude of benevolence," or "gratitude or thanksgiving." Grace thus denotes the graciousness of the giver and the gratitude returned without any instrumental purpose (575–82).

Grace lends itself nicely to the nature of the church's existence as a people called to offer honor, sacrifice, worship, and praise to God. However, this extends beyond Paul's pioneering mission to include our contemporary pluralist and secularizing context, in which churches find themselves needing to rediscover their social, political, and cultural identity, which is all of grace, and thus beautiful. "Taken for granted criteria of value regarding age, ethnicity, social status, education, gender, health, or wealth become in such circumstances the object of critical reevaluation, and churches identify anew what it is about the good news that makes them socially and ideologically distinctive" (573).

Paul writes, "May the God of steadfastness and encouragement grant you to live in harmony with one another, in accordance with Christ Jesus, so that together you may with one voice glorify the God and Father of our Lord Jesus Christ" (Rom. 15:5–6). Doxology—right praise or glory—brackets the body of the letter, which is introduced with these words: "First, I thank my God through Jesus Christ for all of you, because your faith is proclaimed throughout the world" (Rom. 1:8) (459–61). The apostle calls upon Jewish and gentile Christians to welcome one another because Christ has first welcomed them, that they stand together before God on the basis of Christ's welcome alone (Rom. 15:7) (512). Their very existence is due "to the creative mercy of God and to a life created for them, and beyond them, by the resurrection of Jesus. . . . [God's incongruous grace] . . . is the root of Israel's existence and the reality that grounds the identities and loyalties of Jews and Gentiles in Christ" (455).

A Homiletical Aesthetic

Paul affirms that Christ came to serve Israel as a confirmation of God's promises and faithfulness. But Christ also came for the inclusion of the gentiles: specifically, that they might know God's mercy and be joined with Israel in giving glory to God (Rom. 15:7–8). Practical issues such as competing for honor, ethnic conflict, moral pride, and partisan divisions are addressed in light of proclaiming the good news and giving praise to God.[82] In addition to right doctrine or morality, it is doxology, "right praise or glory," that is able to generate

82. Williams, *On Christian Theology*, 255.

and guide the perceptions, dispositions, values, and beauty that are embodied in a community's life and practice.[83]

Preachers would do well to follow Paul's lead by reading Israel's Scripture in light of the gospel to provide a theological basis for the church's mission of proclaiming and showing God's glory to the nations (Rom. 15:9-12).[84] The apostle's commission to proclaim God's work of reconciling Jews and gentiles in Christ is itself a participation in the mystery of God's self-revelation hidden through the ages. Giving glory to God is both the motivation and the goal of proclaiming the gospel of God's righteousness.[85]

Preachers will also benefit from giving careful attention to how the apostle addresses the Christians in Rome as fellow believers and servants of Christ, encouraging them to live in a manner that becomes the gospel they believe and confess. God's glory is manifested in a life of mutual love and harmony that has Christ as its source and norm. "If we accept each other for the glory of God (Rom. 15:7)"—Williams sees this as an essential part of a self-consistency and faithfulness that issue finally in the joy and gratitude of the

83. Barclay, *Paul and the Gift*, 504-5. Barclay draws from the work of Pierre Bourdieu to show that Paul's ethic of Christian community moves at a deeper level than norms and rules, but rather constitutes a culture, or *habitus*, that entails dispositions, sensibilities, and perceptions that are produced by practices and govern practices and are best understood as embodied habits. Barclay points to Paul's language of gift; the Christians in Rome are a "community constructed by unconditioned welcome," so that honor, worth, and glory do not need to be sought and competed for, but have been and will be given by God (508-12). See the excellent discussion of doxology as a way of life in Catherine Mowry LaCugna, *God for Us: The Trinity and Christian Life* (San Francisco: HarperSanFrancisco, 1991), 342-57.

84. Ford and Hardy discuss a way of reading and interpreting Scripture practiced by Israel and the church that centers on the praise of God. "The fact of praise is a particularly good way of getting to the heart of the Bible because in praise there was the supreme attempt to acknowledge to God what was most fundamental for the community: God and God's activity." *Living in Praise*, 31.

85. Williams, *On Christian Theology*, 255-56.

non-Jewish world. Gentiles rejoice in God not only because they have been granted the privilege of grace, but also because the glory of God is made plain to them. "Indeed the gift is inseparable from the delight."[86]

Williams comments, "Giving glory is practically identical with rejoicing in God, being glad that God is God, not merely that God is well-disposed towards us."[87] The intrinsically joyful nature of preaching as an act of faith is grounded in the generosity of God and integrally related to the church's missionary vocation. The starting point and end of mission are offering praise and thanks to God for who God is and for what God has done.[88] The end of preaching is found in knowing and enjoying God's glory, "in seeing something of what God eternally is."[89]

The proclamation of God's righteousness, God's turning in mercy toward both Israel and the gentiles, requires that we attend to its aesthetic and homiletic quality. "Delight in the beauty of God is the goal of our action, what we minister to each other and the human world at large."[90] Our preaching will point away from ourselves to the saving beauty of God's generous self-giving in Christ, which embraces Israel and the nations. The humility of God in Christ will dispose us to acknowledge that our achievement of successful communication cannot itself produce the love of the Father and the Son, which is poured into our hearts by the Holy Spirit.[91] Like the poor widow,

86. Williams, *On Christian Theology*, 254–55.

87. Williams, *On Christian Theology*, 255.

88. Williams, *On Christian Theology*, 255–56. Ford and Hardy, *Living in Praise*, 31, write, "It is of the greatest importance to the whole of Christian communication that it be praise-centered. . . . The essence of mission and evangelism is in the intrinsic worth, beauty, and love of God, and the joy of knowing and trusting in God."

89. Williams, *On Christian Theology*, 255.

90. Williams, *On Christian Theology*, 255.

91. Here Grieb's comments on the calling of the church as perceiving and displaying God's glory are helpful. "Loving the neighbor also has implications

we seek to proclaim and make known the fullness of God's identity and work in Christ that generates a beauty received in Christ, and lived through Christ, as a visible expression of God's glory.[92] *This is the beauty of preaching.*

---

for the Roman Christians in their life together. They ought to welcome one another because God and Christ have already welcomed the other. Paul uses the language of relation to redescribe the neighbor as the 'work of God' and as 'the brother or sister for whom Christ died' in such a way that gratitude to God and Christ for the work of redemption accomplished on the cross is naturally expressed in the serving of the neighbor who is likewise the recipient of the same gracious mercy. Finally, loving the neighbor means imitating the Messiah in whom the Gentiles hope by following him in mission to the Gentiles." Grieb, *The Story of Romans,* 133.

92. Barclay, *Paul and the Gift,* 519.

– two –

SEEING BEAUTY

This chapter is an appreciative remembrance of the evangelical beauty that shines brightly from a narrative in the fourteenth chapter of Mark's Gospel (14:1–9). The setting is a few days before Passover, when the religious leaders are secretly looking to arrest Jesus and hoping to put him to death. This scenario follows the end of Mark 13, a "little apocalypse" in which Jesus calls his followers to be always awake and alert for the arrival of God's reign: "Watch, ye, therefore, for ye know not when the master of the house cometh, at evening, or at midnight, or at cockcrow, or in the morning, lest coming suddenly he finds you sleeping" (13:35–36). Richard Hays comments on the strange gospel of the crucified Christ and the nature of the communities its proclamation creates. "The political posture of the church, then, as it awaits the eschatological disclosure of Jesus' glory as the Son of Man, is one of patient, watchful, endurance. . . . They are simply to proclaim the good news of the kingdom, despite its paradoxical probability, and to accept whatever suffering may come as a result."[1]

---

1. Richard B. Hays, *Echoes of Scripture in the Gospels* (Waco, TX: Baylor University Press, 2016), 97; Oliver O'Donovan writes of the command of wakefulness, which applies to preachers and the ministry of the Word. "And so the command to wake is addressed in the New Testament chiefly to the church, which ought to be able to count, if any agent could, on being awake already. It sets the church in a moment of crisis, put on the spot, by relating the achieved past to the future

Jesus's command to be alert becomes even more urgent when Jesus travels to Bethany, on the outskirts of Jerusalem, where he goes to the home of a man named Simon the Leper. In the Gospels, table fellowship at the homes of social outcasts, sinners, and the excommunicated such as Simon provides surprising appearances of God's reign when Jesus is present. Each of these scenes points to a particular depth in the conditions of people's lives, out of which unexpected expressions of repentant love are opened to God's boundless goodness and mercy. The astonishing implication is that the joy of the messianic banquet, celebrating the time of Israel's restoration, is experienced as women and men are welcomed by Jesus into the fellowship of God's reign without distinctions. Rowan Williams notes how Jesus is himself the defining focus of "a new people, a new citizenship, a new kingdom . . . functioning as the God of Jewish Scripture." He continues,

> He creates a people by covenant . . . and by a summons that makes something radically new. In giving to the outcast, the powerless, the freedom to take their part in renewing the world and setting aside the existing tyranny of faceless powers and human betrayals, God brings life out of emptiness, reality out of nothing: Jesus Christ, as the bodily presence of that summons, the concrete medium for that gift to be given, is the presence in our world of the absolute creative resource of God, God's capacity to make the difference between something and nothing. God has chosen things low and contemptible, mere nothings, to overthrow the

---

of Christ's coming and to the immediate future of attention and action. Wakefulness is anything but a settled state, something we may presume on, as we can usually presume we are awake to go about our business. It brings us sharply back to the task in hand: the deed to be performed, the life to be lived. Waking is thrust on us. We do not consider it. That is why it is not just one metaphor among many for moral experience, but stands guard over the birth of renewed moral responsibility." Oliver O'Donovan, *Self, World, and Time: Ethics as Theology, Volume 1; An Induction* (Grand Rapids: Eerdmans, 2013), 9.

existing order (I Cor. 1:28); Jesus, reaching out to those who are nothing, is the tangible form of God's choosing.[2]

Both in who he is and what he says, does, and suffers, Jesus manifests God's kingdom. "Whoever touches this man, touches God in every instance. . . . Whoever sees or hears this man, sees and hears God himself. Whoever receives this man in his home, shelters God under his roof. Whoever eats and drinks with this man eats and drinks with God . . . in His kingdom."[3]

The meal with Jesus at the home of a leper was enjoyed in stark contrast to an earlier meal in Mark's Gospel: a gathering in the household of King Herod that was an impressive display of wealth, social influence, and political power or "glory" (Mark 6). However, as Gerhard Lohfink notes, "The glory that illuminated Israel through Jesus was not for the purpose of creating a better life for the privileged, but to bring the divine brilliance through Israel to the whole world."[4]

All were seated in Simon's home when an unnamed woman appeared holding an alabaster jar of expensive ointment of nard, something typically associated with luxurious excess and sensuality. The Song of Songs, for example, has the bridegroom describing the charm and beauty of his maiden: "Ah, you are beautiful, my beloved, truly lovely" (1:16). He calls her to accompany him and praises the fragrance of her love:

> How sweet is your love, my sister, my bride! . . .
> Your channel is an orchard of pomegranates
>   with all choicest fruits,
>   henna with nard,

2. Rowan Williams, *On Christian Theology* (Oxford: Blackwell, 2000), 231.

3. Peter Brunner, *Worship in the Name of Jesus*, trans. M. H. Bertram (St. Louis: Concordia, 1968), 64.

4. Gerhard Lohfink, *Does God Need the Church? Toward a Theology of the People of God*, trans. Linda M. Maloney (Collegeville, MN: Liturgical Press, 1999), 146-49, 150.

> nard and saffron, calamus and cinnamon,
>> with all trees of frankincense,
> myrrh and aloes,
>> with all chief spices—
> a garden fountain, a well of living water,
>> and flowing streams from Lebanon. (4:10–15)

When such extravagant praise of the beloved is expressed, its loveliness overflows to affect others.

> Awake, O north wind,
>> and come, O south wind!
> Blow upon my garden
>> that its fragrance may be wafted abroad. (4:16)

Bernard of Clairvaux offers this meditation from the Canticle on the beauty of the Word.

> Thus for the Word to say to the soul, You are beautiful, and to call her friend, is to impart that which empowers her to love and to know she is loved. But for her, in response, to call the Word Beloved and to confess that he is beautiful is to give him, truthfully and sincerely, the credit for her loving and her being loved. It is to marvel at his kindness and to wonder at his grace. Accordingly, the Bridegroom's beauty is his love: which is all the greater for its being prior to the Bride's. Therefore she cries out—with all her heart and with words of deep feeling—that she must love him, and the more fully and fervently because she realizes that he loved her before he was loved by her. Thus the Word's "speech" is the imparting of a gift, and the soul's response is a rendering of thanks accompanied by wonder.[5]

5. *The Song of Songs: Interpreted by Early Christian and Medieval Commentators*, trans. and ed. Richard Norris Jr., Church's Bible (Grand Rapids: Eerdmans, 2003), 82–83.

Breaking open the jar, the woman poured the ointment onto the head of Jesus as an act of love and devotion, anointing him in anticipation of his suffering and death. Some of those present were outraged by this ostensibly foolish, wasteful act, protesting that the value of the nard, approximately one year's wages, should have been used for the poor, as required by the law (cf. Deut. 15). Jesus told them to leave the woman alone, declaring that she had done a *"beautiful thing."*

This was not a time for calculating what could be accomplished given the arrival of God's reign in Jesus. No amount of human action can replace the extravagance of God's mercy displayed in Christ, who pours himself out for the life of the world. Robert Jenson comments on the Song of Songs: "According to the doctrine of the Trinity, God's Word to us is 'true God from true God . . . of one being with the Father.' God's Speech to us is both 'with' the Creator and is the Creator. . . . We are created, and so exist and exist as what we are, by the very Speech of God that tells us we are good and beautiful and righteous."[6]

It has been said of the unnamed woman that she "is one of the archetypal images [in Scripture] of the essence of praise as recognition and sacrificial honoring. Jesus accepts it with a reference to his death, which will justify it."[7] Jesus did not agree with those who insisted the woman sell the ointment to support the disciples' plans. He knew the poor would not be fully satisfied, since the glory of God's rule includes but also exceeds human practicality and needs. Here the comments of Stanley Hauerwas are apt:

> Christianity is a faith of the poor. This woman poured precious ointment on a poor person. The poor that we will always have with us is Jesus. It is to the poor person that all extravagance is to

6. Robert W. Jenson, *Song of Songs*, Interpretation: A Bible Commentary for Teaching and Preaching (Louisville: Westminster John Knox, 2005), 46.

7. David F. Ford and Daniel W. Hardy, *Living in Praise: Worshiping and Knowing God* (Grand Rapids: Baker Academic, 2005), 43.

be given. The wealth of the church is the wealth of the poor. The beauty of a cathedral is a beauty that does not exclude but in fact draws and includes the poor. The beauty of the church's liturgy, its music and its hymns, is a beauty of and for the poor. The literature of the church, its theology and philosophy, are distorted if they do not contribute to our common life, life in which the poor are central, determined by the worship of God. The church's wealth, the precious ointment poured by this woman on Jesus, is never wasted on the poor. . . . This woman, this unnamed woman, has done for Jesus what the church must always be for the world—precious ointment poured lavishly on the poor.[8]

Only the compelling vision of a useless God can transform our imaginations to perceive the beauty of Jesus as the suffering, crucified, and exalted Lord. David Kelsey makes this point clearly. "God conceived functionally is God conceived, however subtly, as a utilitarian adjunct to whatever problem God solves. My intuition is that the only God who could make a difference to evil, sins, and bondage in sin is God conceived in the first instance as useless, an overwhelmingly attractive good in God's own right, quite independently of any differences God might make in relation to us and our problems."[9]

Proclaiming the glory of God incarnate in the vulnerability of Jesus evokes faith well suited for recognizing the "useless" beauty of his self-giving love. Similarly, the unnamed woman's wasteful act of anointing Jesus was not useful for any purpose other than delighting in his presence at the home of a poor leper. *According to Jesus, this was its beauty.* God generously shares the wonder of his glory as a divine gift of gratitude and joy that embodies itself in a responsive way of

8. Stanley Hauerwas, *Matthew*, Brazos Theological Commentary on the Bible (Grand Rapids: Brazos, 2006), 184.

9. David H. Kelsey, *Eccentric Existence: A Theological Anthropology*, vol. 2 (Louisville: Westminster John Knox, 2009), 1037.

speaking and living in the world.[10] Gerhard Lohfink's comments are a stirring invitation to proclaim the beauty of God's reign: "To be so moved by God's cause that one gives everything for its sake is not something one can ultimately do out of a bare awareness of duty, a 'thou shalt!' or certainly 'you must!' That we freely will what God wills is evidently possible only when we behold bodily the beauty of God's cause, so that we take joy in and even lust after what God wants to do in the world, and so that this desire for God and God's cause is greater than all our human self-centeredness."[11]

The measure of who we are and what we do is not our usefulness; rather, it is the joy of sharing the glory of God's self-giving as the Creator and Redeemer of all that is. In loving attentiveness to Jesus, the woman perceived the glory of God's reign shining brightly in and all around him. Similarly, the vocation of the church as worship does not fit into the world of use and efficiency, or achievement and success. Josef Pieper makes this distinction well: "'We praise you, we glorify you; we give you thanks for your great glory.' . . . How can that be understood in the categories of rational usefulness and efficiency . . . ? The lover, too, stands outside the tight claim of efficiency of the working world . . . and is oriented to and concerned with astonishment and wonder."[12]

Despite good intentions and efforts to improve ourselves, grow the church, or change the world, our efforts are insufficient in light of God's extravagant self-giving that is the source of all we are and do. The glory of our life is revealed in the beauty of Christ, freely given and free of all debt or deserving. However, ignoring this truth leads to worship without devotion, knowledge without love, works without faith, action without prayer, obedience without joy, duty without com-

---

10. Mark A. McIntosh, *Divine Teaching: An Introduction to Christian Theology* (Oxford: Blackwell, 2008), 234.

11. Gerhard Lohfink, *Jesus of Nazareth: What He Wanted, Who He Was*, trans. Linda M. Maloney (Collegeville, MN: Liturgical Press, 2012), 235.

12. Josef Pieper, *Leisure: The Basis of Culture*, trans. Gerald Malsbary, introduction by Roger Scruton (South Bend, IN: St. Augustine's, 1998), 68.

passion, goodness without delight, and "morality without doxology."[13] As Michael Hanby comments, "The doxological self is thus able to participate in the life of the Trinity by virtue of a doxological character which it cannot escape, but can only pervert," and "nihilism can arise only when doxology fails, and *all that is not doxology is nihilism.*"[14]

Rather than providing answers, arguments, or solutions, the Spirit raises up communities of prayer and praise whose delight is participating in the Son's offering of himself back to the Father in undivided love. And while it is true that the poor must be served in their need, in God's reign the poor are gladly welcomed by a people whose way of life is shaped by the Spirit according to the dying and rising of Christ. Pope Francis writes of ministry with the poor as requiring such loving attentiveness.

> We may not always be able to reflect adequately the beauty of the gospel, but there is one sign which we should never lack: the option for those who are least, those whom society discards. . . . We are called to find Christ in them, to lend our voices to their causes, but also to be their friends, to listen to them, to speak for them and to embrace the mysterious wisdom which God wishes to share with us through them. . . . This loving attentiveness is the beginning of a true concern for their person which inspires me effectively to see their good. This entails appreciating the poor in their goodness, in their experience of life, in their culture, and in their ways of living the faith. True love is always contemplative, and permits us to serve the other not out of necessity or vanity, but rather because he or she is beautiful above and beyond mere appearances.[15]

13. Alan Kreider and Eleanor Kreider, *Worship and Mission after Christendom* (Scottdale, PA: Herald, 2011), 152.

14. Cited in Marc Nicholas, *Jean Danielou's Doxological Humanism: Trinitarian Contemplation and Humanity's True Vocation* (Eugene, OR: Pickwick, 2012), 161.

15. Pope Francis, *The Joy of the Gospel (Evangelii Gaudium): Apostolic Exhortation* (Vatican City: Libreria Editrice Vaticana, 2013), 99–100.

The splendor of God's great love for the world in Jesus cannot be calculated, commodified, or controlled, since it exceeds what is merely needed and surpasses all intentions, strategies, and efforts. The church thus perceives the truth and goodness of its life in beholding the glory that shines forth from proclaiming the incarnate, crucified, and risen Lord. As Jesus reminded the woman's critics, which included his disciples, while the poor and their needs would always be with them, to share his company generates a life of joy that springs from and moves toward God's generative love. Thus what began as a humble meal at the home of a poor leper was transformed into a glorious banquet radiating the beauty of God's time of salvation in fellowship with Jesus. The truth of God in Christ and in his church remains the foundation of the love of God and neighbor, a love that is the fulfillment of the whole law.

Jesus's approval of the woman's act neither condoned the existence of poverty nor blessed indifference to the poor. Citing Deuteronomy 15, he recalled the identity of Israel as a people called to witness God's justice and mercy in the world, a call to remember their deliverance from Egypt and to provide generously for those in need. As the Torah states, "There will be no poor among you," since you were called to "open your hand to the poor and needy neighbor in your land" (Deut. 15:11, 14).[16] Moreover, Jesus's pleasure in the beauty of the woman's act challenged the ugliness of her critics. The joy of recognizing his presence evokes "doxological gratitude" for God's generous love without regard to prior merit, achievement, status, and health. Ford and Hardy offer this insight:

> All one has and is, all one's energy, freedom, imagination and thought are tested and stretched in adoration of God; yet this supreme effort only rings true as it also acknowledges that God is its initiator and inspirer. All glory goes to God, but as it does so, God works his never-failing but never-to-be-taken-for-granted

---

16. See the discussion in Lohfink, *Does God Need the Church?*, 82–84.

surprise: freedom is returned as a gift which can once again be used to thank God and offer itself joyfully back in amazed praise. The coming together of divine and human freedom is not experienced as a reduction of human responsibility; rather, the call to free self-giving is intensified and empowered, and praise is the experience of this, to which all the rest of life needs to be conformed.[17]

Blinded by preoccupation with their self-importance—standards of religious duty, moral obligation, and social status—the disciples could not see that the law's fulfillment is found in receptivity to the astonishing love present in Jesus.

While they knew the law required God's justice to be extended in solidarity with the poor, they were more concerned with justifying themselves, their plans, and their accomplishments. Here Williams comments on religious performance:

> The life of Jesus—insofar as it can be characterized in a few brief phrases—has to do with proclaiming and enacting a disturbing truth: that achievement in the terms of a religious ordering of things is not of itself decisive in forming the reaction of God to the human world, and that what is decisive is a commitment of trust in God's compassion that shows itself in costly and painful letting go of the obsessions of the self—both the obsessive search for the perfectly satisfying performance and the obsessive search for the perfectly unconstrained experience. Indeed, these two apparently antithetical urges are shown to have an uncomfortable amount in common: the unprincipled rich man, the unreflectively vindictive servant, the person who unquestioningly indulges aggressive or lustful fantasy are close kin to the accumulator of religious merit. . . . To all such, the word of judgment is addressed:

17. Ford and Hardy, *Living in Praise*, 12–13.

the person who faces inner contradiction, failure, the breakdown of performance and the emptiness of gratification, is the person who is capable of hearing and answering the invitation to loss and trust.[18]

Such insensitivity to the wonder of God's mercy belies a failure to imagine the astonishing newness of God's reign arriving in Jesus. Moreover, a calculated concern for not having enough is answered by the presence of Jesus, from whom God's abundant goodness flows beyond all measure. "When at last the one human being appeared who was entirely and completely at one with God's will, the reign of God also appeared in a surprising and even alarming fullness."[19]

The failure of the disciples was aesthetic as well as moral, since to "see" the beautiful is what love is. The problem was not merely lack of knowledge or power, what they needed to know and do, but the impoverishment of their imaginations, an inability to see beyond their own perceptions, calculations, and desires. To "see," "believe," and "enjoy" God's glory require a giving away of one's whole self, since without wholehearted surrender faith remains divided and turned away from God. The nature of Jesus's ministry is the very enactment of God's reconciliation with estranged creatures that draws them into the Trinitarian communion of love. Such love grasps the whole person in single-minded attentiveness and desire, which is a letting go of the self into the self-giving of God.

Love to God enacted in practices of prayer expresses a passionate desire for communion with God. It is contemplative in that it engages all of a living human personal body's powers in a wholehearted single-minded focus on the sheer reality of the

18. Williams, *On Christian Theology*, 269.
19. Lohfink, *Does God Need the Church?*, 140.

community-in-communion that constitutes the triune God's living reality as a good in and of itself, and not for any benefit it might bestow. It is an act of contemplative adoration in that it passionately seeks to participate in its own creaturely way in that same life of community-in-communion. That is the quality of creaturely life that characterizes life in the new creation of God's eschatological reign of transformative justice, deep peace, and lasting joy. It is thus an active presenting of oneself before God, offering oneself to God, acknowledging that one is not self-constituted and therewith letting go of oneself.[20]

Proclaiming the beauty of gospel is expressed in joyful praise for God's foolish generosity displayed in the life and ministry of Christ. Seen from this perspective, the woman's response was supremely fitting for the glory radiating from the presence of Jesus. Her act was also timely for the new age of God's reign of peace that welcomes the poor, the outcast, the unclean, and the brokenhearted. Here Balthasar's insightful comments are helpful.

This ability to be poor is the human person's deepest wealth; this is revealed by the Christ event, in which the essence of being became visible for the very first time: as glory. In giving up his Son, God the Father has opened up the possibility for all. But the Spirit of God is sent to change this possibility into reality. He shows the world that the poverty of the Son, who sought only the glory of the Father and let himself be robbed of everything in utter obedience, was the most exact expression of the absolute fullness, which does not consist of having but of "being = giving." It is in giving that one is and has.[21]

20. Kelsey, *Eccentric Existence*, 2:1032.
21. Hans Urs von Balthasar, *The Glory of the Lord: A Theological Aesthetics*, vol. 7, *Theology: The New Covenant*, ed. John Riches, trans. Brian McNeil, CRV (San Francisco: Ignatius, 1989), 391.

These reflections point to the need for preachers to be attentive to God's abundant goodness in Christ. An imagination shaped by scarcity and need is an imagination that is unable to perceive the sufficiency of God as the source of every good gift, including the use of words in the ministry of the Word that constitutes preaching.

> There is no equivalence between God's abundance and human wealth or happiness. . . . On the contrary, it is a witness that God's gifts are etched most starkly in the face of human poverty and often recognized most distinctly in the face of human suffering. What is the accumulation of wealth but insulation against dependence on the gifts of God? Is the accumulation of wealth not therefore a proclamation of God's scarcity? What is the absence of wealth but a dependence on the gifts of God—friendship, hospitality, the sharing of food? Is the voluntary absence of wealth not therefore a proclamation of the sufficiency of the gifts of God given in the practices of the Church?[22]

The beauty of the unnamed woman's act illumines the "eyes" of our hearts to behold and to proclaim with joy the abundant goodness of God's reign present in Jesus. What she did displayed "a kind of beauty and allure that is almost irresistible. . . . Such ministry has about it a freshness, an improvisatory character, a loveliness that is itself infectious. And thus an imagination that is at its heart a seeing in depth."[23]

Moreover, the beauty of the woman's act was more than decoration or embellishment. It was more than something "added on" but only tangentially related to the desire, substance, and character of her

22. Samuel Wells, *God's Companions: Reimagining Christian Ethics* (Malden, MA: Blackwell, 2006), 8.

23. Craig Dykstra, "Keys to Excellence," in L. Gregory Jones and Kevin R. Armstrong, *Resurrecting Excellence: Shaping Faithful Christian Ministry* (Grand Rapids: Eerdmans, 2006), 125.

gift. The meaning of what she did, what was recognized by Jesus as "beautiful," was intrinsic to the act itself: the joy of sharing friendship with Jesus and all he welcomes into the community of God's reign. Moreover, unlike the unnamed woman who fixed her gaze on Jesus, the disciples were unable to "see" the end-time drama irrupting in their midst. The woman's act was profoundly eschatological, pointing to a fullness that will be revealed in the consummation of all things: the great banquet of God's reign and the wedding supper of the Lamb.[24]

> It really happened, and it constantly happens, that the Church concerns itself for human hunger in admirable aid campaigns but does not thereby change the world's sick society; in fact it cannot hope to change it in this way. But it also happened, and continues to happen, that the church becomes what in God's terms it should be: the eschatological people of God that allows itself to be gathered by Jesus into that new society in which the abundance of the reign of God shines forth. This eschatological form of the people of God was already incorporated by Jesus and after Easter it became a reality through the Crucified and Risen One.[25]

24. Kelsey writes of practices that are expressive of hope in response to the not-yet of God's future actualization of the eschatological consummation prefigured now by the resurrection of crucified Jesus. "They are practices that aim at being responsive to the future oriented liberating triune missio Dei within their . . . proximate contexts by participating in it. They are not practices that aim to bring in or build God's eschatological reign. Nor are they optimistic practices based on realistic analysis that warrants the judgment that given proximate contexts offer the resources and dynamics that would make revolutionary development of communities of transformative justice likely in the future. Rather, they are practices seeking to enact appropriate responses to God's having already inaugurated fulfillment of promised eschatological blessing." *Eccentric Existence*, 2:1030. See the discussion in Lohfink on the superabundance and glory of God's eschatological reign in Jesus's sharing of meals and feeding the multitudes. Lohfink, *Does God Need the Church?*, 143–50.

25. Lohfink, *Does God Need the Church?*, 148.

The unnamed woman's act recalled Israel's election as a people who exist for the praise of God's glory. God established and filled the temple with his glory, uniting Israel's worship with faithful obedience to the law in the conditions of everyday life. The prophet Zechariah (chaps. 9–15) looks forward to the end time when Israel's life will be brought to fullness at the final advent of God's rule over the whole earth, a time when the temple will shine anew. Everything in Jerusalem and Judah will receive its radiance from the temple's holiness as the reign of God is established by the sanctification of all things. In Mark's Gospel the present reality of this "end-time" way of life, voiced and made visible by Jesus, is "proclaimed" by an unnamed woman in the home of a leper. The glory of the temple has become fully incarnate in Jesus. Wherever he is shines brightly with the splendor of God's rule; in him the whole creation has become a dwelling place of God. In the end, moreover, all things will be transfigured and conformed to God's will in the glory of God's reign.[26] As Ford and Hardy note, "The supreme social benefit of praising God is, however, that it helps in discovering the strongest of objective bonds with others; the link through the reality of God. To praise God as Creator and Father giving himself for everyone through Jesus Christ in the Holy Spirit: that is to route all one's relationships through God, and to open them up to God's future for them. Praise actualizes the true relationship between people as well as with God, and it is no accident that in the symbols of heavenly bliss the leading pictures are feasting and praising."[27]

This is the "today" proclaimed in Christian worship: the time of the Spirit whose abundant outpouring of love completes the new creation brought by the life, death, and resurrection of Jesus. Preaching the gospel is an eschatological act: faith comes by hearing God

26. See here Hays, *Echoes of Scripture in the Gospels*, 81–83; see also Lohfink's discussion of the temple and the ministry of Jesus. *Does God Need the Church?*, 187–94.

27. Ford and Hardy, *Living in Praise*, 14.

speaking in the incarnate, crucified, and risen Lord of all things, who is with us and addresses us "today."

> The church, in all its practices of worship and especially in its practices of praise and preaching, is infused with the life of God so that the body of the church itself glows with the Spirit's radiance, as it is permeated with the beauty of God's holiness. This is no static radiance, for the holiness of the people, which is the holiness of God shining through the people, is displayed in the consecrated life of worship, obedience, and sacrifice, a life that has the particular shape and beauty of Jesus, in whose image the church is being formed through the Spirit.[28]

The story of the unnamed woman shows that what we do and say is not different from who we are. She perceived in Jesus a whole new world that is given by the Spirit's outpouring of God's self-giving love. Expressing his pleasure in the woman's act, Jesus honored her for the beautiful thing she had done. Paradoxically, while the beauty of the unnamed woman's act exceeded the conditions of her particular time and place, it honored Jesus as the visible advent of God's rule in a poor leper's home.

Remembering the unnamed woman directs our gaze to the incarnate, crucified, and risen Lord, whose gospel we have heard and proclaim. The risen Lord whose presence we declare pours out the Spirit, who heals, strengthens, and renews the church as a visible sign and expression of the reconciliation of all things. The radiant beauty of God's goodness displayed by Jesus calls forth adoring praise that overflows in the proclamation of the gospel with our whole selves for the sake of the world.

---

28. L. Roger Owens, *The Shape of Participation: A Theology of Church Practices* (Eugene, OR: Cascade, 2010), 15. Owens is commenting on the reflections of Rev. William C. Turner, pastor of Mt. Level Baptist Church in Durham, North Carolina.

Remembering the Beauty of the Unnamed Woman's Act in Preaching

Mark begins the story of Jesus, "The beginning of the gospel of Jesus Christ, the Son of God." As Rowan Williams comments, "Precisely because glory is not something that is capable of being mastered and because beauty is not something which can be domesticated into the self's agenda, encounter with glory and beauty might be said to be more like hearing than some kinds of seeing."[29] Homiletical beauty requires vulnerable receptivity to the Word, who by the Spirit draws us into the Trinitarian economy of love. Moreover, without the Spirit's gift of delight that inspires love for the beauty of the Father's self-sharing in the Son, preaching lacks the life-giving power of the gospel. "God's graciousness, which brings what is not into existence from nothing, is exactly the same as Jesus' death-less self-giving out of love which enables him to break the human culture of death and is a self-giving which is entirely fixed on bringing into being a radiantly living and exuberant culture."[30]

The story of the unnamed woman raises important questions for preachers, since the closest followers of Jesus could not perceive the beauty of her act. Voicing outrage at the wasteful "uselessness" of her generous love, they were unable to recognize the glory of God appearing in a poor leper's home. And while they viewed the woman's gift in light of the law's requirement to serve the poor, her act pointed to the transfiguration of the law in light of the astonishing love that filled the leper's home. It is the Spirit who illumines the "eyes of our hearts" to perceive God's glory in remembering the unnamed woman whose act addresses a deep longing in our time: "A cry for salvation in

---

29. Rowan Williams, "Theology in the Face of Christ," in *Glory Descending: Michael Ramsey and His Writings*, ed. Douglas Dales et al. (Grand Rapids: Eerdmans, 2005), 182-83.

30. James Alison, *Raising Abel: The Recovery of Eschatological Imagination* (New York: Crossroad Herder, 1996), 55.

a technological society properly begins with the prayer for God's own arrival in power and the opening of human eyes and hearts."[31]

The unnamed woman was enraptured by the glory of the Lord, who, taking the form of a slave, became "formless" and emptied himself in order to be formed and filled by the fullness of God (Phil. 2). Challenging the presumption that we are self-made, self-sufficient creatures, this is a way of being that springs from delighting in the Word, a "dispossessed" existence freed from the necessity of grasping for God's favor and hoarding God's gifts. And while we cannot produce the gift of joy, it can be quenched by excessive self-love and pride. But when the truth is spoken in love, joy abounds freely for the praise of God's glory. "Above all, the joy of God needs to be celebrated as the central and embracing reality of the universe, and everything seen in light of this."[32]

Remembering the unnamed woman inspires preachers whose desire is to proclaim the gospel of God's glory. "The [gospel] is the very memorial of the unnamed woman, as if the words were a continued pouring out of her ointment on Jesus' head."[33] Peter Brunner's comments on the analogy between the costly, pure, and genuine ointment poured out by the woman and the use of ornamentation in worship are worth considering. "This ornamentation is not 'superfluous,' it is superfluous only when compared with the bare utility of the implement. To be sure, this ornamentation is something 'overflowing' as beauty in general manifests this element of overflowing. This overflowing element of ornamentation has, in the final analysis, its basis in the special presence of Jesus Christ which eventuates in worship. . . . It is a sign of the joyous surrender of the congregation to its Lord. It is part of the 'loving demeanor of the bride over against the Bridegroom.'"[34]

31. Brian Brock, *Christian Ethics in a Technological Age* (Grand Rapids: Eerdmans, 2010), 174.

32. Ford and Hardy, *Living in Praise*, 17.

33. Gordon W. Lathrop, *The Four Gospels on Sunday: The New Testament and the Reform of Christian Worship* (Minneapolis: Fortress, 2012), 182.

34. Brunner, *Worship in the Name of Jesus*, 278.

God's beauty shines brightly from preaching that is generated by the Spirit of Christ. Attuned to the reality of Christ, hearts and minds are caught up into the Trinitarian mystery that fills all things and graces human existence with the Spirit's gifts. "The practice of delight is the life we perform under the inspiration and full acknowledgement of God's gracious presence in the world, a presence that lets us know we are loved and invites us to extend this same love to others."[35]

The unnamed woman gave freely of herself for no purpose other than offering thankful praise to God. What she did was a "right and good and joyful thing"—the offering of her gifts to the Father through the Son in the Spirit's freedom. Moreover, the Spirit who liberates us from the power of sin is the same Spirit who draws us into the mutual delight of the Father and the Son. Proclaiming the gospel, then, is both a message and way of living by which the Spirit awakens the world to embrace its true self in giving glory to its Creator. "To hear that our chief end in life is to rejoice in what God has done and is doing is to hear a counter-cultural message. . . . It is to acknowledge the wonderful gift that in Jesus Christ the matter of our salvation has been taken care of . . . and we are set free for doxological lives of joy—to see our neighbor . . . to rejoice in creation, and to give thanks to God."[36]

Wholehearted worship of God is the most fitting context for perceiving and proclaiming the beauty of the gospel. The church's worship and mission are inseparable: the witness of our words and example that springs from preaching and hearing the message of the cross, from sharing a meal in communion with the risen Lord, and giving of ourselves freely in service to others. This is all God's gift,

35. Norman Wirzba, *Living the Sabbath: Discovering the Rhythms of Rest and Delight* (Grand Rapids: Brazos, 2008), 62.

36. Thomas W. Currie III, "The Splendid Embarrassment: Theology's Home and the Practice of Ministry," in *The Power to Comprehend with All the Saints: The Formation and Practice of a Pastor-Theologian*, ed. Wallace M. Alston Jr. and Cynthia A. Jarvis (Grand Rapids: Eerdmans, 2009), 380.

God's desire that we give of ourselves freely in the joy of communion. Daniel Bell states this beautifully:

> In the economy of salvation, Christ is given not to pay a debt or appease an angry God but so that God's desire for communion is satisfied. Christ gives, even to the point of death on a cross, that desire might recover its rest, its true end, its enjoyment in the communion of charity that is the divine life. For this purpose, this mission, in Christ we are empowered to give ourselves—all that we are and all that we have—in love of God and service of our neighbor. In Christ our life is so ordered economically that we reflect the divine economy of ceaseless generosity, of unending charity. The Christian economic life is a matter of living life as the gift that it is.[37]

Jesus admonished the woman's critics by announcing that the time of God's salvation for the blessing of the nations had arrived: "Truly I tell you, wherever the good news is proclaimed in the whole world, what she has done will be told in remembrance of her." As Jean-Pierre Torrell comments, "We are neither good nor virtuous if we do not find joy in acting well. To act or speak with joy is to do so with love so that we find delight in it. It is not sufficient to perform good acts and to say good things out of duty, obligation, or by following external rules; it must also be performed, done and said, with joy and delight according to the norm of the gospel itself."[38]

Jesus expressed his delight in the act of an unnamed woman, describing it as a "beautiful thing." Just as God delighted in the goodness of creation, Adam and Eve delighted in creation as a gift and expression of God's goodness. And just as Yahweh delighted in the liberation of Israel, so did Israel delight in the fear of the Lord, in

---

37. Daniel M. Bell Jr., *The Economy of Desire: Christianity and Capitalism in a Postmodern World* (Grand Rapids: Baker Academic, 2012), 159–60.

38. Jean-Pierre Torrell, OP, *Saint Thomas Aquinas: Spiritual Master*, trans. Robert Royal (Washington, DC: Catholic University Press, 2003), 2:166–67.

receiving the gift of the covenant, and in joyful obedience to the law. Just as the Father expressed his pleasure in the Son by anointing him with the Spirit, so the Father and Son delight in pouring out the Spirit for the completion of all things. The fullness of all human desire and delight will be attained when the conditions of this present life are transfigured in the praise of God's glory. "When worship is faithful to its true subject—God incarnate and Spirit-giving—and relevant to our restlessness for God, it will restore us to joy and delight."[39]

Remembering the beauty of the unnamed woman's act is intimately related to the beauty of proclaiming and living the gospel. "Most important is the fact that Mark includes 14:9 where a woman's act of devotion will be proclaimed along with the Gospel in memory of her throughout the world. Here we see [Mark] indicating that a woman's part in the Gospel story is so crucial that her deed is to be celebrated repeatedly in memory of her."[40] The unnamed woman's act is a sign of the transformation effected in preaching when the Spirit "breaks open" what is concealed to make known the glory of Jesus in human words.

Remembering the unnamed woman's act is also intimately related to proclaiming, hearing, and living the gospel in the world. Writing in 2 Corinthians, Saint Paul describes the spiritual and material beauty of the gospel, manifested in Christ and those who proclaim him as Lord and follow his way. By the grace of the Holy Spirit, the proclamation of the "fragrance" of the knowledge of Christ is a sweet "aroma" that overcomes the foul odor of death.

> But thanks be to God, who in Christ always leads us in triumphal procession, and through us spreads in every place the fragrance that comes from knowing him. For we are the aroma of Christ to God among those who are being saved and among those who

39. Don E. Saliers, *Worship Come to Its Senses* (Nashville: Abingdon, 1996), 40.
40. Ben Witherington III, *Women in the Earliest Churches* (Cambridge: Cambridge University Press, 1988), 160.

are perishing; to the one a fragrance from death to death, to the other a fragrance from life to life. Who is sufficient for these things? For we are not peddlers of God's word like so many; but in Christ we speak as persons of sincerity, as persons sent from God and standing in his presence. (2 Cor. 2:14–17)

Proclaiming the gospel of God's glory spreads as a fragrant aroma through the credible witness of preachers. The proclamation of the cross emits the fragrance of the crucified and risen Lord, who is both its message and its medium. Balthasar's comments on this passage are reflective of the real-life conditions in which we preach: "When the 'gospel of the glory of Christ' is disclosed like this, however, it places . . . the whole of humanity after Christ—before the ever new choice and decision: one must become aware of the 'good odor' that leads to life, or of the 'foul odor' that leads to death."[41]

Jesus associated God's reign with an unnamed woman whose self-giving love spread the sweet aroma of the gospel in the home of a leper. At the heart of the triune God is the communion of selfless love revealed in Christ; "the fullness of Christ's humanity displays how self-giving indicates not only what it means to be fully divine but also what it means to be fully human."[42] The act of the unnamed woman, then, was not only "spiritual" but was a prophetic "word" of praise, and therefore social, economic, and political in scope. Gordon Lathrop writes,

Having a beautiful dinner with beautiful food is not enough, certainly not when its abundance and beauty are only for us. What will unite us across our local diversities are the very themes of reform working in the midst of our various meals: that this is a "hungry feast," proclaiming the death of Jesus and the present gift of the risen one, open for all to come and eat and drink, but

---

41. Balthasar, *The Glory of the Lord*, 7:367.
42. Jonathan Tran, *Foucault and Theology* (London: T&T Clark, 2011), 121.

then sending both its participants and its necessary excess into a hungry world as signs of the life-giving and merciful intention of God. The Eucharist will not solve world hunger, but it will make a meaningful sign toward the poor and the hopeless. Such is a reform we still—and continually—need.[43]

The proclamation of such "scandalous" beauty challenges our pride and self-interest with the humble love of Jesus and all he welcomes, blesses, and serves. In such acts of "foolish weakness," God's glory shines brightly through the wisdom of his suffering and death. Moreover, through the power of his resurrection from the dead, God's glory illumines a whole new world for all who desire to follow and proclaim God's way of cruciform love.

In the act of preaching, ordinary human existence is taken up and transfigured by the beauty of the Word revealed in Jesus as both true and good. Thus when the church participates in the graceful self-emptying of the unnamed woman, the beauty of God's forgiveness, mercy, and justice descends visibly and audibly amidst the ugliness of sin and death. Lathrop comments, "That is what the Gospels mean: Jesus Christ in the power of the Spirit comes here, attending to the fearful and the sinful, bringing life, even against all religious strictures. Our assembly is this house."[44]

The unnamed woman's act, then, was both right and good for enjoying the presence of Jesus at a meal in the home of a leper; it anticipated his passion and death. Her wasteful gift was stirred by the joy of God's overflowing mercy present in him.[45] On the one hand, her act was ascetic in nature: a sacrifice of praise that transposed obedience to the law into a selfless offering of love. On the other hand, her act was aesthetic in nature; delighting in the Father's extravagant love for and in the Son, she gave fully of herself in adoring praise. Her

---

43. Lathrop, *The Four Gospels on Sunday*, 170.
44. Lathrop, *The Four Gospels on Sunday*, 162.
45. Wells, *God's Companions*, 24.

devotion to Jesus was shaped by an ascetic discipline and aesthetic perception that were united in single-minded attentiveness to the humble love of God's reign manifested in him. As Graham Ward notes, "In brief, the beauty we apprehend is ultimately the recognition of ourselves and all creation in Christ."[46] Williams adds:

> The divinity of Jesus is what we recognize in finding in him the creative newness of God: his life and death and resurrection as a whole effect the new creation. Thus that life and death and resurrection are in a highly distinctive way the act and speech of God. Because they create by renunciation, by giving away, a letting go; and because the giving away of Jesus is itself a response to the giving of God whom Jesus calls *Abba*, we learn that God's act includes both a giving and a responding; that God's life is itself in movement and in relation with itself. . . . Jesus is the fleshly and historical form of God's act of giving in responsive dimension—God's answer to God, the embodiment of God's own joy in God.[47]

As a means of grace, preaching prepares the church to receive the word of Christ's self-emptying love to which the whole of Scripture attests in a unified but diverse witness to the triune God. When the words of Scripture are "seen" and "heard" with eyes and hears attentive to the astonishing character and acts of God, the Spirit inspires preaching that expresses the beauty of the Word. With her heart and mind illumined by the Spirit of Christ, the unnamed woman beheld the glory of the Lord, who by emptying himself filled others. "God is overflowing Life itself, and because God's whole desire is to share that life, God's love is beyond all measure; God's gifts to human

---

46. Graham Ward, "The Beauty of God," in *Theological Perspectives on God and Beauty*, ed. John Milbank, Graham Ward, and Edith Wyschogrod (Harrisburg, PA: Trinity Press International, 2003), 57.

47. Williams, *On Christian Theology*, 234.

beings are not measured by their good behavior or deservingness."[48] Geoffrey Wainwright points to the glory of the "Word made flesh" that transforms the whole of life and intimately connects worshiping and knowing God in beautiful expressions of a new creation.

> This means that our bodily capacities, by which we ourselves have received the gifts of God, are in turn employed to mediate the gifts to others; as hearers of the Word, we now speak it; as those who have tasted the goodness of the Lord, we minister to the nourishment of others; as those who have glimpsed the glory of the Lord, we endeavor to show it to others; as those anointed with the gospel's fragrance, we become the aroma of Christ to others; as those touched by Christ's healing hand, we seek to extend a blessing to others in their needs.[49]

A Homiletical Aesthetic

Remembering the story of the unnamed woman encourages us to see preaching as an act of praise in the Spirit, who fashions the church into a "beautiful thing"—as a sign or "word" of the presence of Christ in the world. Preaching is both a gift and the response that unites our intellect, desire, and will, calling us to remember the things that are true, right, good, lovely, gracious, honorable, and worthy of praise.[50] A sermon from the early church provides an example of preaching

---

48. Lohfink, *Does God Need the Church?*, 149.

49. Geoffrey Wainwright, *For Our Salvation: Two Approaches to the Work of Christ* (Grand Rapids: Eerdmans/SPCK, 1997), 18.

50. Jean Danielou, *Prayer: The Mission of the Church*, trans. David Louis Schindler Jr. (Grand Rapids: Eerdmans, 1996), 97. "A saint is always someone who has a sense of God's grandeur, who has found joy in God, and who, filled with his love, desires to communicate and share it, just as one would desire to speak of whatever it is that fills one's heart. If we do not speak enough about God, it is because our hearts are not sufficiently filled with him. A heart filled with God speaks of God without effort" (97).

that admonishes Christians to a way of life that is beautiful and
attractive to others.

> When the heathen hear God's oracles on our lips they marvel at
> their beauty and greatness. But afterwards, when they mark that
> our deeds are unworthy of the words we utter, they go from this
> to scoffing, and say that it is a myth and a delusion. When for
> instance, they hear from us that God says "It is no credit to you
> if you love those who love you, but it is to your credit if you love
> your enemies and those who hate you"; when they hear these
> things, they are amazed at such surpassing goodness. But when
> they see that we fail to love not only those who hate us, but even
> those who love us, then they mock at us and scoff at the Name.
> (2 Clement 13.3–4)[51]

The cultivation of homiletic beauty is imperative for the life and
mission of the church as the handiwork of God, the One from whom
all our words and actions spring and to whom they return as offerings
of joyful praise.[52] Our primary motivation for preaching is the sheer
love, enjoyment, and appreciation of God. The most "relevant" form
of Christian communication is praise centered instead of problem
centered, so that "recognizing and responding to this God inevitably leads to evangelism and mission as acts of love and celebration,
longing for others to share in something whose delight increases by
being shared."[53]

The true home of preaching is the eschatological activity of worship: "It is . . . the beauty of holiness, regarded eschatologically, that
is at the heart of authentic [worship]. Every song, every word, every

---

51. "An Ancient Christian Sermon (2 Clement)," in *The Apostolic Fathers*,
trans. J. B. Lightfoot and J. R. Harmer, ed. and rev. Michael W. Holmes, 2nd ed.
(Grand Rapids: Baker Books, 1989), 1.3, 4.

52. Here I am indebted to Ford and Hardy, *Living in Praise*.

53. Daniel W. Hardy and David F. Ford, *Praising and Knowing God* (Philadelphia: Westminster, 1985), 149–50.

prayer, every act of washing, eating, and drinking together, is eschatological—that is, God intends it to point toward completion in the fullness."[54] We preach because we have been enraptured by God's end-time outpouring of the Spirit made visible in the strange, fragile beauty of Christ.[55]

Like the beautiful act of an unnamed woman in Mark's Gospel, preaching is both humbled and exalted in offering "doxological gratitude" for the astonishing love displayed in the "foolish weakness of the Cross."[56] As Wells observes, "God has done everything that needs to be done and requires no assistance or praise; yet in Christ he embodies perfect service as the praise of his glory; thus it is possible for God's people to live lives—eternal lives—of service, made possible by grace and not by need, in which obedience is perfect service."[57] Freed by divine grace from our fears, self-interests, and anxious striving for control, we are caught up by the Spirit in offering our words and selves as a sacrifice of praise to God that is our eternal duty, desire, and delight. *This is the beauty of preaching.*

54. Don E. Saliers, *Worship as Theology: Foretaste of Glory Divine* (Nashville: Abingdon, 1994), 210–11.

55. Here I have benefited from the discussion in Mark A. McIntosh, *Mystical Theology: The Integrity of Spirituality in Theology* (Oxford: Blackwell, 1998).

56. See the excellent discussion in McIntosh, *Mystical Theology*, 47–53.

57. Wells, *God's Companions*, 18.

– three –

A CONVERTING BEAUTY

In this chapter I turn to Augustine of Hippo in North Africa (d. AD 430). The story of Augustine's conversion, as narrated by his *Confessions*, offers deep insight into the transformation required to perceive the beauty of the "Word made flesh" in Christ, the source and goal of all our words as preachers. Augustine's surprising experience of God, whom he discovered in the humble form of Christ, entailed allowing himself to be drawn away from himself into the event of love and delight between the Father and the Son in the Spirit that is disclosed to the church. Bruno Forte's summary of Augustine's mature theological aesthetic is helpful in seeing Christ's beauty as the way of cruciform love that leads to perfect joy in God. "One may thus understand how for Augustine to think about God, and about all things in God, was one with thinking about beauty: when this theologian speaks of God, he speaks of Beauty, and when he speaks of what is beautiful in this world, he constantly points to the One who is the source of all that is beautiful." For Augustine, too, these two themes of God and beauty are held movingly together by the motif of love: in fact, beauty has such power over us because it draws us to itself with the leading strings of love.[1] Augustine's *Confessions*

---

1. Bruno Forte, *The Portal of Beauty: Towards a Theology of Aesthetics*, trans. David Glenday and Paul McPartlan (Grand Rapids: Eerdmans, 2008), 2, 11. See also Aidan Nichols, OP, *Redeeming Beauty: Soundings in Sacral Aesthetics* (Aldershot, UK: Ashgate, 2007), 3–18; Hans Urs von Balthasar, *The Glory of the*

is written in the form of prayer and praise to God by means of the Psalms, which kindled his love for the beauty of Christ's way of living and dying. A humble receptivity opened his heart and mind to the joy of reading and speaking the truth of Scripture, which became his great passion as a preacher and bishop of the church. For Augustine, becoming a preacher is to have the integrity and quality of one's language and life transformed by the truth, beauty, and goodness of Christ with sparkling clarity.

As God's wisdom incarnate, Christ creates who we are, gives substance to what we know and love, informs what we speak and do, and reorders the desires of our heart to what we shall be in communion with God.[2] As Oliver Davies notes, "It is our love of God which is a reflection of God's love for us, and is a transforming power which makes us conform to the beauty of the divine nature."[3]

As a consequence of his conversion, Augustine came to view the work of preachers as participating in the prayer and praise that constitute the church's life, educate its desires, and nurture its delight through the Word spoken in the humanity of Christ: "the Word which is the beginning of all things, the unchanging center within our existence, and the eternal reality which is God's saving will and action."[4] Worship, then, is the ecology of praise in which the Father speaks the Word in the power of the Spirit to create faith as a participation in the beauty and mystery of Christ. Doctrine and life

---

Lord: A Theological Aesthetics, vol. 2, *Studies in Theological Style: Clerical Styles*, ed. John Riches, trans. Andrew Louth, Francis McDonagh, and Brian McNeil, CRV (San Francisco: Ignatius, 1984), 95–143. "Certainly Augustine will also ascend from the beauty and order of the world to eternal beauty, but he far prefers to see in the light of God's beauty the beauty of the world revealing itself to the person who loves God" (100).

2. Augustine, *Teaching Christianity (De doctrina Christiana)*, vol. I/11 in *The Works of Saint Augustine: A Translation for the 21st Century* (Hyde Park, NY: New City Press, 1996), 4.27.59.

3. Oliver Davies, *A Theology of Compassion: Metaphysics of Difference and the Renewal of Tradition* (Grand Rapids: Eerdmans, 2003), 81.

4. Rowan Williams, *On Augustine* (London: Bloomsbury, 2016), 76.

become one in the Spirit, who draws the church to share the Son's self-giving to the Father.[5] Augustine fittingly begins the *Confessions* with a prayer of adoring praise to the triune God as the ground and goal of human thinking, feeling, and speaking.

> Give me, O Lord, to know and understand whether first to call upon you or praise you, and whether first to know you or call upon you. For if I do not know you I may call upon some other rather than you. . . . Yet how will they call upon you, in whom they have not believed? Or how are they to believe without someone preaching? And they will praise the Lord who seek him. For the ones seeking find him, and the ones finding praise him. Let me seek you, Lord, calling upon you, and let me call upon you, believing you. For you have been preached to us! My faith calls upon you, O Lord, the faith, which you have given me, which you have breathed into me through the humanity of your Son, through the ministry of your preacher.[6]

Debra Murphy has suggested that the *Confessions* be read as a liturgical book that renders joyful praise for the truth and goodness revealed in Christ. Knowledge of God and knowledge of the self are received in the activity of worship. "The God who is at the center of our life . . . is a God first prayed to, a God first worshiped, a God revealed to us as a community of persons. . . . Catechesis, then—our coming to know who and whose we are—is inseparable from doxology, the worship of Christ, the praise and adoration of Father, Son, and Holy Spirit."[7]

The *Confessions* tells the story of Augustine's intensive searching prior to his conversion and subsequent ministry as a bishop and

---

5. Here I am following the interpretation of Augustine in Michael Hanby, *Augustine and Modernity* (New York: Routledge, 2003), 90–106.

6. Augustine, *Confessions,* vol. I/1 in *The Works of Saint Augustine: A Translation for the 21st Century* (Hyde Park, NY: New City Press, 1997), 1.1.1.

7. Debra Dean Murphy, *Teaching That Transforms: Worship as the Heart of Christian Education* (Grand Rapids: Brazos, 2004), 112.

preacher. His restless desire for eternal truth, goodness, and beauty drove him on a passionate pursuit of an intellectual, moral, and emotional awakening through the study of ancient wisdom. Following his baptism and incorporation into the church, Augustine reflected on his intellectual vanity, on the prideful illusion that human reason is capable of ascending unaided to wisdom and happiness.[8]

> In a living creature such as this everything is wonderful and worthy of praise, but all these things are gifts from my God. I did not endow myself with them, but they are good, and together they make me what I am. He who made me is good, and he is my good, too; rejoicing, I thank him for all those good gifts which made me what I was, even as a boy. In this lay my sin; that not in him was I seeking pleasures, distinctions and truth, but in myself and the rest of his creatures, and so I fell headlong into pains, confusions, and errors. But I give thanks to you, my sweetness, my honor, my confidence; to you my God, I give thanks for your gifts. [You] preserve them for me. So will you preserve me too, and what you have given me will grow and reach perfection, and I will be with you; because this too is your gift to me—that I exist.[9]

Augustine would learn a new way of using the superior knowledge and skill he displayed as arguably Rome's most renowned teacher of rhetoric. This entailed subordinating his learning and experience to

8. William Mallard, *Language and Love: Introducing Augustine's Religious Thought through the Confessions Story* (University Park: Pennsylvania State University Press, 1994); see also Ellen T. Charry, *By the Renewing of Your Minds: The Pastoral Function of Christian Doctrine* (Oxford: Oxford University Press, 1997), 120–52; Peter Brown writes, "The *Confessions* is very much a book of a man who had come to regard his past as a training for his present career. Thus, Augustine will select as important, incidents and problems that immediately betray the new Bishop of Hippo. He had come to believe that the understanding and exposition of the Scriptures was the heart of a bishop's life." Peter Brown, *Augustine of Hippo: A Biography* (Berkeley: University of California Press, 2000), 155.

9. Augustine, *Confessions* 1.20.31.

the wisdom of the incarnation, the "Word made flesh" who is the subject of the church's "folly of preaching" and correlative cruciform way of life. Augustine began a new vocation in the use of words, a conversion from speaking to win the praise of people to speaking that gives praise to God. His calling was to proclaim Christ as God's incarnate Wisdom, the principle of creation as well as the means and goal of its redemption.[10] "That is how the Wisdom of God treats the ills of humanity, presenting herself for our healing, herself the physician, herself the physic. So because man had fallen through pride, she applied humility to his cure. We were deceived by the wisdom of the serpent; we are set free by the folly of God. On the one hand, while her true name was Wisdom, she was folly to those who took no notice of God; on the other hand, while this is called folly, it is in fact Wisdom to those who overcome the devil."[11]

Seeking Beauty

The *Confessions* tells the story of Augustine's seeking for wisdom and his deep longing for the pleasure of beauty. This was an intense struggle, since he loved the enjoyment of natural, sensuous beauty, deriving immense pleasure from the loveliness of created things. He acknowledged his frustration in his search for happiness, and he would later confess that the goal of this searching was God himself.

> Far be it, Lord, far be it from the heart of your servant who confesses to you; far be it from me to think that enjoyment of any and every kind could make me happy. A joy there is not granted to the godless, but to those only who worship you without looking for reward, because you yourself are their joy. This is the happy life,

10. See here Rowan Williams, "Wisdom in Person: Augustine's Christology" and "Sapientia: Wisdom and the Trinitarian Relations," in Williams, *On Augustine*, 141–54, 171–90.

11. Augustine, *Teaching Christianity* 1.12–14.

and this alone: to rejoice in you, about you, and because of you. This is the life of happiness, and it is not to be found anywhere else. Whoever thinks there can be some other is chasing a joy that is not the true one; yet such a person's will has not been turned away from all notion of joy.[12]

Augustine confessed that God is rightly to be praised for the beauty of all that is. He concluded that all our love for the beauty of created forms and expressions is to be referred to God as their Creator. He discovered that the pleasure derived from loving creatures was actually a participation in the pleasure and delight of God. "If sensuous beauty delights you, praise God for the beauty of corporeal things, and channel the love you feel for them onto their Maker, lest the things that please you lead you to displease him" (4.12.18). Created beauty is good and sweet when praise is given to God as Creator. Yet he long resisted giving himself to the humble way of Christ.

He who is our very life came down and took our death upon himself. He slew our death by his obedient life and summoned us in a voice of thunder to return to him in his hidden place, that place from which he set out to come to us when he first entered the Virgin's womb. There a human creature, mortal flesh, was wedded to him that it might not remain mortal forever, and from there he came forth like a bridegroom, from his nuptial chamber, leaping with joy like a giant to run his course. Impatient of delay he ran, shouting by his words, his deeds, his death and his life, his descent to hell and his ascension to heaven, shouting his demand that we return to him. . . . Life has come down to you, and are you reluctant to ascend and live? But what room is there for you to ascend, you with your high-flown ways and lofty talk? (4.12.19)

12. Augustine, *Confessions* 10.22.32. Hereafter, references from this work will be placed in parentheses in the text.

Augustine was immersed "to the depths" in love for the beauty of created things. As he inquired of his friends, "Do we love anything save the beautiful? . . . Indeed, what is beauty? What is it that entices and attracts us in the things we love?" (4.13.20).

The delights of beauty presented an irresistible pull. His attraction to the harmony of creation was "background music" preventing him from hearing the inner melody of God. His disordered loves and enjoyments prevented him from recognizing the voice of the One who is the source of all human loves and joy. Moreover, his love of and capacity for human wisdom and eloquent speech continued to satiate his desire for honor and praise. Because he was in love with the attention and approval of others, ambitious for the "delight of human vanity," the joy of the Word was unable to reach his ears. Distracted by the clamor of his desires, and dragged down by the weight of self-love, he was unable to rise up and give praise to God since he had not yet been so humbled. He imagined God speaking to him, "But what room is there for you to ascend, you with your high-flown ways and lofty talk?" (4.12.19).

A Humble Word

Augustine's conversion set him on the path of prayer, of vulnerable receptivity to God, whose grace is received in the form of Christ's humble love. He slowly came to understand how hearing is also seeing, that the primary obstacle to hearing and seeing is pride—in loving created things more than their Creator. Although he possessed a keen appreciation for the beauty of created things, he continued to long for the pleasure of Beauty itself. And while he delighted in the beauty of the many things that brought him happiness, he longed for the delight of knowing their Creator. He was not yet able to "see" the beauty of Christ, to recognize Christ as the "Word made flesh." He had not yet grasped the "fittingness" of Christ, the beauty of humbling himself to effect God's will for creation (7.7.11–9.13). Dorothy Day, cofounder of the Catholic Worker Movement, wrote of a similar experience on her "long way home" to conversion. "Natural goodness, natural beauty, brings joy and a lifting of the spirit, but it is not enough, it is not the same. The special emotions I am speaking of came only at hearing the word of God. It was as though each time I heard our Lord spoken of, a warm feeling of joy filled me. It was hearing of someone you love and who loves you."[13]

Augustine's confusion carried over into his reading of the Christian Scriptures. He was offended by the Bible's humble style, its moral horrors, and the strange story of a weak, suffering, and dying savior. While he sought to find beauty in its words, he was unable to perceive the splendor of a Lord who humbled himself and became a servant. His confusion was as much spiritual and moral as theological and philosophical. What he longed to possess exceeded his unaided intellectual capacities—a life ordered by love of divine Wisdom, which transforms one's whole self by divine grace (3.5.9).

This confusion was exacerbated when he heard Christ proclaimed by preachers whose way of life pointed to the truth of Christ's self-giving that he desired for himself. Augustine had begun the *Confessions* in this manner: "The thirteen books of my *Confessions* concern both my bad and my good actions, for which they praise our just and good God. In so doing they arouse the human mind and affections toward him."[14] He confessed that the desire and capacity for confession is a gift "which you have breathed into me through the humanity of your Son, through the ministry of your preacher" (1.1.1). It is not coincidental that the *Confessions* is written in the form of prayer that draws from the language of the Psalms.[15] Augustine desires to tell his story as a song of praise to God, who in the preaching of the

13. *Dorothy Day: Selected Writings*, edited and introduction by Robert Ellsberg (Maryknoll, NY: Orbis, 2011), 13.

14. Augustine, *Confessions: Revisions* II, 6.32.

15. Brown, *Augustine of Hippo*, 168.

word of Christ grants faith perfected in love.[16] It is fitting, then, that Augustine should refer to the words of Saint Paul: "And how can they hear without a preacher?" (1.1.1).

Confession entails praise for the identity and activity of God revealed to faith that comes by hearing rather than by speculation or imagination. Since God is not a part of the creation, the triune mystery cannot be contained by creatures or created things. Contemplating the wonder of God's mystery moved Augustine to prayer. His words point to the freedom and inexhaustibility of God whose identity and activity we seek to name in our preaching.

> What are you, then, my God? What are you, I ask, but the Lord God? For who else is lord except the Lord, or who is god if not our God? You are most high, excellent, most powerful, omnipotent, supremely merciful and infinitely just, most hidden yet intimately present, infinitely beautiful and infinitely strong, steadfast yet elusive, unchanging yourself though you control the change in all things, never new, never old, renewing all things yet wearing down the proud though they know it not, ever active, ever at rest, gathering while knowing no need, supporting and filling and guarding, creating and nurturing and perfecting, seeking although you lack nothing. You love without frenzy, you are jealous yet secure, you regret without sadness, you grow angry yet remain

16. Murphy, *Teaching That Transforms*, 112. Williams writes, "Thus, the most spiritual reading for Augustine will always lead us most directly to humility. Where literalism is to be rejected, it is because it proposes to us a static object of knowledge capable of possession and thereby fails to stir us to longing for the greater fullness of God. So there is a paradoxical dimension to this hermeneutics: what most locates us in our earthly experience in all its reality is what most opens up the fuller sense because it most prompts desire." Williams, *On Augustine*, 33. See here the insightful comments on reading the *Confessions* as a song of praise, incompletion, and unlikeness that engages readers in Augustine's desire for the praise of God and examination of one's life before God. Catherine Conybeare, "Reading the *Confessions*," in *A Companion to Augustine*, ed. Mark Vessey, with the assistance of Shelley Reid (Oxford: Wiley-Blackwell, 2015), 99–110.

tranquil, you alter your works but never your plan, you take back
what you find although you never lose it, you are never in need
yet you rejoice in your gains, never avaricious yet you demand
profits. You allow us to pay you more than you demand, and so
you become our debtor, yet which of us possesses anything that
does not already belong to you? You owe us nothing, yet you pay
your debts; you write off our debts to you, yet you lose nothing
thereby. (1.4.4)

The prayer gives thanks for human speech as God's gift. "After saying
all that, what have we said, my God, my life, my holy sweetness? What
does anyone who speaks of you really say? Yet woe betide those who fail
to speak, while the chatterboxes go on saying nothing" (1.4.4).

Augustine longed to be filled with God's peace, to be "inebriated"
by God's grace. But he was unable to turn from his errant ways to
embrace God as his true end and joy. He prayed for knowledge of
God, and of himself, as known by God. "Through your own merciful
dealings with me, O Lord my God, tell me what you are to me. Say
to my soul, I am your salvation. Say it so that I can hear it. My heart
is listening, Lord; open the ears of my heart and say to my soul, I am
your salvation. Let me run toward this voice and seize hold of you.
Do not hide your face from me, let me die so that I may see it, for
not to see it would be death to me indeed" (1.5.5).

Augustine did not yet understand that God's beauty must be
embraced for its own sake to be rightly enjoyed. Seeking God and
sensual pleasure continued to bring him misery instead of happiness;
his desire for God was weighed down by pride and self-love.

He identified at last a critical turning point in his life, pointing
to a change effected by "the mediator between God and humankind,
the man Christ Jesus." The divine weakness revealed in Jesus drew
him to the humble God who teaches the wisdom that draws us up
to heaven. This heavenly wisdom, however, is not an object of vision
that can be possessed or controlled but is a way of moving through
time and is acquired by following Christ's lowly way.

> Not yet was I humble enough to grasp the humble Jesus as my God, nor did I know what his weakness had to teach. Your Word, the eternal Truth who towers above the higher spheres of our creation, raises up to himself those creatures who bow before him, but in those lower regions he has built himself a humble dwelling from our clay, and used it to cast down from their pretentious selves those who do not bow before him, and make a bridge to bring them to himself. He breaks their swollen pride and nourishes their love, that they may not wander even farther away through self-confidence, but rather weaken as they see before their feet the Godhead grown weak, by sharing our garments of skin, and wearily fling themselves down upon him so that he may arise and lift them up. (7.18.25)

Knowledge of God is given in the weakness and humility of Christ, through which the "eyes of the heart" are purified to trust the love of God made known in the "Word made flesh." Rowan Williams comments on the nature of Augustine's turn from pride and false self-confidence to God revealed in the form of Christ's humanity. "Christ assumes the form of an earthly, temporal identity, vulnerable to loss and suffering: it is the centerpiece of God's 'rhetoric' in communicating with us, God's persuasion of us, not in argument but fleshly life. The weakness of God, the presence of God in a moral life, undermines whatever we take for strength. . . . In the world of faith, meanings are found not by appeal to eternal truth as content of the mind's processes but by assimilation to God's own acceptance of the limits of time and body."[17]

Augustine's conversion entailed a reeducation of desire, a reorientation of his intellect and will to the love of God. Rest, the happiness he had long sought in vain, came in being freed from the perverse habits of thinking and feeling that had controlled him. Surprisingly,

17. Williams, *On Augustine*, 11.

he discovered that the humility of Christ provided a new way of knowing and being in love with God's Truth. "In your unfathomable mercy you first gave the humble certain pointers to the true Mediator; and then sent him, that by his example they might learn even a humility like his. . . . Only in virtue of his humanity is he the Mediator; in nature as the Word he does not stand between us as God, for he is God's equal, God with God, and with him one only God" (10.43.68).

John Cavadini notes in commenting on Augustine's *Confessions*, "The universe is invested in wonder because its intelligibility comes from the self-emptying love of Christ. In such love is freedom to behold the wonder of God's good creation, to see all things from the perspective of the love in which it was created, and which it expresses." This is the paradox of love. We ascend by descending; we are exalted by humbling ourselves, by true self-knowledge, confession, and repentance of our pride. The way is the incarnate Lord, who is also its goal. The Word was made flesh in the form of self-giving love, which is the wisdom of all that is. This is the marvel of God's creative and redemptive works, the beauty that draws us to see the One who is the source and end of all things. It is the Lord who gives freedom from the "useless and obsessive quest for glory, honor, and prestige."[18]

Augustine returned to God in prayer: "I love you, Lord, with no doubtful mind but with absolute certainty. You pierced my heart with your word, and I fell in love with you" (10.6.8). He confessed that the whole creation spoke to him: the sky, the earth, and all created things. They proclaimed God's glory and called him to surrender to God's love. He reflected on loving God in light of the loveliness of creation and pleasures of sensual experience—to the eyes, the ears, the smell, the taste and touch. Although these were not what he

---

18. John Cavadini, "The Anatomy of Wonder: An Augustinian Taxonomy," *Augustinian Studies* 42, no. 2 (2011): 161, 166.

loved when he loved God, they were not to be rejected. His love of sensual beauty was transformed by "seeing" created things in the glory of God's love.

> And yet I do love a kind of light, a kind of voice, a certain fragrance, a food and an embrace when I love my God: a light, voice, fragrance, food and embrace for my inmost self, where something limited to no place shines into my mind, where something is not led away by possessing time sings for me, where something no breath blows away yields to me its scent, where there is savor undiminished by famished eating and where I am clasped in a union from which no satiety can tear me away. That is what I love when I love my God. (10.6.8)

The goodness and beauty of created things speak as eloquent "words" of God. Recalling years of questioning the earth, the sea, the living creatures, the winds, the sky, the sun, moon, and stars, and all the wonders of God's handiwork, he confessed, "My questioning was my attentive spirit, and their reply, their beauty." He continues,

> Therefore they cry out that they did not make themselves. We are, because of this: that we were made. Therefore, we were not, before we were, in any way as to be able to be made by ourselves: And the voice of those things speaking is self-evidence! You therefore, Lord, you make these things, you who are beautiful, for they are beautiful, you also are good, for they are good; you also are, for they are. Yet they are not as beautiful, they are not as good, indeed they are not, in the same way as you, their Creator, are. Compared to you they are neither beautiful, nor good, nor are. We know these things, thanks be to you—and our knowing is ignorance compared to your knowing. (11.4.6)

Augustine concluded that God cannot be found through the senses only. Seeing God's beauty requires a spiritual capacity awakened by the One who, although existing beyond the self, is always present to the self. "To rejoice in you. This is the life of happiness that cannot be found anywhere else. Whoever thinks there can be some other is chasing a joy that is not the true one; yet such a person's will has not turned away from all notion of joy" (10.22.32).

Surprised by Beauty

Much to his surprise, Augustine discovered that God had pursued him through his search for happiness. However, God had remained hidden to him because he had hidden himself from God. Augustine meditated on his past in light of the story of Christ, which prompted him to confess, "This is why you have dwelt in my memory ever since I learned to know you, and it is there I find you when I remember and delight in you. These are my holy delights, and they are your gift to me, for in your mercy you look graciously upon my poverty" (10.24.35).

Confessing enabled him to connect hearing God with seeing God, since God, or Truth, is revealed in the Word made flesh. However, many people do not hear God speaking, since they hear only what they desire to hear. Those who desire to serve God rather than themselves will desire to hear what God wills instead of what they will. Augustine applied this truth to preaching. Truth will engender hatred, while a life of happiness is a rejoicing in the truth, in learning to love the wisdom incarnate in Christ (10.24.34).

Augustine saw how people love what they will and hear what they want. They love truth if it serves their desires, but they hate truth when it challenges and accuses them. Although they love what truth reveals, they hate it when it reveals their deceitfulness. The consequence is that Truth, God himself, continues to elude them in their blindness and weakness, in their disrepute and shabbiness, and in their desire to hide themselves. On the other hand, Beauty is found in the Truth of God and the world disclosed in the humble love of Christ. This humble love freed Augustine to rejoice in and embrace

Truth, to delight in the One who had lovingly pursued him in his searching and wandering.

> *Late, have I loved you, Beauty so ancient and so new; late have I loved you!* Lo, you were within, but I outside, seeking there for you, and upon the shapely things you have made I rushed headlong. I, misshapen. You were with me, but I was not with you. They held me back from you, these things which would have no being were they not in you. You called, you shouted, broke through my deafness; you flared, blazed, lavished my blindness; you lavished your fragrance, I gasped, and now I pant for you; I tasted you, and I hunger and thirst; you touched me, and I burned for peace. (10.27.38 [emphasis added])

The eyes of his heart were enlightened to see Beauty in the Word made flesh, an awakening that opened his heart to the humble love of Christ. But he continued to struggle with understanding how the pleasures of created beauty he loved and enjoyed were signs directing his gaze to Beauty: "O my God, for me you are loveliness itself; yet for all these things too I sing a hymn and offer a sacrifice of praise." Giving praise to God stirred him to meditate on the hidden depths of creation that point beyond themselves to the beauty and love of God. "O lightsome house, so fair of form, I have fallen in love with your beauty, loved you as the place where dwells the glory of my Lord, who fashioned you and claims you as his own" (10.24.53).

Augustine's capacity to "see" Beauty was integral to being restored to the image of Christ. "Like a lost sheep I have gone astray, but on the shoulders of my shepherd . . . I hope to be carried to you" (12.15.21). His desire was to be made whole, his scattered loves and desires united, his whole self refashioned to reflect God's beauty. Just as important for Augustine was a new love and appreciation for the Word, which would become the basis of his faith and work as a preacher.

To Love the Beauty of the Word

This wholeness he sought is found only in the Word. Augustine's new desire, then, was to allow the Word to do its work; the Word who gave creation being; the living Word who converts human creatures to the One who made them; the Word who is the light of their illumination; the Word who by his love reorients the desires of their hearts to himself. It is he who, being in the form of God, is equal to God but assumed the form of a servant. To be, however, is not merely to be beautiful. To be is simply to cling to God in humility and love, the transformation of the ugliness of sin into the beauty of God's goodness. "Our true place is where we find rest. We are borne toward it by love, and it is your good Spirit who lifts up our swollen nature from the gates of death" (13.9.10).

Seeing God's beauty in created things is intimately related to loving the Word made flesh in Christ. To hear the Word and to see the world rightly cannot be separated from speaking the truth in love and is a gift of the Spirit, who bestows the gift of seeing. To see the goodness of things is to see them in God, to delight in them in God, to enjoy them in God, to understand them in God, and to proclaim them in God. Moreover, to love all things in God, who has created them in love, is a disposition of grace, the "eyes" of faith through which God sees their goodness and delights in their beauty. God is thus loved and given glory by what he has made, "But he could not be loved were it not through the Spirit he has given us, because the love of God has been poured into our hearts through the Holy Spirit bestowed upon us" (13.31.40).[19]

19. Williams writes, "Existing 'in God's truth' is, in the *Confessions,* primarily to do with existing in reality rather than fantasy, and (consequently) existing in coherence: that is to say, the transparency of the world to the prior reality of God lies in the perception of things actively existing and maintaining a pattern of interaction that we can follow or chart in certain ways, a pattern of interaction that leaves no room for a final self-fragmentation, a chaos of ordinary events. This

There is radiant beauty in all that is. "Your creation sings praise to you so that we may love you, and we love so that praise may be offered to you by your creation." At the same time, this is a fragile beauty. Since all created things have their morning and evening, the whole order of exceedingly good things in their beauty will pass away when God's purpose has been served. Creation thus exists only because God knows or sees it. But we are blessed in seeing the goodness of creation with "eyes of the heart" conceived by the Spirit in knowing and enjoying the Creator, the source and end of all that is (13.33.48).

The "eyes" of Augustine's heart were cleansed by love for the Word made flesh: "Late have I loved you, Beauty, so ancient and so new!" A consequence of this conversion was new habits of thinking, loving, and speaking. A prominent figure in the profession of rhetoric, he had enjoyed fame and celebrity in Rome, acclaimed for his superior intellect and persuasive rhetorical skills. His conversion and calling to the priesthood set him on a path of relearning how to "use" the skills that had satisfied his desire for the praise of others.

His insatiable desire for attention and approval was transformed by giving himself to the humble Jesus as God. He discovered how a fitting use of words in preaching is capable of making known God's glory in the weak, dying Christ. Instead of speaking for the praise of others, Christian preaching praises the glory of the crucified Lord, who fills the church with the Spirit's gifts and love. Yet such praise of God in our words, actions, feelings, and thoughts is both a gift and a vocation that takes a lifetime to grow and deepen.[20]

Augustine's conversion also awakened him to perceive the beauty of the church's Scriptures. He had long despised the style of the

---

orderliness is the essence of what we call beauty; and our ability to make judgments about beauty, our instinctive appeal to a standard of ideal harmony, is one of Augustine's most familiar grounds for asserting an innate God directedness in the mind." Williams, *On Augustine*, 62.

20. Catherine Mowry LaCugna, *God for Us: The Trinity and Christian Life* (San Francisco: HarperSanFrancisco, 1991), 344.

Bible's humble writings and unlearned writers in comparison to the elegance of Greek and Roman literature. "My swollen pride recoiled from its style and my intelligence failed to penetrate its inner meaning; scripture is a reality that grows along with little children, but I disdained to be a little child and in my high and mighty arrogance regarded myself as a grown up" (3.5.9).

His mind was gradually changed by divine grace affecting his heart. He confessed that God's "most gentle and merciful hand" turned his disposition toward the Word he had begun to believe in and cling to as God's truth. His change of mind was assisted by hearing the preaching of Ambrose, bishop of Milan in Italy, whose elegant sermons drew his attention to the letter and spirit of Scripture. The change in his understanding of Scripture was accompanied by an awareness of the mystery that exceeds the senses, of the God whom to know purifies the mind and heart in order to apprehend the truth, beauty, and goodness found in Christ (6.3.3–4).

Healing occurs in believing, while love enables seeing. Although Augustine had regarded the Scriptures as ugly, at times even repelling, he began to perceive the church's writings as holy and profound, worthy of his reverence and faith, accessible and mysterious. He was astonished by the plain words and humble expressions of the Bible. The church's Scriptures welcomed all comers and stretched the understanding of all attracted by its narrow way. "Scripture does so by speaking with both noble authority and holy humility," which is echoed in the speech of preachers. He perceived both Scripture and creation as words of God to those who have ears to hear and eyes to see. Hearing and seeing God, however, require constancy in seeking God and calling upon God. Reading, praying, and speaking are therefore united in and for the love of God (6.5.6–8). He confessed, "And to whom should I confess my stupidity with greater profit than you, who do not weary of my intense burning interest in your Scriptures?" (11.22.28).

Augustine prayed that God would enlighten his understanding of the Word. "Speak to me yourself, converse with me. I have believed your Scriptures, but those words are filled with hidden meaning" (12.10.10). As his attention to God was increasingly focused by the Spirit's love, so was his delight in hearing God speak: "How amazing is the profundity of your words! We are confronted with a superficial meaning that offers every access to the unlettered, yet how amazing their profundity, O my God, how amazingly deep they are. To look upon that depth makes me shudder, but it is the shudder of trembling love" (12.14.17).

Seeing the Beauty of the Creator in the Creation

Augustine's conversion, his change of mind, invites preachers to a way of seeing visible things, including human actions and words, as signs pointing to what is invisible: "for finite 'bodies' of all kinds indicate by their grandeur some conception of the infinite, divine Being."[21] For example, the book of Genesis is "a summary account of the sheer gift of finite existence, a doxological invitation rather than a full philosophical or scientific exposition of origins" (47). The study of creation, gaining knowledge and understanding of its wisdom and ways, evokes wonder and amazement leading to worship of the Creator. Reading creation is as much a liturgical task as is the study of Scripture. The Word proclaimed in Scripture, and the Word incarnate in Christ, is the same Word that resounds through all that is in declaring God's glory. "Christian theology affirmed that God had accommodated the divine self to the limitations of human language and our creaturely existence, both in Scripture and the Incarnation; an accommodation which necessarily involved symbolism—metaphor and type that pointed beyond itself" (72).

Theology leads to wisdom and discernment for choosing language that is fitting for speaking the word of God in Christ. Truth, good-

---

21. Frances M. Young, *God's Presence: A Contemporary Recapitulation of Early Christianity* (Cambridge: Cambridge University Press, 2013), 46. Hereafter, page references from this work will be given in parentheses in the text.

ness, and beauty are revealed in Scripture and creation as "words" of God. Because there is more than meets the eye in the world, the way of spiritual assent, humble receptivity to God, must enlarge and purify our capacity to see, love, know, and understand (72).

Discernment will also be required if we are to worship the Creator rather than created things, including ourselves. "The true God transcends the cosmos and attracts creatures toward transcendent truth, beauty, and goodness through the truth, beauty, and goodness immanent in the harmony of the cosmos" (79–81). Beauty is not merely a gift to the eye of the beholder; "what God esteems beautiful is the capacity of a thing to fulfill its divinely intended purpose" (72). Young describes this as a "sacramental perspective" that unites the incarnation, the Scriptures, the Eucharist, and the life of the church. The gift of enlarged and purified vision enables perception of "the Creator through the creation, the Spirit through ordinary physical disclosure, of God in God's human image and the human community in the Body of Christ" (5).

God's work of creation and re-creation in Christ are one. Augustine's vision of the new creation does not leave the created order behind but rather offers a robust affirmation of God's generous love displayed in the goodness and beauty of created things (103–4). In his handbook for preachers, Augustine writes of loving created things in God rather than in the place of God. "We should be making use of [God's providence in the ordering of all things to God in love] with a certain love and delight that is not, so to say, permanently settled in, but transitory, rather, and casual, like love and delight in a road, or in vehicles, or any other tools and gadgets you like, or if you can think of any better way of putting it, so that we love the means by which we are being carried along, on account of the goal to which we are being carried."[22]

There is a particular beauty and goodness, a loveliness and harmony, an intelligibility and order of creation that is perceived

---

22. Augustine, *Teaching Christianity* 1.35.39.

in attending to the wonder of God's radiant glory in all things (102–3). Young describes Augustine's vision as a call to "doxology in the everyday, thanksgiving for the sheer gift of existence" (133). The language of preaching is most fully Christian in attending to this "creatureliness and doxological imperative." The right "use" of words in preaching is an expression of love for God and a way of recognizing, honoring, and proclaiming God in the whole of life (133).

Augustine's exposition of Psalm 103 provides a reading of creation's beauty as a "word" pointing to its Creator.[23] He states that the psalm is composed with "figurative statements and mysterious expressions." His use of the text shows that God's creative works possess a sacramental quality by which the invisible reality of God is discerned through visible things (Rev. 1:20). The fabric of sky and earth, the grandeur of all God has fashioned, gives an inkling of the greatness and beauty of the Creator. "We do not yet see him, but we already love him." Although purity of heart, which makes human beings fit to see God, has not yet been attained, God does not cease to display his works "so that through seeing what we can see we may love him where we cannot see and be enabled to see him eventually in virtue of his love" (*Expositions*, 5:107).

The psalmist blesses God for creation's gifts and favors. Augustine calls upon the church to listen with alert minds and the "eyes of pure hearts," to be attentive to the "glorious gifts of God; gifts, joyous and beautiful, desirable and full of gladness." Listeners are invited to share the delight that moved the psalmist to write: "Bless the Lord, O my soul!" When the things of the created order are seen with the purity of Christians' eyes, God is also seen truly. "If nothing is pure, or holy, to [unbelievers], even God cannot be, [but] . . . if he seems pure in your eyes, let him delight you, let him be praised, but if he

---

23. Augustine, *Expositions of the Psalms*, vol. 5 (Pss. 99–120), vol. III/19 in *The Works of Saint Augustine: A Translation for the 21st Century* (Hyde Park, NY: New City Press, 2003). Hereafter, page references from this work will be given in parentheses in the text and abbreviated as *Expositions*.

is blasphemed, it must be because you take no delight in him, and if you do not find him delightful, how can he appear pure to you?" (*Expositions*, 5:109).

Loving God the Creator and loving the creation in God are inseparable. "O Lord, my God, you are exceedingly magnified." God reveals the knowledge of himself and his works as wonderful in our eyes, a vision that accompanies the renewal of our minds in Christ. As Augustine confesses, "You have clothed yourself in confession and seemliness." Seemliness is beauty, and to seek beauty is to seek something good. In the ugliness of our sin, we are given to see the love of the Bridegroom, beautiful and fair beyond all the children of men. "He is more beautiful than any of humankind" (*Expositions*, 5:109–10). Augustine inquires this of the congregation: "Do you want to please him? You cannot please him as long as you are ugly, but what would you do to become beautiful? First of all you must find your deformity displeasing, and then you will receive beauty from him whom you hope to please by being beautiful. He who formed you in the beginning will reform you" (*Expositions*, 5:110).

Creation and redemption are one in Christ. Proclaiming the formation and reformation of human life in Christ begins with confession, with praising God for the magnificent works of creation while acknowledging the reality of sin. Such confession is the truth of the church. "To render her beautiful he loved her even when she was ugly." Christ is beautiful, "fair of form beyond all humankind," who came to the ugly one to make her beautiful. "To make her beautiful he became ugly himself. Christ died for the ungodly" (*Expositions*, 5:111).

This is the good news of God's loving presence in Christ. "The Son of God who was in the form of God took the form of a slave" (Phil. 2). God is "seen" because the Son is discerned in the created things that are seen. "He was fair of form beyond all humankind. But we saw him, and there was no fair form or seemliness in him" (Isa. 53). Christ was devoid of beauty and majesty. Humbling himself, he was obedient to the point of death, even death on a cross. Augustine adds,

"He did not come down from the cross, but he rose from the tomb" (*Expositions*, 5:111–12). The beauty of preaching consists of confession and praise to the end that Christ's beauty will become the very beauty of the church. The beauty of creation and Creator has been reconciled in Christ, just as the first creation and the new creation are one in Christ and his body the church (*Expositions*, 5:113).

The church's praise of God invites the world to an extravagance beyond justice, to a homecoming that embraces those who have been divided, dishonored, disfigured, and dismissed. There is a particular foolishness in this, the foolishness of God, the beauty of useless love, and the wonder of grace, which is the radiant glory that is "the anatomy of the Body of Christ." This is a "new way of doing business in the world, a new way of assessing worth, and so a new way of assessing wonder." For Augustine, the whole creation bears traces of such gratuitous love, which preachers make known in Christ indwelling his people, the living Word who summons the church to a life of thanks and praise, to "doxology as a way of life" in grateful response to the wonder of God's self-giving in him.[24]

A Homiletical Aesthetic

The *Confessions* tells the story of Augustine's conversion and subsequent transformation that led him into the vocation of preaching. His search for God is expressed in the form of confession, an offering of prayer and praise that reflects his desire for language fitting for God. If God is great and worthy to be praised, the happiness of human creatures depends upon acquiring a language of truth and praise worthy of God. By telling the story of his conversion, from an acclaimed intellectual and rhetorician to the calling of pastor and preacher of the Word, Augustine confesses and proclaims the glory

24. Cavadini, "The Anatomy of Wonder," 170–71. On doxology as a way of life, see the excellent discussion in LaCugna, *God for Us*.

and wonder of God, which made it possible to confess both his sin and God's goodness.[25]

As a community of praise, the church is taken up by the Spirit in offering extravagant shouts of glad acclamation that "participate in the movement of God and celebrate his abundance while being shaped by his word and opened to a new future."[26]

Augustine's love of beauty reflects this deep longing for a life made whole and undivided in what it knows, loves, and speaks. As William Mallard suggests, "When Augustine realized and began to yearn for the Incarnation in the church, he grasped an authoritative language of Incarnation that responded to his dilemma concerning language across many years. This language was of course scripture, was 'other,' strange, rough-hewn, the mystery of the Word made flesh; yet it was simple, accessible, largely in story form, concerning the coming and the doings of the Son of God. . . . It told a story of divine activity and humble sacrifice accessible to all."[27]

Augustine's love of truth became a path guided by the wisdom of Christ, which also leads to Christ as goal. Intellectual integrity requires love, and love means a kind of illumination of the heart and mind that is wisdom. What Augustine arrived at was not a theory of preaching but rather a way of loving God with his thoughts, affections, and words, a way of thinking and speaking that delights in the beauty of God's love in all things. This led to his most important discovery: the disposition of humble love displayed in the lowliness of Christ, the "Word made flesh." As Williams sees this, "Becoming a creature is learning humility, not as submission to an alien will, but as the acceptance of limit and death; for that acceptance, with all that it means in terms of our moral imagination and action, we are equipped by learning through the grace of Christ and the concrete fellowship of the Spirit."[28]

25. Mallard, *Language and Love*, 231–33.
26. Daniel W. Hardy and David F. Ford, *Praising and Knowing God* (Philadelphia: Westminster, 1985), 120.
27. Mallard, *Language and Love*, 135–36.
28. Williams, *On Christian Theology*, 78.

Augustine confessed that to move into a sphere of knowledge that does not begin with the Creator is never to arrive at the Creator. "To see all things in the light of God is to see them as they really are and to include the reality of God from the outset." By sharing Christ's humility, we are drawn into a way of perceiving reality marked by dispossession, incompleteness, and weakness.[29] Mallard's summary describes Augustine's way of perceiving and speaking of the Creator, the vulnerability of creatures, and the fragile nature of beauty. "Thus emerges one of the West's surest aesthetic instincts. To see beauty is important in itself; but to see beauty and know that it is only transient is more richly full of wonder. The superbly beautiful is only the more amazing in its fragility."[30]

The discovery that shaped Augustine's practice as a preacher is immensely illuminating of our work as preachers. As part of the created order, our language is a gift of the Creator, and therefore fragile, limited, and incomplete. Moreover, as a gift of the Creator, our language is to be offered back in praise to its Giver. Like Augustine, we need to learn to "use" the language of Scripture as an offering of love and praise to God for the beauty of Christ, which is hidden and revealed in all things. "This language of praise was words he had always known, but now they came with the two gifts of integrity and humility that enabled him to use them. The language of praise and Incarnation had two sides: discipline and call, rule and passion. Love was both ordering and energizing; faith was both public and private. The language of authority, the two-sided language of Incarnation, was the language of love."[31]

What is at stake for preachers is discerning a truthful vision of "God's glory" that is capable of capturing the imagination and affection of their listeners. Augustine was aware of rival versions of honor, worth, and "glory" existing side by side in the church. He observed

29. Mallard, *Language and Love*, 87, 219–21.
30. Mallard, *Language and Love*, 94.
31. Mallard, *Language and Love*, 162.

the effect on leaders and prominent members who were drawn to a vision exalting the beauty of pride and self-importance in their own desire to win social approval. Augustine was compelled, theologically and pastorally, to address these false forms of "beauty" with a homiletical aesthetic inspired by Christ's humility and love.[32]

In a sermon preached shortly after the sack of Rome (AD 410), Augustine proclaimed the cross of Christ and its wisdom, calling the church to conform itself to the crucified Lord as the way and goal of its life.[33] He began by affirming the reality of God's grace displayed in sending the Son, who was born as a human being and who died at the hands of human beings. This astonishing news is the basis of Christian memory and hope, "that God died for the sake of human beings." This assertion, moreover, is grounded in the truth of the incarnation, the "Word which was in the beginning; that was with God and was God: this Word became flesh and dwelt among us" (194).

By adhering to the story of the incarnate Word, Augustine affirms the "great exchange" by which Christ assumed the condition of humanity and death to bestow his life upon dying humanity. "Accordingly, he struck a wonderful bargain, a mutual give and take; ours was what he died by; his was what we might live by." Christian people are to take pride in the cross and place maximum trust in it. By his death, Christ fully engaged himself with our humanity to give us life in himself, thus showing how much he loves us through a great act of divine wisdom and justice (195).

In the aftermath of the sack of Rome, Augustine was responsible for preaching to Christian people in North Africa who were witnessing the surprising and disruptive ending of a familiar, known

---

32. Peter Brown, *Through the Eye of a Needle: Wealth, the Fall of Rome, and the Making of Christianity in the West, 350–550 AD* (Princeton: Princeton University Press, 2012), 308–84.

33. Augustine, *Sermons on the Liturgical Seasons*, vol. III/6 in *The Works of Saint Augustine: A Translation for the 21st Century* (New Rochelle, NY: New City Press, 1993). Hereafter, page references from this work will be given in parentheses in the text.

world. As a pastor and bishop, he sought to encourage a Christian community that was the object of ridicule by pagans and educated despisers for "worshiping a crucified Lord" instead of the gods esteemed by Rome (195).

The homily concludes by returning to the Lord's passion. Augustine remembers the gift of baptism as a sign of the cross and gives thanks for the church's cruciform identity in Christ. "So let us take pride in the cross of our Lord Jesus Christ, through whom the world may be crucified to us and we to the world. It was to save us from being ashamed of that cross that we placed it right on our foreheads, that is, on the dwelling place of shame" (196).

Augustine's exemplary response to this pastoral challenge offers encouragement to preachers who are called to proclaim the cross as the source of hope and promise of glory that sustain the church as a pilgrim people during "the time of the world." Since God, in the ministry of Christ, teaches integrity and humility by his word and example, so too may the church, by its words and actions, show its love for God by sharing itself with the world in the humility of the crucified Lord. Augustine concludes with an exhortation to love the beauty of God's humble way in Christ as more precious than life itself. "*Accordingly, since the apostle urges us not to have big ideas, but to go along with humble folk, we should consider, as far as we can, over what precipice we human beings may tumble if we don't go along with a humble God*" (196 [emphasis added]).

– *four* –

A SPOKEN BEAUTY

In a sermon on Psalm 44, Augustine provides an eloquent reading of the beauty of Christ, the "Word made flesh." His christological interpretation demonstrates a spiritually awakened aesthetic sensibility that points us to consider seriously the possibility of "joining the content of the gospel and the concept of beauty."[1]

He is Beautiful as God, as the Word who is with God, he is beautiful in the Virgin's womb, where he did not lose his godhead but assumed our humanity. Beauty he is as a baby, as the Word unable to speak, because while he was still without speech, still a baby in arms, and nourished at his mother's breast, the heavens spoke for him, a star guiding the magi, and he was adored in the manger as food for the humble. He was beautiful in heaven, then, and beautiful on earth; beautiful in the womb, and beautiful in his parents' arms. He was beautiful in his miracles, but just as beautiful under the scourges, beautiful in laying down his life, and beautiful in taking it up again, beautiful on the cross, beautiful in the tomb and beautiful in heaven.[2]

1. Aidan Nichols, OP, *Redeeming Beauty: Soundings in Sacral Aesthetics* (Aldershot, UK: Ashgate, 2007), 4.
2. Augustine, *Expositions of the Psalms*, vol. 2 (Pss. 33–50), vol. III/16 in *The Works of Saint Augustine: A Translation for the 21st Century* (Hyde Park, NY: New City Press, 2000), 283.

Augustine's maturing vision of preaching acknowledged the fragile and incomplete nature of homiletical beauty in light of Christ's weakness and vulnerability.[3] Communication in the church finds its true source and end in the love of God, drawing its inspiration and truth from the reality of Christ. His desire was for preaching that proclaims God's truth with wisdom and eloquence "fitting" for the splendor of divine beauty taking humble human form.[4]

Unlike his career as a highly successful rhetorician, a "peddler of words" for whom creating persuasive affect was an end in itself, Augustine viewed preaching as possessing a particular wisdom and eloquence shaped by the "evangelical beauty" of Christ. As Carol Harrison writes, the cultural significance of rhetoric in the Roman Empire carried with it social respect, prestige, power, and authority.[5] The rhetorical tradition could easily become self-absorbed, lapsing into "frivolous aestheticism" that emphasized style over truth, seeking mere entertainment and showmanship.[6] Peter Brown comments on Augustine's ambivalent attitude toward the difficulty of communicating the mystery of God in Christ, which exceeds human imagining, feeling, and understanding. He describes a challenge faced by preachers both in his time and ours.

---

3. William Harmless, SJ, *Augustine and the Catechumenate* (Collegeville, MN: Liturgical Press, 1996), 349–50.

4. Rowan Williams, *On Augustine* (London: Bloomsbury, 2016), 75–76.

5. Carol Harrison, "The Rhetoric of Scripture and Preaching: Classical Decadence or Christian Aesthetic?" in *Augustine and His Critics: Essays in Honor of Gerald Bonner*, ed. Robert Dodaro and George Lawless (London: Routledge, 2000), 216.

6. In Harmless, *Augustine and the Catechumenate*, Harmless addresses our contemporary situation in light of Augustine's experience. "In an era in which thinking, whether political or religious, threatens to be reduced to TV sound bites, this drift should not be underestimated. Given the contemporary milieu, it becomes even more imperative that [preachers], whatever their rhetorical gifts, be well informed, that they have at their fingertips the best that scholarship has to offer" (358). See also the study of Augustine's preaching as "psychagogy, or the cure of souls," a "therapy of the affections," in Paul R. Kolbet, *Augustine and the Cure of Souls: Revising a Classical Ideal* (Notre Dame: University of Notre Dame Press, 2010), 167–209.

The huge pressure built up by the need to communicate does nothing less than seep away the elaborate scaffolding of ancient rhetoric. For, as Augustine came to see it at the end of his life, rhetoric had consisted of polishing an end product, the speech itself, according to elaborate and highly self-conscious rules. It ignored the basic problem of communication: the problems faced by a man burning to get across a message, or by a teacher wanting his class to share his ideas. Immediacy was Augustine's new criterion. Given something worth saying, the way of saying it would follow naturally, and inevitable and unobtrusive accompaniment to the speaker's own intensity. . . . The impact was also immediate; for the speaker's style was not thought of as a harmonious assemblage of prefabricated parts, which the connoisseur might take to pieces, but rather as the inseparable welding of form and content in the heat of the message, so that "it is a waste of time to tell someone what to admire, if he does not himself sense it."[7]

Augustine viewed preaching as a form of Christian rhetoric, speaking the truth with wisdom and eloquence cultivated in contemplating Scripture's witness to Christ. Being a preacher requires humility and love, just as preaching is conducted as an act of humble love.[8] The speaker and that which is spoken are shaped by God's wisdom manifested in the humility and love of Christ. "But a good listener warms to it as by pronouncing it energetically. For these words were not devised by human industry, but were poured forth from the divine mind both wisely and eloquently, not in such a way that wisdom was directed toward eloquence, but in such a way that eloquence did not abandon wisdom."[9]

7. Peter Brown, *Augustine of Hippo: A Biography* (Berkeley: University of California Press, 2000), 253.

8. Harrison, "The Rhetoric of Scripture and Preaching," 216, 222.

9. Augustine, *Teaching Christianity (De doctrina Christiana)*, vol. I/11 in *The Works of Saint Augustine: A Translation for the 21st Century* (Hyde Park, NY: New City Press, 1996), 4.7.21.

Harrison describes Augustine's preaching as a "Christian aesthetic" in which a preacher's words, in service of the Word, hold a central place. Language is transformed from speaking that seeks to please and persuade in itself to infusing love for and the practice of the truth that is brought to clarity in the person of Christ. Preaching works with a theological assumption; "the will itself has no motive unless something presents itself to delight and stir the mind."[10] That something is God's revelation of himself to sinful human creatures to inspire delight, to please and move so that it is loved and performed as the good.[11] Augustine states this clearly: "So we love those things by which we are carried along for the sake of that toward which we are carried."[12] Harrison summarizes Augustine's homiletical aesthetic: "Truth is beautiful; if beauty is delightful; if delight is the way in which God chooses to orient the fallen will towards himself, there is nothing artificial, arbitrary, misleading, superficial or decadent about describing Scripture as a work of literature, or using rhetoric to preach."[13]

The beauty of preaching is displayed by speaking the truth of God as aesthetically pleasing, accessible, and clear. Rather than beginning with matters related to style, strategy, or skill, Augustine began with the conviction that human beings long for and love truth as it is presented in Scripture. Love is inspired by delight, which is inspired by beauty, and beauty is inspired by truth. "It is, therefore, essential for Augustine that Scripture be shown to be beautiful, be made delightful, if its true end is to be attained."[14]

Although Scripture matters greatly in preaching, knowing and loving God matter even more. Scripture remains secondary, as a gift

---

10. Harrison, "The Rhetoric of Scripture and Preaching," 223.

11. See here the excellent discussion in Harrison, "The Rhetoric of Scripture and Preaching," 223–27; see also Harrison, *Augustine: Christian Truth and Fractured Humanity* (Oxford: Oxford University Press, 2000), 75–76.

12. Augustine, *Teaching Christianity* 1.35.39.

13. Harrison, "The Rhetoric of Scripture and Preaching," 224.

14. Harrison, *Augustine*, 76.

and means of grace that is "used" with right intention and the inspiration of love received from God. Faithfulness in "biblical preaching" requires forming preachers in the wisdom, language, idiom, and movement of Scripture that points beyond itself to Christ. This is a particular form of learning that draws a preacher into a conversion of the "heart," from delighting in created things, including words, to delighting in the beauty of Christ and desiring what God wills to make of the church as a "word" to the world.[15]

Trinitarian Beauty and Preaching

For Augustine, preaching springs from delighting in the Word by the inspiration of the Spirit. Christ is the form of God's beauty; the Son is the Father's eloquence.[16] The Word possesses a particular splendor by which the Spirit moves us to love of the triune love itself. As the fullness and end of all signs, the Word delights and captivates in love. As Michael Hanby comments, Augustine "understands Christ's passion as a manifestation of the beauty of divine love that restores the harmony between creature and Creator." The cross is the beauty of divine love generously poured out, which in its radiance purifies the "eyes of our hearts" to see the truth of this love itself (61).

Augustine's vision was shaped by the church's confession of Christ, the fully divine and human Son of the Father. Because the Trinity is transcendent love, the creation unfolds and flourishes

15. Harrison, "The Rhetoric of Scripture and Preaching," 226–28. See also the good introduction to the use of Scripture in the early church in Robert Wilken, *The Spirit of Early Christian Thought: Seeking the Face of God* (New Haven: Yale University Press, 2003), xiv–xvii, 3, 24. "In the sermon the preacher sought not only to explain the words but also invited the congregation to enter into the reality itself, the mystery of Christ, by the use of words" (43–44). See the excellent discussion of the incarnation as the humble form of God's self-communication in Williams, *On Augustine*, 48–49.

16. For this next section, I am drawing from the work of Michael Hanby, *Augustine and Modernity* (New York: Routledge, 2003). Hereafter, page references from this work will be given in parentheses in the text.

within the love that is shared by the Father and the Son. Christology is central, in that Christ manifests the eternal beauty of God in time and history, just as time and history unfold in the eternal beauty of God. As Hanby concludes, "Christ's function is one whereby he reincorporates an estranged creation into the Trinitarian life of God . . . the manifestation of the divine beauty in creation, or rather, the restoration of creation as a manifestation of the beauty of divine love . . . and our apprehension of it" (28).

This love is God *and* God's gift. Divine love transforms our deformed loves into the form of Christ's beauty, who draws us into the generous love he exemplifies and pours out in his passion. Salvation is aesthetic: the reformation of what is deformed in and through the divine love, which incites love and attracts by the compelling power of delight in its transcendent source. The incarnation of Christ is the visible manifestation of the Father's beauty, while the Spirit is the gift of love that attests, delights, and persuades by that beauty. The visible things of the world, including use of words in preaching, function as signs that have their source and end in the delight of the Father and the Son (30–32).

As human creatures, we are just to the extent that we participate in God's doxological beauty, which is the sum of Scripture. That we love God with all we are, have, and do, and love our neighbors as we ourselves are loved by God, is simply beautiful. Love for God and neighbor is the true form of the church, the beauty of Christ and his body made visible in the world. Manifesting the love of the Father and the Son, the church is the creation on the way to restoration in the image and movement of that love. The beauty of Christ thus renders our life as creatures, as living signs and "words" of God's glory, which is proclaimed by our participation in the beauty of creation (37–38). Augustine states this eloquently: "'He had no form or comeliness that we should look at him.' The deformity of Christ forms you. For if He had not wished to be deformed you would not have received back the form that you lost. Therefore, He hung deformed upon the cross, but His deformity was our beauty" (quoted at 46).

Trinitarian love is true and good, but it also requires the fruit of
love, joy, delight, and blessedness, which is the Holy Spirit. God's
truth and goodness must delight us to move us by inciting our desire and stirring our affections. Fully divine and fully human, Christ
manifests and mediates the beauty of divine love and our participation in it. As the Son, he is the beauty of the Father in whom the
Father delights.

Moreover, as the Son, he is both Savior and Mediator, the One
in whom our life as human creatures unfolds and finds its fullness.
Hanby comments, "Our conversion will be a participation in the
Father's delight in the beauty of the Son's responsive vision of the
Father." Because conversion is all of divine grace, this participation
is itself a reception, and as a reception it is self-giving. "Our apprehension of this vision will be inseparable from our manifestation as
love and doxology" (54–55).

Trinitarian beauty is intrinsic to preaching as the Spirit's gift,
since preaching is itself an expression of doxological love for God
in the form of Christ. And our hearing, by which faith comes, is a
letting go, a gift that makes us partakers in the Son's answer to the
Father in the joy of his knowledge that is the Spirit's love (55). Hanby
writes, "Only the saint truly is. But she only is, and is as an image of
God, paradoxically, because of her very difference from God, because
she can receive the gift whereby she can become most fully herself
in God's love of, delight in, and giving of himself. She can become
herself only in becoming God's" (66).

Preaching is an act of human speech in which our words are signs
by which the Spirit inspires delight in Christ, the full expression
of God's self-giving love. Moreover, Christ is himself the form of
divine love that is the reality of God in creation, and creation in the
reality of God. This beauty is displayed to the world by the church
as a people conformed to his image through the faith that comes by
hearing (68–70).

We preachers will benefit by attending to how Augustine's homiletical aesthetic is intimately related to the art of speaking, which

informed his work as a pastor and bishop. Writing in *Instructing Beginners in Faith*, he addresses concerns related to the difficulty preachers experience in learning to understand and speak the language of Scripture.[17] Augustine was convinced that the clarity of what is preached—the knowledge and love of God—should delight and inspire. A preacher's use of words will be inspired by love of the truth, which, in its goodness and beauty, evokes the desire and pleasure of both speaker and hearers. Pope Francis states this purpose clearly: "Proclaiming Christ means showing that to believe in him and to follow him is not only something right and good, but also something beautiful, capable of filling life with new splendor and profound joy, even in the midst of difficulties."[18] Preaching the truth, then, draws listeners to the beauty of divine love as manifested, although partially and incompletely, in the preacher's thinking, loving, and speaking as a "sign" of Christ. Francis adds this comment on the preacher's life:

> We are not asked to be flawless, but to keep growing and wanting to grow as we advance along the path of the Gospel; our arms must never grow slack. What is essential is that the preacher be certain that God loves him, that Jesus Christ has saved him and that his love has always the last word. Encountering such beauty, he will often feel his life does not glorify God as it should, and he will sincerely desire to respond more fully to so great a love. Yet if he does not take time to hear God's word with an open heart, if he does not allow it to touch his life, to challenge him, to impel him, and if he does not devote time to pray with that word, then he will indeed be a false prophet, a fraud, a shallow imposter. . . . The Lord wants to make use of us as living, free, and creative be-

17. Augustine, *Instructing Beginners in Faith (De catechizandis rudibus)*, The Augustine Series, vol. 5 (Hyde Park, NY: New City Press, 2006). See the insightful discussion of the treatise in Harmless, *Augustine and the Catechumenate*, 106–54.

18. Pope Francis, *The Joy of the Gospel (Evangelii Gaudium): Apostolic Exhortation* (Vatican City: Libreria Editrice Vaticana, 2013), 84.

ings who let his word enter their own hearts before then passing it on to others. Christ's message must truly penetrate and possess the preacher, not just intellectually, but in his entire being.[19]

Preaching as the Beauty of Wisdom

Augustine wrote *Instructing Beginners in Faith* as a response to a fellow pastor who sought his help for the task of instructing inquirers and new Christians in the faith.[20] He summarizes the problem. "You have also admitted—and what's more, lamented the fact—that even when your address is lengthy and delivered without enthusiasm you have often had the feeling of being trifling and distasteful to yourself, not to mention the one to whom you were speaking in the course of his intial instruction, or the others who were there to listen" (prologue, 1.1). Augustine responds by offering an honest confession, pointing to his own limited success as a preacher. "It is the same with me too: I am nearly always dissatisfied with the address I give. For the address I am so eager to offer is the superior one which I enjoy again and again in my inner being before I formulate it in spoken words" (prologue, 1.2).

Augustine understood well that our tongues cannot keep pace with our intellects. There is always a gap, a difference, between what one speaks and the flashes of insight that occur in the intellect and are left in the memory. This gap, however, is not a matter of poor insight or lack of desire. Preachers often feel a sense of incompleteness, inadequacy, and even failure. "And then we feel distressed at our failure and, like people expending effort to no avail, we become limp with disgust and, as a result of this very disgust, our speech becomes even more sluggish and colorless than when it first gave rise to that feeling of disgust in us" (prologue, 2.3).

---

19. Pope Francis, *Joy of the Gospel*, 76.
20. Augustine, *Instructing Beginners in Faith*, introduction, prologue, 1, 1. Hereafter, references from this work will be given in parentheses in the text.

The language of preaching can become bland and listless, unable to inspire, delight, and move those who speak and listen. Augustine acknowledged that the enthusiasm of those to whom he preached was, at times, greater than his—a situation he found encouraging. But the reality of preaching still remains. What is spoken often falls short of what a preacher intends to say, and may actually be distasteful, uninspiring, uninteresting, and unattractive. What is a preacher to do?

> And in actual fact, we are given a much more appreciative hearing when we ourselves enjoy performing our task. Then the texture of our speech is suffused with the very delight that we take in speaking, and our words flow more easily and pleasingly. Hence the difficult part of our task is not in giving rules about where to begin and where to end the historical exposition in which the content of faith is communicated. . . . No, our greatest concern is much more about how to make it possible for those who offer instruction in faith to do so with joy. For the more they succeed in this, the more appealing they will be. And, indeed, in this regard, there is a teaching ready to hand. "For God loves a cheerful giver" (II Cor. 9:7) in matters of material wealth, how much more in matters of spiritual wealth? But for such cheerfulness to be present at the opportune time depends on the confession of the One whose teaching it is. (prologue, 2.4)

This is a homiletic aesthetic, generated by the beauty of divine love and drawn by the motivating energy of human delight in God. It is a vision of preaching inspired by the story of the gospel. Augustine begins with Christ, who came so people might learn how much God loves them, and might learn this so that they would catch fire with love for him who first loved them, and so they would also love their neighbors as he commanded and showed by his example of humility—Christ who made himself their neighbor by loving them when they were not close to him, wandering far from him (part one, 4.8).

William Harmless summarizes this well: "Augustine believed the heart of the matter lay in the heart. As he saw it, the core of Scripture was a message aimed at the human heart: the love of God and love of neighbor, for God, in Christ, had shown how much he loved us and, in Christ, had made himself our neighbor. The message shaped the pedagogy; inquirers needed to have a first taste of this love of God and neighbor."[21]

Preaching requires wisdom and humility that love the truth and desire the goodness of what is spoken. Augustine viewed the gap between those who preach and what is preached in light of Christ, "who though himself was equal with God, embodied the pattern of preaching in his self-emptying and death" (part one, 10.15). He also saw the pattern of Christ's self-emptying manifested in the ministry of the apostle Paul, who in his desire for the salvation of those to whom he preached delighted in giving himself for the sake of the gospel. Augustine viewed this as a matter of cultivating delight generated by a passion for the gospel. "Thus if our understanding finds its delight within, let it also delight in the following insight into the ways of love: the more love goes down in a spirit of service to the ranks of the lowest people, the more surely it rediscovers the secret that is within when its good conscience testifies that it seeks nothing of those to whom it goes down but eternal salvation" (part one, 10.15).

Because preaching springs from delight in God and seeks the delight of listeners in God, preachers may find relief from the anxiety of performing and not knowing how people may respond to their preaching. Augustine claims that relief for anxious preachers is found in the love of God and neighbor, which includes those who listen, as the end or purpose of a preacher's life and speech. "A work is truly good when the will of the one who performed is struck with a shaft of love" (part one, 11.16).

Augustine believed that the love of God, as the end and purpose of preaching, is more important than a preacher's personal success,

21. Harmless, *Augustine and the Catechumenate*, 153–54.

satisfaction, or comfort. Attention to God is intrinsic to the task of introducing listeners to the purpose of creation as given by its Creator, for inspiring and elevating hearts of listeners in praise to God. Moreover, there is joy in sharing of oneself, one's knowledge and love, in the bonds of compassion and affection that are life-giving for all. Augustine defines preaching as an act of friendship, a particular way of speaking that seeks the joy and delight of all who hear the Word. As a pastor, he had discovered that the work of showing the way to others evokes an eager and glad spirit, a cheerful mood, and at times, even awe and astonishment. He had also learned that the limitations and incompleteness of preaching bring grief and sadness, since "we are doing this on the orders of the One who has given this peace to us" (part one, 12.17).

Since preachers speak as those who are called to be disciples like all Christians, the efficacy of preaching is dependent upon God's transformative power. Augustine points to the need for divine grace to heal human ignorance and weakness, acknowledging that preachers are subject to the weaknesses and failures of all human beings: depression, sadness, disinterest, lack of enthusiasm, self-centeredness, pity, self-interest, excessive pride, confusion, discouragement, anxiety, moral failure, irritability, boredom, dullness of heart, and spiritual exhaustion. At the same time, he viewed the nature of preaching as a sign or "word" pointing beyond itself to the knowledge of God that exceeds a preacher's temptations and failures. "Fluent and cheerful words will stream out from an abundance of love and are drunk with pleasure. For it is not so much I who say these words to you as it is love itself that says them to us all, the love *that has been poured out in our hearts by the Holy Spirit who has been given to us* (Rom. 5:5)" (part one, 14.21, 22; emphasis in the original). Harrison writes, "*De catechizandis rudibus* [*Instructing Beginners in Faith*] might aptly be described as a treatise on the nature of love; it is love that ought to form the preacher's attitude and words; love that forms the subject of the discourse, and is the central lesson of Christian history as it is narrated in Scripture and expressed in the Church; love the discourse [that] inspires

and that motivates [a preacher's] actions. Love, therefore, informs the
nature, practice, and goal of exegesis and preaching."[22]

For Augustine, preaching addresses the need of human beings
to be addressed by God's Word, which evokes awe, wonder, and joy.
Preaching inspires praise and joy in God by the drawing of the Spirit
into ever-deepening delight in the knowledge and love of Christ
(part one, 13.18, 19). Rather than turning the church away from the
realities of life, delighting in God through hearing the Word is the
way of human participation in the "central and embracing reality of
the universe and everything else seen in light of this."[23] David Ford
and Daniel Hardy summarize this way of living well. "At the heart of
ordinary Christian life is recognition of the love of God. All creation
is a work of God's love. Jesus Christ is God's giving of himself in
love to restore and fulfill all creation. The Holy Spirit is the pouring
out of this love in endless transformation and fresh creativity. Praise
of God recognizes all of this [the divine beauty] and first enjoys and
celebrates it. Praise is therefore an attempt to cope with the abundance of God's love."[24]

Augustine's homiletical wisdom—delighting in the Word of
God—invites preachers to clearer recognition of God, to deeper capacities of thinking and feeling, to more generous ways of perceiving
and speaking the "language of love."[25]

The Delight of Preaching

Augustine addressed the significance of delight in *The Spirit and the
Letter*.[26] This work is typically remembered as a theological defense

22. Harrison, "The Rhetoric of Scripture and Preaching," 228.
23. David F. Ford and Daniel W. Hardy, *Living in Praise: Worshiping and
Knowing God* (Grand Rapids: Baker Academic, 2005), 15.
24. Ford and Hardy, *Living in Praise*, 2.
25. Ford and Hardy, *Living in Praise*, 13. See the section entitled "The Language of Love" in Harrison, *Augustine*, 65–78. Harrison later refers to the transformation of the intellect and will by love as the "passionate intellect" (93).
26. Augustine, *The Spirit and the Letter*, in *Augustine: Later Works*, selected and

of divine grace in opposing the teaching of Pelagius. *The Spirit and the Letter*, however, contributes to understanding Augustine's views on the assistance provided to the human will by the endowment of human freedom, the teaching of the law, and the gift of the Holy Spirit.[27] He arrives at the important conclusion that it is the Spirit who evokes love and delight in God as the supreme Good. Robert Wilken's comment on this treatise points to the significance of love and delight for preaching. "For Augustine, love, poured into our hearts by the Holy Spirit, is the soul's movement, the will's energy, the wind that fills the sails of virtue and leads us to embrace the good."[28]

As God's gift, the Spirit is imparted in abundance, kindling the heart's affection and adherence to God while illumining the mind to discern right speech and action in relation to God who is its true end. Rowan Williams notes, "This is why love of God and love of neighbor are not really to be distinguished: love of the neighbor is love of the actual or possible presence of loving generosity in him (either we see it and approve it or don't see it and long for it to be there); but to love loving generosity as the goal and standard of our humanity is to love it as the good . . . which is to love it as God."[29]

There is much wisdom here for preachers. Telling listeners what they need to know and do is not sufficient for human beings who have been created to enjoy the communion of love with each other in God. We must be changed from within by the work of the Spirit, who engenders love for God and others. "We do not have to confront a God who sets before us demands that must be met by our free choices; we have to surrender to sovereign love, so that we become new, and our own activity is opened up to the Spirit who is supremely the gift of love."[30]

---

translated with introductions by John Burnaby, Library of Christian Classics 8 (Philadelphia: Westminster, 1965), 195–250.

27. Augustine, *Spirit and the Letter*, 198.

28. Wilken, *The Spirit of Early Christian Thought*, 288.

29. Williams, *On Augustine*, 160–61.

30. Williams, *On Augustine*, 140.

Augustine believed there is no life of devotion to God, or the good life, unless it be delighted and lived. Love is a gift of the Spirit, "the love of God shed abroad in our hearts, not by the free choice whose spring is in ourselves, but through the Holy Spirit which is given us" (Rom. 5:5).[31] This is delight in not sinning, but it is also delight in the law, which has been written on the heart by the Spirit, the delight of living by faith and doing good works through love that is of the Spirit.[32] As Augustine summarizes, "There can be no better good, no happiness than this; life for God, life from God, with whom is the well of life, in whose light we shall see light."[33] Rowan Williams's discussion of the triune relations is helpful in understanding the Spirit as agent of human transformation and of our participation in the life of God as love. "In other words, the Spirit's godhead is precisely that of the Father and the Son: the loving wisdom of self-giving. But we may say of the Spirit in particular what is true of divinity in general . . . because it is through the Spirit that the life of love and gift which is God lovingly given in the specific history of our salvation and to concrete and diverse individuals. . . . The Spirit as God gives God, gives the reality of self-sharing [wisdom] that exists eternally as the Father's generation of the Word."[34]

Augustine viewed the fear of God evoked by the old covenant as having been transposed into delight, inspired by the new covenant in which the Spirit transforms believers into lovers of God. "For it is the work of the Spirit of grace to renew in us the image of God, in which 'by nature' we were made."[35] Since the Spirit's work will exceed our thoughts and actions, knowing God and God's will is worthy of our devotion and desire, as delighted in and loved.[36] The more we know of God, the more we know God is pleased with faith that

---

31. Augustine, *Spirit and the Letter*, 197–98.
32. Augustine, *Spirit and the Letter*, 198.
33. Augustine, *Spirit and the Letter*, 222.
34. Williams, *On Augustine*, 182–83.
35. Augustine, *Spirit and the Letter*, 226.
36. Augustine, *Spirit and the Letter*, 247.

works through love—for God and neighbor—which is the beauty of holiness with which the Spirit suffuses our preaching.[37] As Harrison observes, disfigured humanity is transfigured in "awareness, knowledge, and love of the gracious redemptive activity of [our] Trinitarian Creator, revealed . . . in the incarnation of the Son, and loved in the inspiration of the Holy Spirit."[38]

Incarnate Beauty

Delighting in the Word occupies a central place in Augustine's Christmas sermons as exemplifications of homiletical beauty.[39] The sermons demonstrate Christian preaching as adoring praise through which the church is summoned to behold the wonder of the incarnate Son of God, the Son of God who manifests God's humble love in the world. Augustine begins by announcing "The birthday of our Lord and Savior, Jesus Christ, the day on which Truth sprang from the earth." This reference to Psalm 85 is read in light of Christ, who is the Truth of God in person. This Truth in person has dawned upon the church "today" in its celebration of his promised coming and birth. Augustine identifies what the church is celebrating and why: in Christ the lowliness of God's greatness has been bestowed upon it as a precious gift that is received by faith. He acknowledges that this is a mystery, recalling the words of Saint Paul that point to God's self-giving in Christ. "God has hidden these things from the wise and prudent, and revealed them to the little ones" (242).

Augustine's reference to Paul does not function as a proof text in support of the sermon. It is a word of pastoral wisdom, a way of using Scripture to interpret Scripture for confessing the "style" of

---

37. Augustine, *Spirit and the Letter*, 247.

38. Harrison, *Augustine*, 44.

39. Here I am drawing from Augustine, *Essential Sermons*, vol. III/25 in *The Works of Saint Augustine: A Translation for the 21st Century* (Hyde Park, NY: New City Press, 2007), 242–53. Hereafter, references to this work will be given in parentheses in the text.

Christ's coming in proclaiming the Word. "So let the humble hold fast to the humility of God, in order that, helped by this wonderful conveyance as by a kind of vehicle for their weakness, they may arrive at the heights of God. As for the wise and prudent there, they aim at the loftiness of God without believing in his humble lowliness, and so, by overstepping this and not reaching that, they have remained empty, weightless, inflated and elated" (242).

Augustine reflects on the reconciliation of God and humanity in Christ, offering a diagnosis of the intellectual, moral, and spiritual effects of sin that prevent human beings from "seeing" the beauty of God's self-giving. This is a matter of perception, of receiving the capacity to "see" God's wisdom in the person of Jesus Christ. Moreover, the reality of God's wisdom in Christ is the basis of the church's rejoicing: "So, then, let us celebrate the birthday of the Lord with all due festive gatherings," a celebration embracing all humanity. Because Christ has been born a man and born of a woman, both male and female have been honored and blessed by his coming. The expansive scope of God's work in Christ prompts Augustine's pastoral exhortation in light of Christ's humble birth. Augustine encourages all manner of people, and in all sorts of conditions and circumstances, to rejoice and be filled with gladness upon hearing the news of God's abundant goodness given in Christ (243–44).

Augustine's manner, or "style" of preaching, is doxological—delighting in the Word, praising God, and giving glory to Christ, who makes visible and restores the glory of humanity in relation to God. Augustine's manner of speaking is therefore "fitting" for the mystery of God's grace revealed in Christ. He does not attempt to explain the doctrine of the virgin birth, nor does he try to reduce the mystery of Christ to make it easier to understand. He does, however, take great care in attending to God revealed in the humanity of Christ, inviting the church to participate by faith in what God has done and continues to do "today." Augustine's delightful conclusion proclaims the One of whom Scripture speaks, to whom it points, and in whom it finds its purpose and end: the God whose glory shines brightly in Christ.

Rightly therefore did the prophets foretell that he would be born, while the heavens and angels announced that he had already been. The one who holds the world in being was lying in a manger; he was both speechless infant and Word. The heavens cannot contain him, a woman carried him in her bosom. She was ruling our ruler, carrying the one in whom we are, suckling our bread. O manifest infirmity and wondrous humility in which was there concealed total divinity! Omnipotence was ruling the mother on whom infancy was depending; was nourishing on truth the mother whose breasts it was suckling. May he bring his gifts to perfection in us, since he did not shrink from making his own our tiny beginnings, and may he make us into children of God, since for our sake he was willing to be made a child of man. (244)

Augustine was neither original nor creative in his preaching. Indeed, his proclamation of the birth of Christ is orthodox in its theology. His commitment to the Trinitarian faith confessed by the church is expressed in the introduction to a sermon preached from Psalm 96 on the occasion of Christ's birth. "This day has been sanctified for us by the Day of all Days, about whom the psalm sings; 'Sing to the Lord a new song, sing to the Lord all the earth. Sing to the Lord and proclaim the goodness of the day from the day.'" According to Augustine, the day is the Son from the Father and Light from Light (248). He marvels at the reconciliation of God and humanity in light of the incarnation; Christ was born so that human creatures might be reborn in him. "The Lord Christ is forever, without beginning, with the Father. And yet ask what today is, it's a birthday. Whose? The Lord's. Has he really got a birthday? He has. The Word in the beginning, God with God has a birthday? Yes, he has. Unless he had a human birth we would never attain to the divine rebirth. He was born that we might be reborn. Let nobody hesitate to be reborn; Christ has been born, born, but with no need of being reborn!" (249).

Augustine's words are a "showing" of God's wonder through a play of words. "The only ones in need of rebirth are those who have been condemned in their first birth. So let his mercy come to be in our hearts. His mother bore him in her womb but we have him in our hearts. The virgin was big with the incarnation of Christ; let our bosoms open big with the faith of Christ. She gave birth to the Savior; let us give birth to praise—we mustn't be barren, our souls must be fruitful with God" (249).

The sermon delights in the wonder of Christ, God's humble love becoming incarnate for the life of the world. God's extravagant self-giving evokes amazement. "It's a great thing, you are astonished. He is God, don't be astonished, let astonishment give way to praise and thanksgiving. Let faith be present, believe that it happened. If you don't believe, it still happened, but you remain unbelieving." Sharing in this astonishment, Augustine invites the congregation to consider what more they could want from God. Answering his own question, he declares what God has already done in humbling himself and becoming human, being laid in a crowded, cramped manger and wrapped in rags. Augustine invites his listeners to join him in "seeing" where this is found: "You heard it when the gospel was read." This news is astonishing indeed. "The one who filled the universe could find no room in a lodging house; he was laid in a feeding trough; he became our food" (250).

Augustine's Christmas sermons are a persuasive invitation to delight in the beauty of Christ as God's incarnate Word. The scope of the sermons is fitting for the abundant goodness of God, and also for the depth of human weakness and neediness before God. The beauty of the sermons shines brightly from the truth of their subject: God's glory and salvation, the goodness of creation, the redemption of humanity in Christ, the church as the visible sign of a new creation. By his careful attentiveness to the "Word made flesh," Augustine unites the praise of God, the faith of the church, and the language of preaching. Preaching is intelligent and adoring praise for God, who speaks to address the church "today." The gospel is good news for the world that makes known the dependence and weakness of Christ's human form, or beauty, as "God with us." Finally, preaching is a public act of worship set on getting the Word into the world through the visibility of the church, a community whose faith and life participate in the beauty of Christ's humble love.

> So let us proclaim the good news from day to day, his salvation; let us proclaim among the nations his glory, among all peoples his wonders (Ps. 96:2–3). He lies in a manger, but he holds the whole world in his hands; he sucks his mother's breasts, but feeds the angels; he is swaddled in rags, but clothes us in immortality; he is suckled, but also worshiped; he could find no room in the inn, but makes a temple for himself in the hearts of believers. It was in order, you see, that weakness might become strong, that strength became weak. Let us therefore rather wonder at than make light of his birth in the flesh and there recognize the lowliness on our behalf of such loftiness. From there let us kindle charity in ourselves, in order to attain his eternity. (253)

Preaching as Humble Speech

Erich Auerbach has traced the roots of the *sermo humilis* (humble speech) to the fathers, with Augustine being its most outstanding proponent in his defense and practice of the biblical writers' lowliness.[40] Ironically, *humilis* is related to *humus*, the soil, and literally means low-lying, of small stature, an allusion to the preacher who embodies the humility of the incarnation in both her speech and her life. This is a voluntary humiliation illustrated by a life on earth among the lowest social classes, among the materially and spiritually poor, and reflecting the whole character of Christ's acts and teachings.[41]

40. Erich Auerbach, *Literary Language and Its Public in Late Antiquity and in the Middle Ages*, trans. Ralph Manheim (New York: Bollingen, 1965), 31–66.
41. See here the insightful discussion of *sermo humilis* in John N. King, *English Reformation Literature: The Tudor Origins of the Protestant Tradition* (Princeton: Princeton University Press, 1982), 319–39.

The purpose of humility, the *ethos* of the preacher and sermon, is to make the message of the Word, its inward and spiritual truth, available to all without intimidating or repelling the unlearned. In popular preaching, the lowly, earthy style that was incarnate in Christ and is embodied in Scripture demonstrates a humility capable of overcoming barriers that impede hearing. Such vulnerability evokes a world of the divine accommodating itself to the weak and lowly in the plain, humble Word through preachers who exemplify Christ's character and wisdom.[42] Here Rowan Williams's comments are apt: "Central to nearly all of Augustine's theology is the assumption that we speak about God and speak to God only from our setting within time and the body. . . . Christian rhetoric is distinctive in that it gives unarguable place to stumbling or derivative performance. Such performance reminds us of the fact that this rhetoric seeks to persuade us not of this or that case or party in the world but of God's 'case.' Faithful discourse insists on its own inadequacy in unambiguous ways."[43]

The paradox of preaching is that God is supremely magnified in the lowly, humble figure of Christ. Moreover, if Christ, the Lord and Son of God, is encountered in the ordinariness of Scripture and sermons, we may be confident that Christ will also be encountered in the ordinary times, places, people, and circumstances of everyday life. In the proclamation of the gospel, the lives of ordinary folk are dignified and granted a place of honor in God's realm of humble service that worships Christ as the Lord of heaven who has come to earth. Augustine's wisdom helps us to see that proclaiming Christ both requires and creates an imagination enlightened and shaped by Scripture. This is a way of seeing reality through the images, figures, and events in Scripture, read by the light of the church's confession of faith in the "Word made flesh." Jason Byassee describes Augus-

---

42. Auerbach, *Literary Language*, 39–47; see the excellent discussion by Peter Auski, *Christian Plain Style: The Evolution of a Spiritual Ideal* (Montreal: McGill-Queen's University Press, 1995), 13–67, 232–66.

43. Williams, *On Augustine*, 32, 34.

tine's approach to Scripture as providing a basis for discerning the appropriateness of biblical interpretation in preaching: "Namely . . . whether it is beautiful. By this we mean whether it is 'fitting' with the words on the page, with the figure of Christ, and with the need of the congregation present to have its affections redirected aright once more."[44]

The reconciliation of humanity by the grace of Christ impels the church to reimagine its life in light of Scripture's story of God and the world—past, present, and future. This remarkable news is proclaimed with thankful praise for God's abundant generosity made visible in and to the world through Christ. The gospel of Jesus Christ unites things high and low, things lofty and simple, so that the most mundane tasks may be seen as joyful service of the neighbor, as fulfilling of the church's calling to show the beauty of Christ in the whole of life.[45] As William Mallard comments on this, "So with Augustine and other church fathers, the Incarnation celebrated the style called *sermo humilis* . . . the unadorned words of and about Christ, yet passionately declared—a summons to a public, yet hidden mystery of salvation."[46]

Debora Shuger argues persuasively that Augustine's vision of preaching transfigures the use of words in the practice of a Christian rhetoric. One learns to speak well of God, that is, with wisdom and eloquence, by hearing and reading exemplary models. While human wisdom and eloquence are necessary for preaching, they are not sufficient, since the Christian speaker must be a person of prayer and love in all she thinks, speaks, and does. Devotion to God, which involves the offering of one's whole self to God, is most important

44. Jason Byassee, *Praise Seeking Understanding: Reading the Psalms with Augustine* (Grand Rapids: Eerdmans, 2007), 152–53; on fittingness, see also Jonathan King, *The Beauty of the Lord: Theology as Aesthetics* (Bellingham, WA: Lexham, 2018), 9–12.

45. Auerbach, *Literary Language*, 48–60.

46. William Mallard, *Language and Love: Introducing Augustine's Religious Thought through the Confessions Story* (University Park: Pennsylvania State University Press, 1994), 165.

and provides the appropriate environment for developing homiletical skill and technique.[47]

Since the Word and human words are reconciled in Christ, nature and grace are not divided. Preaching does not work by the exercise of a distant "cause and effect" power but must be seen as a "working together" for the good as given by God. In a paradoxical way, God's sovereignty and human freedom are bound by the integrity of divine love, which is the source and end of all human delights and love—for God and the neighbor.[48]

Preaching the Melody of Love

The end of preaching for Augustine is that the world should be drawn into the joy of communion, which is the beauty of Trinitarian love. This entails reading Scripture and preaching as the practice of a "pedagogy of love." As Rowan Williams notes, Augustine sees interpretation as an act of love that moves us to a more radical love for God. This is the activity of God, God's own love taking root in us, so that in our way of thinking, feeling, and speaking we become signs of that love, a living "text" or "sermon" that others may read and hear.[49]

As a preacher, Augustine sought to bring his words into harmony with Christ; an attunement to the astonishing love poured out in his humility, weakness, suffering, and death. This attunement lends itself to understanding Augustine's preaching as a form of singing God's praise, since Augustine's practice of preaching was inseparable from his training in classical rhetoric. The art of rhetoric taught him to value imaginative and flexible improvisations that flow from a well-stocked memory, cultivated by disciplined study and practice. William Harmless has written of Augustine's theology and preaching

47. Debora K. Shuger, *Sacred Rhetoric: The Christian Grand Style in the English Renaissance* (Princeton: Princeton University Press, 1988), 42.

48. Shuger, *Sacred Rhetoric*, 42–43.

49. Williams, *On Augustine*, 56.

as a form of "jazz" that is profoundly improvisational. He describes this in four elements: (1) prayer-inspired improvisation; (2) conversation with his audiences; (3) creative reworking of stock themes around the central melody of Christ; and (4) inspiring the hearts and desires of listeners to know, love, and enjoy God in all of life.[50]

In his sermons Augustine aimed to instruct, delight, and move hearts toward a truer and deeper love for God in communion with others. This way of preaching was fitting for a pilgrim church seeking integrity, uniting the means and end of faith, refusing to separate the present and the future, and stirring the affections toward Christ's self-giving love in the whole of life. This is "preaching as a moral pedagogy for earthly pilgrims."[51] The beauty of the gospel is communicated best by the poetic speech of praise, a blending of exegesis, ecclesiology, and eschatology in clear, graceful performances of the Word. Transformed by the Word, the church is made pleasing to God by the beauty of Christ's goodness and love filling and restoring its life.[52]

Augustine's preaching exemplifies the sensibilities of a consummate improviser.[53] The primary focus of preaching is not the perfor-

50. William Harmless, SJ, "A Love Supreme: Augustine's 'Jazz' of Theology," *Augustinian Studies* 43, no. 1–2 (2012): 150. I am indebted to Harmless's fine essay for the construction of the next several paragraphs on Augustine's preaching.

51. Shinji Kayama, "Augustine and Preaching: A Christian Moral Pedagogy," in *The Authority of the Gospel: Explorations in Moral and Political Theology in Honor of Oliver O'Donovan*, ed. Robert Son and Brent Waters (Grand Rapids: Eerdmans, 2015), 102.

52. Harmless, "A Love Supreme," 151.

53. On improvisation, see Samuel Wells, *Improvisation: The Drama of Christian Ethics* (Grand Rapids: Brazos, 2004): "The Bible is not so much a script that the church learns and performs as it is a training school that shapes the habits and practices of the community. This community learns to take the right things for granted, and on the basis of this faithfulness, it trusts itself to improvise within its tradition. Improvisation means a community formed in the right habits trusting itself to embody its tradition in new and often challenging circumstances; and this is exactly what the church is called to do" (12). I would add that Augustine's *City of God* narrates the church's improvisation of the gospel in time and history, thus depicting habits of faithfulness formed by reading, preaching, and living

mance of the preacher but rather the speech and action of God, who manifests himself in the beauty of Christ. For this a particular kind of "attunement" is required: an affective love of God that seeks to perceive God's providential activity in particular times, places, and circumstances. Harmless comments that for Augustine, the preacher is more "played" by delight in the music of revelation than he or she plays. Preachers are human "instruments" whose improvised words are inspired by God to touch and move hearts in the ways God wills.[54]

The primary task of a preacher is to listen with exacting, loving attentiveness to the word of God in Christ, through whom the Spirit renews humanity in the divine image. Augustine focused on that which is lovely, grand, and attractive, following the melody line that resounds through the whole of Scripture to praise the beauty of divine love expressed in Christ.[55] His preaching offered variations on Scripture's words, images, and feelings to display the beauty of Christian faith and life made visible in the world.

Scripture is the primary inspiration for Augustine's homiletic aesthetic, as in-spirited discourse attentive to the smallest details in light of the whole by which he sought "to tease out hidden melodies in the divine biblical chorus."[56] This homiletic aesthetic was deeply pastoral and was performed in partnership with live assemblies of worship. Augustine's preaching was participatory, capable of drawing shouts, applause, groans, and penitential tears responsive to Christ, who speaks through fresh improvisations of Scripture offered up by preachers as acts of praise and love.[57] Jason Byassee writes, "It would be difficult to overstate the importance of this theme—of God's beauty, human desire, and the growth of the latter toward the

---

Scripture. Augustine tells the story of the past to inspire hope in God's promised future that illumines the humble way of Christ in the present.

54. Harmless, "A Love Supreme," 152–53.
55. Harmless, "A Love Supreme," 156.
56. Harmless, "A Love Supreme," 157.
57. Harmless, "A Love Supreme," 158.

former—in Augustine's exegetical work. The entire purpose of biblical interpretation is to move those who attend the liturgy to love of God. The active verb—move—is important, for those present are all pilgrims on the way somewhere, and need to be helped along."[58]

Harmless describes this as "lived" theology, a conversation inspired by the beauty of Christ, the source, content, and form of the church's confession, prayer, and praise. Augustine understood this liturgical context well. Pathos matters as much as words, ideas, and concepts that instruct the mind but do not delight and move the heart to love God and to desire the beauty of God's will in the form of Christ.[59] "Christ's saving work took the form it did precisely to convert our affections, to change our loves and fears, to draw us into the divine beauty."[60]

A deep sense of love and delight in the beauty of Christ perceived in creation, Scripture, and the church characterizes Augustine's sermons as offerings of praise for the wisdom of God's ordering of all things in love.[61] Love is the constant refrain that runs through his preaching; love as the heart of Christian life and faith, love as the heart of God and the world, love as the glory of Scripture, and love

58. Byassee, *Praise Seeking Understanding*, 125.

59. Harmless, "A Love Supreme," 161.

60. Byassee, *Praise Seeking Understanding*, 141. Hildegund Muller points to the "concrete topographical element to Augustine's preaching." She calls attention to the "moving" metaphor and the recurring imagery of movement in his sermons. "This is the image of our pilgrimage on a road toward the heavenly city. Our whole life as Christians is defined by this journey, as is shown by many variations on the formula . . . 'we are on the way. . . .' In many instances . . . the movement from one subject to another actually maps out the path of salvation narrative through history, and thus the path of the church to its ultimate fulfillment." Hildegund Muller, "Preacher: Augustine and His Congregation," in *A Companion to Augustine*, ed. Mark Vessey, with the assistance of Shelley Reid (Oxford: Blackwell, 2012), 307. Here I would see the *City of God* as providing a larger biblical framework for the "topography" of preaching as a theological and pastoral practice of the church on pilgrimage through time.

61. On the beauty of creation as the "signature-style" of God, see Paul J. Griffiths, *Intellectual Appetite: A Theological Grammar* (Washington, DC: Catholic University of America Press, 2009).

as the beauty of the church. Augustine spoke with profound gratitude for the glory of God's love that incites desire and delight in the divine melody resounding in Christ.[62] This way of preaching was radiant, luminous, and deeply felt, a fitting union of heavenly beauty and human affection capable of evoking awe and wonder in making known the glory of God's love poured out for the church and the world.[63]

Augustine does not provide "how to" steps or a formula for successful preaching. Instead, he offers us a vision of the wisdom of preaching that serves the church on pilgrimage toward its final completion in knowing, praising, and loving God. By attending to Christ as the primary focus of Scripture, our life and speech as preachers are rightly ordered to discern what is fitting for building up the church to delight in God's justice and love in particular times, places, and circumstances. Augustine thus "used" Scripture to form the eschatological imagination of the church in preaching to orient the heart and mind to a future unfolding in the present. His is an exemplary homiletical aesthetic that begins with, is guided by, and is oriented toward contemplating the evangelical beauty of Christ, the "Word made flesh."

62. Harmless, "A Love Supreme," 167.
63. Harmless, "A Love Supreme," 167.

– five –

A SIMPLE BEAUTY

My interest in the beauty of preaching was inspired in part by the practice of the Trinitarian faith within the tradition bearing the name "Wesleyan." For John Wesley, preaching is generated by the Father's sending of the Son in the power of the Spirit, who breathes the beauty of holy love into hearers at particular times, places, and circumstances—"to the right person, to the right extent, at the right time, with the right aim, and in the right way . . . the love of God and man not only filling my heart, but shining through my whole conversation."[1]

The message of the gospel creates its own medium; the calling and formation of witnesses whose life and speech make known the humble receptivity and generous self-giving of Christ, the Incarnate Word of the Father and the source and goal of genuine Christian preaching.[2] As Thomas Langford clarifies, "Christian holiness is first a gospel, and only then a quality of life."[3] Preachers are called to the holy and happy task of proclaiming Christ, the crucified and risen Lord whose beauty reverberates through one's being, as the heart,

---

1. John Wesley, "An Address to the Clergy," in *The Works of John Wesley*, 3rd ed. (Grand Rapids: Baker Books, 1978), 485, 499.

2. See the informative account in David Hempton, *Methodism: Empire of the Spirit* (New Haven: Yale University Press, 2005), 53–85.

3. Thomas A. Langford, *Practical Divinity: Theology in the Wesleyan Tradition*, vol. 1, rev. ed. (Nashville: Abingdon, 1998), 35.

soul, mind, and strength are filled with the love of God and the neighbors with whom we are called to speak.[4]

Wesley spoke of God's "design" in raising up the preachers called "Methodists," which was "to reform the nation, and in particular, the Church: to spread scriptural holiness over the land."[5] There is a compelling attractiveness to the design, the moral beauty of scriptural holiness taking form in the worship and witness of the church.[6] However, evangelization by the Wesleyans was the fruit of participating in a larger purpose: the proclamation and enactment of the gospel within an economy of creating, justifying, and sanctifying grace through faith in Christ that is energized by the Spirit's love.[7] Charles Wesley gives voice to the desire, devotion, and direction of early Methodist prayer, praise, and preaching.

> Love divine, all loves excelling,
> > joy of heaven, to earth come down;
> > fix in us thy humble dwelling;
> > > all thy faithful mercies crown!
> Jesus, thou art all compassion,
> > pure, unbounded love thou art;
> > visit us with thy salvation;
> > > enter into every trembling heart.[8]

---

4. Albert C. Outler, *Evangelism and Theology in the Wesleyan Spirit* (Nashville: Discipleship Resources, 2004), 104.

5. *The Works of John Wesley*, bicentennial ed., 32 vols. (Nashville: Abingdon, 1984–), 10:854. Hereafter, this edition will be cited as *WJW* in the notes; sermons cited from these works will contain the sermon title, volume, and page number.

6. See the discussion of the Christian plain style of speaking and spiritual beauty in Peter Auski, *Christian Plain Style: The Evolution of a Spiritual Ideal* (Montreal: McGill-Queen's University Press, 1995), 309–10.

7. On the ecclesial implications of sanctification, see Randy Maddox, *Responsible Grace: John Wesley's Practical Theology* (Nashville: Kingswood Books, 1994).

8. Charles Wesley, "Love Divine, All Loves Excelling," in *The United Methodist Hymnal: Book of United Methodist Worship* (Nashville: United Methodist Publishing House, 2002), 384.

The joy of preaching, singing, and celebrating the good news of God's love for the world in Christ was the fruit of prayerful attentiveness to the canon of Scripture, Christian tradition, and lives of the saints within the sacramental life of the church.[9] Sermons and songs were public acclamations of praise in response to the extravagant love of the Father, who, by sending the Son in the power of the Spirit, calls and creates a holy people in the world.[10]

Jason Vickers's study of eighteenth-century Protestant theology in England helps to clarify the significance of the Wesleys' ministry of teaching and assisting people to know and love God through prayer, worship, preaching, and the sacraments. He shows that the Trinity was not an abstract doctrine in early Methodism but rather the name of God people needed to know to respond rightly in acts of prayer and praise for the saving activities of the Father, Son, and Holy Spirit. To this end, Wesleyan sermons and hymns were living reminders of the rightful home of Trinitarian language in giving glory to God. This entailed participating in "the invocation, worship, and praise of God that the church encountered initially in the coming of Jesus Christ and of the Holy Spirit and presently in her worshiping life."[11]

Contrary to the widely held opinion of many contemporary Wesleyans, numerical growth and social change were not the primary end or goal. These were celebrated as the fruition of the Spirit's grace made visible in personal and social holiness, as grace-induced signs of God's reign coming on earth through faith in Christ that is active in

9. See Ryan Danker's discussion of Wesley's expectation that early Methodists would share his love for the established church and its liturgical and sacramental ethos, functioning as an "evangelical order" within a surrounding environment of catholicity. Danker's discussion shows how Wesley's evangelical passion and strategies served to work against his desire that Methodism be a renewal movement within the Church of England. Ryan Nicholas Danker, *Wesley and the Anglicans: Political Division in Early Evangelicalism* (Downers Grove, IL: IVP Academic, 2016), 98–110.

10. Kenneth Wilson, *Methodist Theology* (London: T&T Clark, 2011), 19–38.

11. Jason E. Vickers, *Invocation and Assent: The Making and Remaking of Trinitarian Theology* (Grand Rapids: Eerdmans, 2008), 169–70.

love.[12] Charles Wesley gives elegant expression to the simple beauty of proclaiming Christ in the following hymn:

> Ye servants of God, your Master proclaim,
> and publish abroad his wonderful name;
> the name all victorious of Jesus extol,
> his kingdom is glorious and rules over all.[13]

John Wesley identified preaching as "offering Christ" in his prophetic, priestly, and kingly offices, through which sinners are convicted, sins are pardoned, and the capacity for God's goodness is restored.[14] Preachers must not lose sight of God's beauty revealed in the holiness of Christ, which means that the fullness and harmony of Holy Scripture must be proclaimed with words carefully chosen with conviction and clarity. Wesley summarizes the task of preaching Christ in a passage that shows the intimate relation of the law and gospel.

> To preach Christ as a workman that needeth not to be ashamed is preaching him not only as our great "High Priest, pertaining to God," as such, "reconciling us to God by his blood," and "ever living to make intercession for us," but likewise as the Prophet of the Lord, "who of God is made unto us wisdom," who by his word and his Spirit "is with us always," "guiding us into all truth," yea, and as remaining King forever; as giving laws to all whom

---

12. L. Faye Short and Kathryn D. Kiser write, "Personal and social holiness work together in a synergistic and cooperative relationship. They act together to increase the effect of one another. Personal growth in holiness combines with outward good works. Increased zeal and performance of outward good works increases one's zeal for personal experience of inner growth in grace and holiness." L. Faye Short and Kathryn D. Kiser, *Reclaiming the Wesleyan Social Witness: Offering Christ* (Franklin, TN: Providence House Publishers, 2008), 11.

13. Charles Wesley, "Ye Servants of God," in *The United Methodist Hymnal*, 181.

14. See Wesley's sermons "The Law Established by Faith I and II," in *WJW*, 2:37–38.

he has bought with his blood; as restoring those to the image of God whom he has first reinstated to his favour; as reigning in all believing hearts until he has "subdued all things to himself"; until he hath utterly cast out all sin, and "brought everlasting righteousness."[15]

The preaching of the gospel tells the story of God who creates and redeems the world so that God's holiness might be shared by a people empowered by grace to live holy lives. Wesley's preaching was fired by the conviction that all people can be adorned by the beauty of divine love through the work of the Holy Spirit in whom the life of God is "a continual action of God upon the soul, the reaction of the soul upon God; an unceasing presence of God, the loving, pardoning God, manifested in the heart, and perceived by faith; and an unceasing return of love, praise, and prayer, offering up all the thoughts of our hearts, all the words of our tongues, all the works of our hands, all our body, soul, and spirit, to be an holy sacrifice, acceptable unto God in Christ Jesus."[16]

Wesley has been called a "Protestant Francis of Assisi." The simple beauty of his preaching is not found in its eloquent, elaborate, or entertaining oratory, but rather in the breadth of its reach *ad populum* to eighteenth-century coal miners, laborers, mill workers, scrubwomen, prisoners, soldiers, and in general, large crowds of common people.[17] Wesley proclaimed the beauty of the gospel plainly and with conviction and compassion: justification by faith, the sanctification of life, the new birth, and the assurance of salvation's fullness in communion with the triune God.[18]

Such homiletical simplicity requires profound familiarity with the

15. John Wesley, "The Law Established by Faith II," in *WJW*, 2:37–38.

16. John Wesley, "The Great Privilege of Those That Are Born of God," in *WJW*, 1:442.

17. Hughes Oliphant Old, *Moderation, Pietism, and Awakening*, vol. 5 in *The Reading and Preaching of the Scriptures in the Worship of the Christian Church* (Grand Rapids: Eerdmans, 2004), 111.

18. Wesley, despite his commitment to plain speech for preaching to common people, is to be understood as seeking to restore the Church of England to a vision of "vital religion" that, according to Ryan Danker, was "based on the church

language of Scripture, as well as the exercise of practical wisdom for carefully rendering its images in a "fresh, vivid, and arresting" manner with humility and love.[19] A hymn by Charles Wesley, "Before Reading the Scriptures," offers a poetic invocation of the Holy Spirit's presence to illumine the reading and preaching of the word of God in Scripture. The transforming work of the Spirit radiates the beauty of God's life and love that forms the basis of a Wesleyan aesthetic.

> Come, Holy Ghost, our hearts inspire,
>   Let us thine influence prove,
> Source of the old prophetic fire,
>   Fountain of life and love.
> Come, Holy Ghost (for moved by thee
>   The Prophets wrote and spoke);
> Unlock the truth, thyself the key,
>   Unseal the sacred book.
> Expand thy wings, celestial dove,
>   Brood o'er our nature's night;
> On our disordered spirits move,
>   And let there now be light.
> God through himself we then shall know,
>   If thou within us shine;
> And sound, with all thy saints below,
>   The depths of love divine.[20]

---

fathers as read through high church Anglicanism and the Caroline divines." Danker, *Wesley and the Anglicans*, 249.

19. Old, *Moderation, Pietism, and Awakening*, 131; Debora Shuger identifies a plain, passionate style of preaching in the medieval period that was fitting for popular audiences. It emphasized the preacher's character or virtue, prayer and preparation, and evangelical purpose. Sermons were simple since verbal eloquence would detract from the pressing need of seeking the spiritual good of hearers through the "impassionating Word." Shuger concludes, "The passion of the sermon arises from the speaker's own ardor and from the activity of the Holy Spirit arousing his heart and giving efficacy to his words." Debora K. Shuger, *Sacred Rhetoric: The Christian Grand Style in the English Renaissance* (Princeton: Princeton University Press, 1988), 51–53.

20. Charles Wesley, "Before Reading the Scriptures," in *A Collection of Hymns*

The End of Preaching: Holiness and Happiness in God

Wesley was a teleological thinker, which means he understood that all such truly human aspirations are oriented toward a life of holiness and happiness by becoming like God in goodness.[21] This restless hunger can only be satisfied by following the way of Jesus Christ, who embodies fully the beauty of a new creation.[22] Happiness is found in enjoying the gracious presence of God, in returning our deepest self to God as we are moved by the affections that spring from loving desire that is responsive to God's self-gift in Christ. As Debora Shuger comments on the role of the affections in preaching: "The direction of our love determines who we are."[23] This entails a purification of the heart by the disciplining of our passions and prejudices so that we may perceive clearly the truth, goodness, and beauty of God revealed in Jesus Christ.

Methodist preaching thus aimed to spread holiness and happiness, and participation in a fellowship of holy living and dying in communion with God both in this life and in the life to come. This is the nature of "true religion," the knowledge and love of God, which is the religion of Christ. Wesley clarifies this important matter in his sermon from Mark 1:15, "The Way to the Kingdom," which shows the beauty of the Christian life. He announces at the outset that true religion consists of "righteousness, peace, and joy in the Holy Ghost." However, what true religion is not must also be clarified. True religion is not merely an outward thing such as forms of worship, rites, and ceremonies. True religion is not merely abstaining from evil and doing good works such as feeding the hungry and clothing the

---

for the Use of the People Called Methodists, ed. Franz Hildebrandt and Oliver A. Beckerlegge (Nashville: Abingdon, 1983), 7:185.

21. In writing the following section, I have benefited from D. Stephen Long, *John Wesley's Moral Theology: The Quest for God and Goodness* (Nashville: Abingdon, 2005).

22. John Wesley, "The Great Privilege of Those That Are Born of God," in *WJW*, 1:442.

23. Shuger, *Sacred Rhetoric*, 254.

naked. True religion is not merely adhering to orthodoxy or having right opinions, including about the incarnation and the Trinity, and holding to the Apostles', Nicene, and Athanasian Creeds.[24]

True religion is giving one's heart to God, as declared by the apostle Paul in Romans 14:17; it is "righteousness and peace and joy in the Holy Spirit." Wesley saw this light of the Great Commandment with its "two grand branches," to love God with all we are and have, and to love our neighbor as ourselves. Of loving God, Wesley affirms, "Thou shalt delight thyself in the Lord thy God; thou shalt seek and find all happiness in him. . . . Thou shalt hear and fulfill his word who saith, 'My son, give me thy heart.' And having given him thy heart, thy inmost soul, to reign without rival, thou mayest well cry out in the fullness of thy heart, 'I will love thee, O Lord, my strength. The Lord is my strong rock and my defence: my Savior, my God, and my might, in whom I trust, my buckler, the horn also of my salvation, and my refuge."[25]

And of loving our neighbors, Wesley has much to say. "Thou shalt love—thou shalt embrace with the most tender good-will, the most earnest and cordial affection, the most inflamed desires of preventing or removing all evil and of procuring for him every possible good." He then clarifies just who is "thy neighbor." Our neighbor is not only our friends, family members, or acquaintances; it is not only the virtuous and the friendly, those that love us, and those that return our kindness. Our neighbor is every human being, every soul God has made. Loving our neighbor means not excepting those we have never met, those we do not recognize by appearance or name; it also means not excepting those we know to be evil and unthankful, even those that still use and persecute us. Wesley concludes, "Him thou shalt 'love as thyself'; with the same invariable thirst after his happiness in every kind, the same unwearied care to screen him from whatever might grieve or hurt either his soul or body."[26]

True religion of the heart ordered rightly by the love of God and

24. John Wesley, "The Way to the Kingdom," in *WJW*, 1:220.
25. John Wesley, "The Way to the Kingdom," in *WJW*, 1:221.
26. John Wesley, "The Way to the Kingdom," in *WJW*, 1:221–22.

love of others implies both holiness and happiness in God.[27] Preaching becomes a holy and happy activity as we are taken up by the Spirit in the joy of proclaiming the presence of God's self-giving love in Christ, who is freely received with the gift of faith. As Albert Outler explains, for Wesley "faith is a means in order to love, just as love is in order to goodness, just as goodness is in order to happiness—which is what God made us for in this world and the next."[28]

Wesley drew from the wisdom of a tradition influenced by early Christian moral thinking, which took root in the soil of ancient moral philosophy; it was marked by imitation, the virtues, interior dispositions, character, and transformation into the divine image and likeness. This tradition was not rejected by the early church; rather, its framework was maintained and adapted to fit the truth, goodness, and beauty of the triune God's self-revelation in Christ. For this the Sermon on the Mount provided the fundamental call to be holy, to be "perfect . . . as your heavenly Father is perfect" (Matt. 5:48).[29]

Christians understood their life in light of the promised fulfillment of God's promises through Christ by the Spirit's power. Christian speech and action were assessed and judged when directed to the most praiseworthy of all ends—the flourishing of human lives through participation in the life of the triune God, who is the supreme good; a good, however, that is not a means to other ends.[30]

The aim of this vision was to lead people to a good and happy life in God, which is fitting for our truest and deepest aspirations as human creatures. It is significant, then, that the Beatitudes begin with "blessed" or "happy," so that Jesus is heard as the Teacher of God's Wisdom and

27. John Wesley, "The Way to the Kingdom," in *WJW*, 1:219–22.

28. Outler, *Evangelism and Theology in the Wesleyan Spirit*, 130.

29. See here the discussion of Wesley's moral theology in Long, *John Wesley's Moral Theology*, 125–202.

30. Robert L. Wilken, *The Spirit of Early Christian Thought: Seeking the Face of God* (New Haven: Yale University Press, 2003), 262–72; Servais Pinckaers, OP, *The Sources of Christian Ethics*, trans. Sr. Mary Thomas Noble, OP (Washington, DC: Catholic University Press of America, 1995), 1–44.

followed as the Way leading to happiness and holiness as the goal of human life in God. The Beatitudes were thus read as depicting both the character and the wisdom leading to that end. Because God is the highest good of human life, nothing else is sufficient for human creatures made in God's image. Only communion with God, consisting of knowledge, love, and delight, can bring fulfillment to human life. Moreover, in returning to God by the work of divine grace, we are drawn into fellowship with others and brought into genuine happiness. As Robert Wilken observes, for the early Christians holy and happy were one: "For Christians, the moral life and the religious life were complementary. Although thinking about the moral life moved within a conceptual framework inherited from Greek and Latin moralists, Christian thinkers redefined the good by making fellowship with the living God the end; revised the beginning by introducing the teaching that we are made in the image of God, and complicated the middle with talk of the intractability and inevitability of sin."[31]

Holiness and happiness are the "more" for which human beings long, and which are received as gifts through the revelatory action of the triune God. Since the Christian life is itself Trinitarian, goodness and happiness are possessed in Christ and bestowed by the Holy Spirit, who grants a new identity in the fellowship of the church.

Holy Preaching, Holy Living

Because Wesley was firmly rooted in the wisdom of Christian tradition, he understood that the life of faith, hope, and love is hard, mysterious, and grand beyond telling. At the same time, he labored to educate and equip preachers for proclaiming Christ in plain, passionate speech that communicates the joy of knowing and loving God. He expected preachers to have a good grasp of human nature as created in the image of God, and the virtues, spiritual fruits, and

---

31. Wilken, *The Spirit of Early Christian Thought*, 275.

Christian means of grace that lead to real human happiness and a good human life in Christ.

This involved preachers in rigorous training within an ecclesial environment constituted by doctrine, devotion, and discipline that dispose one's thoughts, words, and affections toward sound judgment, wise discernment, and good taste in the ministry of the Word. Vicki Tolar Burton summarizes Wesley's development of preachers in the following manner: "Wesley brought plain-style, gospel-based, heart-centered preaching delivered by passionate, plain-speaking, gospel-reading men, and . . . by passionate, plain-speaking, gospel-reading women as well."[32]

Homiletical beauty, Christian speech that is wise and good, is akin to "love speaking well." Uniting knowledge and affection, homiletical wisdom is shaped by single-minded devotion to the beauty of God's holiness displayed in the whole narrative of Jesus Christ.[33] As Wesley observes, "It is wisdom to aim at the best end by the best means. Now the best end which any creature can pursue is happiness in God. And the best end a fallen creature can pursue is the recovery of the favor and image of God, which is better than life itself. And this is by the righteousness of faith, believing in the only-begotten Son of God."[34] Wesley saw this truth summed up beautifully by a petition that seeks to know, love, and glorify God. "Cleanse the thoughts of our hearts by the inspiration of thy Holy Spirit, that we may perfectly love thee, and worthily magnify thy holy name."[35] Here Geoffrey Wainwright's summary of a Wesleyan hermeneutic of holy love

32. Vicki Tolar Burton, *Spiritual Literacy in John Wesley's Methodism: Reading, Writing, and Speaking to Believe* (Waco, TX: Baylor University Press, 2008), 149. See the excellent historical introduction to a "passionate, plain style" of preaching in Shuger, *Sacred Rhetoric*.

33. Michael S. Sherwin, *By Knowledge and by Love: Charity and Morality in the Moral Theology of St. Thomas Aquinas* (Washington, DC: Catholic University of America Press, 2005), 106–18.

34. John Wesley, "The Righteousness of Faith," in *WJW*, 1:213–14.

35. John Wesley, "On Laying the Foundation of the New Chapel," in *WJW*, 3:586.

is helpful for seeing the intimate connection between the message and its messengers. "Study of the Scriptures in the Spirit, by whom they were divinely written, conveys the incarnate Christ, who gives knowledge of the Father who sent him, so that we may love the Father and thus be conformed to the Son and enjoy the holiness which the Spirit gives."[36]

Wesley perceived the intimate link between our homiletical practice and holy living. At the same time, he recognized that the holiness of preachers cannot be separated from the life of a holy people raised up by the love of the Father and the Son in the Spirit through the means of grace. "Holy preaching," then, will be faithful to the wisdom of Scripture *and* fitting for communities called to repentance and maturing toward God through the perfection of love.[37] Here it is important to note that Wesley's doctrine of God and his doctrine of Christian perfection are vitally connected. Kenneth Loyer's comments help us understand this intimate relation that is also significant for thinking about the beauty of preaching and a preacher's formation by that beauty. We cannot preach that in which we do not participate through the work of the Holy Spirit. "Wesley's conception of perfect love can be said to have a trinitarian basis by virtue of its firm grounding in God's saving action in and for the world. . . . As Christians experience God through their spiritual senses, they come to a deeper knowledge of God and a greater love for God and neighbor, unto the perfection that is attainable by God's grace. In other words, through the work of the Holy Spirit they are renewed in the divine image and drawn increasingly into the life of the God *whose 'darling attribute' is love: Father, Son, and Holy Spirit*."[38]

---

36. Geoffrey Wainwright, "The Trinitarian Hermeneutic of John Wesley," in *Reading the Bible in Wesleyan Ways: Some Constructive Proposals*, ed. Barry L. Callen and Richard P. Thompson (Kansas City, MO: Beacon Hill, 2004), 23.

37. Ellen F. Davis, with Austin McIver Dennis, *Preaching the Luminous Word: Biblical Sermons and Homiletical Essays* (Grand Rapids: Eerdmans, 2016), 90.

38. Kenneth M. Loyer, *God's Love through the Spirit: The Holy Spirit in Thomas*

Such human flourishing requires an ecclesial culture sufficiently capable of inspiring the holiness without which we cannot see the triune God, who is the source and goal of our life. When oriented to this end, holy preaching calls the church to immerse itself in the grand story of Scripture's witness to God's creative and redemptive works that find their fullness in the knowledge and love of Christ.[39] As Robert Wall notes, "Wesley's sermons were centered by the grand themes of the *ordo salutis* [order of salvation] and became theological commentaries on how God's salvation related to its audience in practical ways."[40]

Holy preaching draws us into a participatory vision of salvation through the Spirit's workings of divine grace. And by divine grace, "God dwells among us in order to bring about our reconciliation; our sanctification; even our transfiguration."[41] Here Debra Dean Murphy's comments are illuminating: "Christ draws us into the beauty of the triune God and summons from us outward expressions of what we already are: sharers in the divine nature. For Wesley, love of God and neighbor is the centerpiece of Christian perfection which he clarifies in the following manner, 'By perfection, I mean the humble, gentle, patient love of God, and our neighbor, ruling our tempers, words, and actions.'"[42] While Wesleyan preaching declares the triumph of God's beauty in Christ's death and resurrection, it has no place for a Christian "triumphalism" that is ugly.

Aquinas and John Wesley (Washington, DC: Catholic University Press of America, 2014), 61; emphasis added.

39. See the excellent discussion in Rowan Williams, *On Christian Theology* (Oxford: Blackwell, 2000), 142–48.

40. Robert W. Wall, "Toward a Wesleyan Hermeneutic of Scripture," in Callen and Thompson, *Reading the Bible in Wesleyan Ways*, 54.

41. Horton Davies, *Worship and Theology in England*, vol. 2, *From Watts to Wesley to Martineau, 1690–1900* (Grand Rapids: Eerdmans, 1996), 194–97.

42. Debra Dean Murphy, *Happiness, Health, and Beauty: The Christian Life in Everyday Terms*, with Questions for Consideration by Andrew Kinsey (Eugene, OR: Cascade, 2015), 84.

The Beauty of Preaching and the Poor

Because the church has no outward beauty in itself, we need to remember the means of grace, particularly the intimate connection of the works of piety and mercy that participate in the humility of Christ.[43] Wesley saw these as necessary to sanctification, the working out of full salvation, the holiness that shows forth Christ's beauty in acts of self-giving love for God and neighbors. For example, as works of mercy, preaching and ministering to the poor are not merely a matter of social activism or moral obligation. God has so made this ministry to have a unifying, even "beautifying" effect on those who experience the joy of mutual giving and receiving by sharing in Christ's love and goodness.[44]

A hymn by Charles Wesley invites us to see the significance of the poor as Christ's beloved.

> The poor, as Jesus' bosom-friends,
>> The poor he makes his latest care,
> To all his successors commends,
>> And wills us on our hands to bear:
> The poor our dearest care we make,
>> Aspiring to superior bliss,
> And cherish for their Saviour's sake,
>> And love them with a love like his.[45]

43. Here I have benefited from the excellent essays in Richard P. Heitzenrater, ed., *The Poor and the People Called Methodists, 1729–1999* (Nashville: Abingdon, 2002).

44. See Richard Heitzenrater, "The Poor and the People Called Methodists," in Heitzenrater, *The Poor and the People Called Methodists, 1729–1999*, 15–38. "Wesley theologized the motivation for charitable activities. His basic goal in this regard was for Methodists to imitate the life of Christ, not improve the national economy. He conceived of the problem theologically in terms of love of God and love of neighbor rather than in terms of defining minimum wage, improving the country's wealth, or solving a social problem. Everyone in every level of society was a child of God and deserved to be treated as such" (36).

45. Cited in Ted A. Campbell, "The Image of Christ in the Poor: On the

The poor, then, are intimately connected to Christ and central to preaching and living the gospel, since the fulfillment of Christian living remains conformity to the mind of Christ which is a sharing in his way of self-emptying love. In the particular story of early Methodism, the gospel was a message quite often spoken and heard by humble people who lived and served out of love for Christ and who rejoiced in the gift of his abundant grace and goodness.[46] They saw Christ's ministry with the poor, including his preaching, as attending to both physical and spiritual needs in his mission as the incarnate Son of God.[47] As a preacher himself, Charles Wesley hymned the intimate connection of preaching the gospel *and* serving the poor as the measure of participation in the joy of Christ's mission.

> On us, O Christ, thy mission prove,
> Thy full authority to heal,
> The blindness of our hearts remove,
> The lameness of our feeble will,
> Open our faith's obedient ear,
> Our filthy, leprous nature cure,
> And preach Perfection to the poor.[48]

Works of piety—activities such as prayer, reading Scripture, preaching, worship, and the sacraments—are joined with works of

---

Medieval Roots of the Wesleys' Ministry with the Poor," in Heitzenrater, *The Poor and the People Called Methodists, 1729–1999*, 51.

46. Hempton, *Methodism*, 85.

47. Randy Maddox, "'Visiting the Poor': John Wesley, the Poor, and the Sanctification of Believers," in Heitzenrater, *The Poor and the People Called Methodists, 1729–1999*, 68: "The integral connection Wesley makes between works of mercy and the sanctified life reflects deep disagreement with any such merely instrumental valuation of works of mercy and with the spiritualized view of salvation that underlies it."

48. Charles Wesley, *Unpublished Poetry*, 2:100, cited in S. T. Kimbrough, "Perfection Revisited," in Heitzenrater, *The Poor and the People Called Methodists, 1729–1999*, 105.

mercy such as ministry with the poor, the sick, the destitute, the imprisoned, widows, and orphans. The Wesleys viewed works of mercy as means of grace that contribute to nurturing virtue and devotion in all who share themselves with others in mutual love and service. Loving the poor and needy, then, has a revelatory rather than merely functional effect, since such ministry is a place of meeting the risen Lord by participating in his self-giving love for humanity.[49] Charles Wesley gives lovely expression to this in poetic form:

> Thus fit us, Savior, for heav'n,
> as with gladness we restore
> all that God has freely giv'n
> to his deputies, the poor.
> God has chosen the simple poor
> as the followers of his Son,
> rich in faith, of glory sure,
> they shall win the heav'nly crown.[50]

Following the way of selfless love and poverty of spirit directs our attention to the humble image of Christ with and among the poor, which is inherent to the simple beauty of speaking and living the gospel. Because the poor are both recipients and images of Christ's grace and mercy, they occupy a central place in the Spirit's renewing of our minds in the knowledge and love of God whose glory we perceive and proclaim in Christ.[51]

Preachers lead by following the pattern of Christ's holiness honored in the humility of the poor. This is inseparable from poverty of spirit, or lowliness of heart. For John Wesley, genuine Christian humility flows from "a sense of the love of God, reconciled to us in

49. Maddox, "'Visiting the Poor,'" 69–76.

50. Charles Wesley, "Ambitious, covetous, vain," in *Help Us to Help Each Other: Hymns for Life and Ministry with the Poor*, ed. S. T. Kimbrough Jr., music editor, and Carlton R. Young (Madison, NJ: Charles Wesley Society, 2010), 22–23.

51. See the discussion in Campbell, "The Image of Christ in the Poor," 39–58.

Christ Jesus . . . as a continual sense of our total dependence on him for every good thought or word or work."[52] Here it is also important to remember that the way of humility and self-denial for the sake of recognizing the poor as recipients of God's perfect love was central for Jesus in his ministry of proclaiming and enacting God's reign. A hymn by Charles Wesley calls upon God to pour out an abundance of the Spirit's renewing love, which is received in opening oneself to love and serve others in God.

> Come, thou holy God and true!
> Come, and my whole heart renew;
> Take me now, possess me whole,
> Form the Savior in my soul:
> In my heart thy name reveal.
> Stamp me with the Spirit's seal,
> Change my nature into thine,
> In me thy whole image shine.
> Love immense, and unconfined,
> Love to all of humankind.[53]

Beautiful preaching entails glad receptivity to the immensity *and* humility of God's love in Christ, who stoops to dwell among the poor and lowly. The Holy Spirit conforms us to Christ's moral excellence with his gifts, grace, and fruit, by which we mature in faith, advance in hope, and embody "a beauty, a love, a, holiness."[54] Wesley provides a fitting description of preaching that highlights the simple beauty of Christ's humble love displayed in communicating the gospel. "Nor is it a little advantage . . . to hear a preacher whom you know to live as he speaks, speaking the genuine gospel of present salvation through

52. John Wesley, "Sermon on the Mount I," in *WJW*, 1:482.

53. Charles Wesley, "Come, Thou Holy God and True," in *Help Us to Help Each Other: Hymns for Life and Ministry with the Poor*, ed. S. T. Kimbrough and Carlton R. Young (Drew, NJ: Charles Wesley Society, 2010), 44–45.

54. Eugene H. Peterson, *Under the Unpredictable Plant: An Exploration in Vocational Holiness* (Grand Rapids: Eerdmans/Gracewing, 1992), 21.

faith, wrought in the heart by the Holy Ghost, declaring present, free, full justification, and enforcing every branch of inward and outward holiness. And this you hear done in the most clear plain, simple, unaffected language, yet with an earnestness becoming the importance of the subject and with the demonstration of the Spirit."[55] As Burton notes, this is a "rhetoric for the common people."[56]

To this end, Wesley directed Methodist preachers to cultivate habits of daily prayer and study in order to contemplate the fullness of Scripture's saving wisdom and to speak its truth in love with great care. The aim of such learning is vocational holiness, the formation of preachers endued with a joy expressed in gratitude to God, devotion to God, and generous love for all listeners without discriminations.[57] A good example of this can be seen in Samuel Bradburn, a younger contemporary of Wesley and fellow Methodist minister who used a prayer by Thomas Aquinas before his studies to seek God's guidance in preaching.

> Ineffably wise and good Creator, illustrious origin, true fountain of light and wisdom, vouchsafe to infuse into my understanding some ray of thy brightness, thereby removing that two fold darkness under which I was born of sin and ignorance. . . . Thou that makest the tongues of infants eloquent, instruct, I pray thee, my tongue like-wise: and pour upon my lips the grace of thy benediction. Give me quickness to comprehend; and memory to retain; give me a happiness in expounding; a facility in learning; and a copious eloquence in speaking. Prepare my entrance into learning, direct me in my journey, and render the event of it complete, through Jesus Christ, our Lord. Amen.[58]

55. Cited in Karen B. Westerfield Tucker, "Wesley's Emphasis on Worship and the Means of Grace," in *The Cambridge Companion to John Wesley*, ed. Randy L. Maddox and Jason E. Vickers (Cambridge: Cambridge University Press, 2010), 236.

56. Burton, *Spiritual Literacy in John Wesley's Methodism*, 23.

57. See the excellent discussion of Wesley's method of educating preachers in Burton, *Spiritual Literacy in John Wesley's Methodism*, 105–13.

58. Cited in Burton, *Spiritual Literacy in John Wesley's Methodism*, 136. See also the larger discussion of Bradburn's formation and practice of preaching (134–43).

This kind of learning cultivates an attunement of one's heart and mind to the witness of the Spirit as the wellspring of prayer, love, and gratitude in proclaiming the gospel of Jesus Christ. Wesley saw this as entailing a reordering of our affections and perception by which we increase in the knowledge and enjoyment of God. As he states, "[He or she] that delights and rejoices in [God] with an humble joy, and holy delight, and an obedient love—is a child of God."[59]

The minutes of the 1746 Methodist conference of preachers preserves a series of questions devoted to the examination or "trying" of those who believed they had been led by the Spirit and called to preach. The questions address a preacher's faith, love, and devotion, as well as the quality of one's knowledge and judgment appropriate to the task of preaching and discerning the spiritual and moral condition of listeners.

This will require cultivating the wisdom and virtue that enable a preacher to "see" and name the world in light of God's past, present, and future work in Christ. The Wesleyan examination of preachers to discern their calling and "fitness" provides an insightful depiction of homiletical beauty that is intimately related to the holiness of one's life and speech. It also raises important questions regarding the purpose of theological education, and particularly the formation of preachers.

> Do they know in whom they have believed?; Have they the love of God in their hearts?; Do they desire and seek nothing but God?; And are they holy in all manner of conversation?; Have they a clear understanding?; Have they a right judgment in the things of God?; Have they a just conception of the salvation by faith?; And has God given them any degree of utterance? Do they speak justly, readily, clearly?; . . . Do they not only speak as generally either to convince or affect the hearts—but have any received remission of sins by their preaching—a clear and lasting

59. John Wesley, "The Witness of the Spirit I," in *WJW*, 1:276.

sense of the love of God?; As long as these . . . marks undeniably concur in any, we allow him to be called of God to preach. These we receive as sufficient evidence that he is moved thereto by the Holy Ghost.[60]

Preaching in the Beauty of Holiness

The witness of the Spirit bears fruit in holy desire that adorns our thoughts, words, and actions with the beauty of the gospel. Wesley summarizes this as a formation of the heart that occurs by walking after the Spirit. He provides a beautiful sketch of those called to preach and minister in the church.

They who "walk after the Spirit" are also led by him into all holiness of conversation. Their speech is "always in grace, seasoned with salt," with "the love and fear of God." "No corrupt communication comes out of their mouth, but (only) that which is good," that which is "to the use of edifying," which is "meet to minister grace to hearers." And herein likewise do they exercise themselves day and night to do only the things which please God; in all their outward behavior to follow him who "left us an example that we might tread in his steps," in all their intercourse with their neighbor to walk in justice, mercy, and truth; and "whatsoever they do," in every circumstance of life, to "do all to the glory of God."[61]

At the center of Wesley's homiletical wisdom are thirteen *Discourses on the Sermon on the Mount* that depict the beauty of the knowledge and love of God communicated by and in Christ. The *Discourses* are significant in that they provide a rich description of

60. "Doctrines and Discipline in the Minutes of the Annual Conferences, 1744–47," in *John Wesley*, ed. Albert C. Outler (New York: Oxford University Press, 1980), 160–61.
61. John Wesley, "The First Fruits of the Spirit," in *WJW*, 1:237.

the beauty of Christian faith and life as proclaimed by Christ, the Wisdom of God incarnate. Wesley's commentary invites us to see the intrinsic meaning of Christ and his teaching as a whole, to perceive the form of God appearing in him, which demands a commitment of one's whole self in an "aesthetic, moral, and spiritual sensitivity to the whole of things."[62]

Wesley perceived a beauty, wholeness, and symmetry in Christ's teaching, in that each part is proportioned in harmony with the others. He viewed the teaching of the Sermon on the Mount as lovely in its holiness, truthful in its form, and desirable in its goodness. God's love communicates itself in Christ for our reception and witness to its beauty. Wesley states this clearly: "*The beauty of holiness, of that inward manner of the heart, which is renewed after the image of God, cannot but strike every eye which God hath opened; every enlightened understanding.*"[63]

The beauty of holiness shines forth with the brightness of the Father's love as manifested in the Son, the express image of his person in whom the divine glory dwells in human form. Wesley writes, "He is the character and the stamp, the living impression of his person who is the fountain of beauty and love, the original source of excellence and perfection."[64] The "eyes" of our hearts are thus illumined by the light of Christ's glorious love, through which we perceive God in human form and present for our imitation.[65]

Wesley delighted in the harmony and proportion of the parts and whole of Christ's teaching: "How desirable is the happiness here described, how venerable; how lovely the holiness!" Christ's blessings or beatitudes are transcribed in the heart till "we are holy as he who hath called us is holy."[66] The life and teaching of Jesus, the incarnate Son of God, radiates a beauty that, uniting his truth and goodness, is diffused

62. Wilson, *Methodist Theology*, 15.
63. John Wesley, "Sermon on the Mount IV," in *WJW*, 1:531 (emphasis added).
64. John Wesley, "Sermon on the Mount IV," in *WJW*, 1:531–32.
65. John Wesley, "Sermon on the Mount III," in *WJW*, 1:530.
66. John Wesley, "Sermon on the Mount III," in *WJW*, 1:530.

through the whole of Scripture. Here Wesley calls attention to the intricate design of the Bible: "The main lines of this picture are beautifully drawn in many passages of the Old Testament. These are filled up in the New, retouched and finished with all the art of God."[67]

Jason Byassee comments that this approach to Scripture in preaching will "seek to show its conformity, its fittingness, its beauty in relationship to the words on the page, the flourishing of human lives, and the beauty of the Son who reflects the Father's beauty with us in the Spirit drawn body of Christ."[68] This is a participatory way of knowing that reorients how we perceive God, ourselves, and others in light of the Father's love, which shines brightly from the human righteousness of Christ. In the sermon "Scriptural Christianity," Wesley sums this up as "'the mind that was in Christ,' whose holy 'fruits of the Spirit' [work] to fill them with 'love, joy, peace, long-suffering, gentleness, goodness'; to endue them with 'faith,' with 'meekness and temperance'; to enable them to 'crucify the flesh with its affections and lusts,' its passions and desires; and in consequence of that inward change, to fulfill all outward righteousness, 'to walk as Christ also walked,' in the 'work of faith, the patience of hope, the labour of love.'"[69]

This practical wisdom is formed by participating in Christ's goodness: having the "mind that was in Christ," which reorients our thinking, feeling, and speaking according to the truth as received in him.[70] Practical wisdom, then, directs the intellect, affections, and will in preaching that is faithful to the gospel and fitting for building up communities in the virtues of faith, hope, and love, and the fruits of the Spirit.[71]

---

67. Cited in Scott J. Jones, *John Wesley's Conception and Use of Scripture* (Nashville: Abingdon, 1995), 58.

68. Jason Byassee, *Praise Seeking Understanding: Reading the Psalms with Augustine* (Grand Rapids: Eerdmans, 2007), 146.

69. John Wesley, "Scriptural Christianity," in *WJW*, 1:160-61.

70. Long, *John Wesley's Moral Theology*, 171-202.

71. John Wesley, "The Reformation of Manners," in *WJW*, 2:318; see here the

This change is effected by an awakening of the spiritual senses that transforms our perception of God, the world, and ourselves. Wesley describes this as being made "sensible of God" by the Holy Spirit, who gives "spiritual respiration" and "spiritual life," which is received through faith in Christ. The "eyes of the understanding" are opened to perceive the glory and majesty of God in Christ, while the "ears are opened" to hear and obey the voice of God in Christ. Wesley summarizes this awakening as one in which the veil is removed and God's light and voice, God's knowledge and love in Christ, are imparted by the Spirit—God's life-giving breath—which is returned in unceasing love, prayer, and praise.[72]

The beauty of Christ, moreover, cannot be apprehended only by a process of reasoning but will require the gift of purified sight and the affective recognition of love. This way of seeing accompanies the transforming work of the Holy Spirit, who restores us to the beauty, health, and happiness for which we have been created in Christ.[73] In his sermon "The Circumcision of the Heart," Wesley offers a vision of the triune character that inspires a preacher's passions and directs her desires, words, and actions toward enjoying and giving glory to God both in the present and the promised end of all things in God.

> The one perfect good shall be your ultimate end. One thing shall ye desire for its own sake—the fruition of him that is all in all. One happiness shall you propose to your souls, even a union with him that made them, the having fellowship with the Father and the Son, the being joined to the "Lord in one Spirit." One design ye are to pursue to the end of time—the enjoyment of God in time and eternity—desire other things so far as they tend to this. Love the creature—as it leads to the Creator. But in every step

excellent discussion in Jason E. Vickers, *Minding the Good Ground: A Theology of Church Renewal* (Grand Rapids: Baker Academic, 2011), 99.

72. John Wesley, "The Great Privilege of Those That Are Born of God," in *WJW*, 1:434-35.

73. Murphy, *Happiness, Health, and Beauty*, 83.

you take be it this glorious point that terminates your view. Let every affection, and thought, and word, and work be subordinate to this. Whatever ye desire or fear, whatever ye seek or shun, whatever ye think, speak, or do, be it in order to your happiness in God, the sole end as well as the source of your being.[74]

William Abraham has described Wesley's sermons as an experiment in ascetic theology; the disciplined love of Christian wisdom communicated as a homiletical art by which disoriented and darkened souls are healed by the knowledge and love of God.[75]

I would add that this requires a homiletical aesthetic that attunes both preachers and hearers to the Spirit's love, which draws us to share in Christ's evangelical beauty.[76] As Wesley himself affirmed, it is the Holy Spirit that disposes the person who preaches to delight in "be[ing] a steward of the mysteries of God, and shepherd of the souls for whom Christ died," and thus "to be endued with an eminent measure of love to God, and love to all his brethren."[77]

Proclaiming the gospel is a holy vocation, a work of great beauty that makes known the glory of its true subject and object; the God of infinite love who is the source and end of all things. Our words are made beautiful as offerings of adoring praise to the Father, through the Son, in the Spirit, the Holy Trinity who is known, loved, and

---

74. John Wesley, "The Circumcision of the Heart," in *WJW*, 1:408.

75. William J. Abraham, "Wesley as Preacher," in Maddox and Vickers, *The Cambridge Companion to John Wesley*, 109–12. "[Wesley] can be allowed to stand as he is, that is, as a modest and attractive figure in the history of preaching and spiritual direction. Wesley lived by preaching; he gave himself totally to mastering a practice that has a unique and lasting place in the life of the church. His greatest joy was to see people find God for themselves, not least when he was the agent of the Holy Spirit in the awakening of faith and the fostering of holiness. The whole life is standing testimony to the beauty of a spiritual art that can bring lasting healing to disoriented and hurting souls" (112).

76. See the helpful discussion of a Wesleyan aesthetic in Murphy, *Happiness, Health, and Beauty*, 77–83.

77. John Wesley, "Sermon on the Mount II," in *WJW*, 1:486–87.

enjoyed for his own sake—rather than as a means to other ends.[78] Preaching as a homiletical art is inspired by the Spirit of God, who suffuses our whole being with the beauty of divine love, thus orienting our hearts, minds, and wills toward God and God's purpose to redeem the creation in Christ. Debra Dean Murphy summarizes nicely Wesley's vision of human life that communicates God's beauty in love: "To live a beautiful life, then, is to love as we are loved by God—freely, without strings or conditions, extravagantly, without counting the cost or keeping score, fully, with joyful abandon, holding nothing back. It is to be caught up in the drama of divine love and intimacy and mutuality and generosity."[79]

Beautiful preaching springs from the faith and love of preachers who have been swept up by the Spirit in the church's offering of itself in prayer and praise to God through the ministry of Christ. Such preaching does not seek to stir emotion for emotion's sake; rather, preaching embraces and expresses an affectivity that moves the heart to a holy delight in what is truly worthy of love: God, who is worshiped in the "beauty of holiness."

A Homiletical Aesthetic

This is a homiletical aesthetic based on God as the unique subject matter of preaching and the distinctive qualities of a preacher's heart and affections that are formed in the worship of God.[80] As Wesley states, "to worship God in spirit and in truth means to love him, to delight in him, to desire him, with all our heart and mind and soul and strength, to imitate him whom we love by purifying ourselves, even as he is pure; and to obey him whom we love, and in whom we believe, both in thought and word and work."[81] Wesley notes

78. On the centrality of worship for Wesley, see the discussion in Tucker, "Wesley's Emphasis on Worship and the Means of Grace."

79. Murphy, *Happiness, Health, and Beauty*, 84.

80. Shuger, *Sacred Rhetoric*, 60.

81. John Wesley, "Sermon on the Mount IV," in *WJW*, 1:544.

elsewhere that "serving God is to resemble or imitate him." Or, as he quotes from Saint Augustine, "It is the best worship or service of God, to imitate him you adore."[82]

Here it is important to note Wesley's way of tracing the worship of God. He begins with love, desire, and delight, moves to imitation and obedience, and concludes with the formulation and confession of belief: beauty, goodness, and truth. Perceiving, acting, and thinking are taken up into a movement of self-giving that is also a receiving of Christ's self-emptying love. Passion for the Word is inspired by the Spirit, who links our thoughts, affections, and words with the gracious activity of God in Christ for the spiritual good of hearers. Burton calls attention to an important element in such preaching: that the source of much Methodist rhetoric is named in Wesley's affirmation "The best of all, God is with us." She continues, "The marginalized men and women of Methodism spoke and wrote not because their gendered or classed position qualified them to do so, not because of talent within themselves—though many had such talent—and not because they were educated in public address, for few were. They spoke and wrote because they believed God had called them from their lives into speech and because their fellow Methodists affirmed their call by listening, reading, and believing. Rhetors gained agency from the belief that God was with them."[83] The beauty of the Word resounds through preachers enraptured by the unreserved love of God mediated in Christ's living, dying, and rising. Wesley marvels at this reality, in that we are "amazed and humbled to the dust by the love of God which is in Christ Jesus."[84] By God's grace, our sermons may become sacraments that serve as "means for the body of Christ to ingest the sacred words and to experience in

---

82. Cited in Geoffrey Wainwright, "Trinitarian Theology and Wesleyan Holiness," in *Orthodox and Wesleyan Spirituality*, ed. S. T. Kimbrough Jr. (Crestwood, NY: St. Vladimir's Seminary Press, 2002), 59.

83. Burton, *Spiritual Literacy in John Wesley's Methodism*, 300.

84. John Wesley, "The Sermon on the Mount XIII," in *WJW*, 1:698.

them afresh the Holy Spirit's active presence in our hearts."[85] Such preaching is sustained by a holy desire to see God's glory revealed in the beauty of creation perfectly restored and transfigured in the Creator. Charles Wesley expresses this desire beautifully in a poetic form of prayer and praise.

> Finish, then, thy new creation,
>   pure and spotless let us be.
> Let us see thy great salvation
>   perfectly restored in thee;
> changed from glory into glory,
>   till in heaven we take our place,
> till we cast our crowns before thee,
>   lost in wonder, love, and praise.[86]

My Wesleyan reflections have highlighted habits of humble receptivity and generous self-giving for a homiletical aesthetic based on the Spirit's refashioning of disfigured lives to the beauty of God's image appearing in Christ. By this I mean preaching as an act of intelligent and adoring praise inspired by the Spirit, who transforms human beings deformed by sin to bear the beauty of Christ's holy love and happy obedience in the world.[87]

This is a theology of beauty for preachers that revolves around grateful receptivity to "the sheer generosity and gratuity of the Father, Son, and Holy Spirit in rescuing, redeeming, and rehabilitating fallen humanity."[88] The whole of our life in Christ is a pilgrimage of the affections during which the Holy Spirit produces in us the fruits of

---

85. Robert W. Wall, "Wesley as Biblical Interpreter," in Maddox and Vickers, *The Cambridge Companion to John Wesley*, 128.

86. Charles Wesley, "Love Divine, All Loves Excelling," 384.

87. I am indebted to Murphy's discussion of a Wesleyan aesthetic as bearing God's beauty. *Happiness, Health, and Beauty*, 83–85.

88. Jason E. Vickers, *Wesley: A Guide for the Perplexed* (London: T&T Clark, 2009), 105.

"love, joy, peace, long suffering, gentleness, goodness, fidelity, meekness, temperance, and whatsoever is lovely or praiseworthy." This is the beauty of holiness manifested in those who "adorn in all things the gospel of God our Saviour."[89]

A sermon by John Wesley from Revelation 21:5 directs our gaze to the beauty of holiness brought to glorious perfection in the everlasting joy of communion with the Holy Trinity: "And to crown all, there will be a deep, an intimate, and uninterrupted union with God; a constant communion with the Father and his Son Jesus Christ, through the Spirit; a continual enjoyment of the Three-One God, and of all the creatures in him!"[90]

---

89. John Wesley, "The First-Fruits of the Spirit," in *WJW*, 1:237.

90. John Wesley, "The New Creation," in *WJW*, 2:510. See also the extended discussion in Patrick Sherry, *Spirit and Beauty: An Introduction to Theological Beauty* (London: SCM, 2002). Although Sherry does not refer to the Wesleys in his discussion of spiritual and moral beauty, they would have been fitting for the sections covering Jonathan Edwards; the Holy Spirit and the Trinity; and beauty, sanctification, and the Spirit as "Perfecter."

– *six* –

A STRANGE BEAUTY

For Martin Luther, the proclamation of the gospel sparkles with the beauty of Jesus Christ, the crucified and risen Lord of heaven and earth. The good news is that the "Beautiful Savior" became ugly so that sinners made ugly through sin might be made beautiful through the work of divine grace.[1] This "strange beauty"[2] is imparted as an extravagant but "useless" gift through preaching that praises the Father for his saving work in the Son by the Spirit's power. "The Reformation saw a great renewal of preaching as word-centered praise, especially in the form of prophetic preaching. The aim of this was above all to glorify God by proclaiming what he has done, with the response expressed supremely in lives of thanks and praise."[3]

For example, commenting on Isaiah 52, Luther rejoiced in the beauty of God's reign that resounds through those sent to preach the gospel.

---

1. I am alluding to the hymn "Beautiful Savior," which can be found in *Evangelical Lutheran Worship* (Minneapolis: Augsburg Fortress, 2006), 838. Stanza 4: "Beautiful Savior, Lord of the nations, Son of God and Son of Man! Glory and honor, praise, adoration, now and forever more be thine!"

2. For the description of "strange beauty" I am indebted to Mark C. Mattes, *Martin Luther's Theology of Beauty: A Reappraisal* (Grand Rapids: Baker Academic, 2017).

3. David F. Ford and Daniel W. Hardy, *Living in Praise: Worshiping and Knowing God* (Grand Rapids: Baker Academic, 2005), 19.

Here the prophet describes for us what kind of word it is that the speaker will speak. It is not wailing but gentle and doxological. Behold how attractive, how pleasant are the feet of him who publishes peace. . . . By means of personification he pictures the apostles running over the mountains, that is kings, princes, peoples, nations, tribes. Over these the Gospel runs. . . . Good tidings mean joy and happiness, and the fruits of the Spirit. . . . Your God reigns. This is the voice of the Gospel, as if to say "Receive your king." Whom? "God, who has his eyes on you." Turn now to this King, Christ, who is true God and man, since it is Christ Himself who preaches and teaches.[4]

"It is . . . gentle and doxological. Behold how attractive, how pleasant are the feet of him who publishes." Matthew Boulton has written of Luther's use of doxological language for expressing his desire to see the worship of the church reformed and renewed.[5] Luther was criticizing the liturgical ceremonies, rituals, times, and places that are most vulnerable to expressing a "theology of glory" rather than a "theology of the cross" (81–82).

According to Luther, sin can be manifested in religious, spiritual, and liturgical forms that are inseparable from everyday speaking, thinking, and acting. Even the worship of God, the source of the church's life through the ministry of Word and sacrament, is subject to excessive self-interest by which "the holy things of Christianity" can be turned toward ends lesser than God. Luther viewed this as human nature turned in upon itself: the effect of sin that seeks to use the enjoyment of God and God's gifts for human advantage rather than God's service. Christian living and ministry may indeed

---

4. Martin Luther, *Lectures on Isaiah* (40–66), vol. 17 in *Luther's Works*, ed. Jaroslav Pelikan (St. Louis: Concordia, 1972), 232.

5. Matthew Myer Boulton, "Angels of Light: Luther's Liturgical Attack on Christendom," in *Luther Refracted: The Reformer's Ecumenical Legacy*, ed. Piotr J. Malysz and Derek R. Nelson (Minneapolis: Fortress, 2015), 77–92. Hereafter, page references from this work will be given in parentheses in the text.

be oriented by self-serving aims rather than seeking after "God and neighbor-serving gifts" (83–85).

Luther saw such self-love having severe consequences that must be addressed in an "orthodox" manner. Boulton helps us to see how Luther was deeply committed to "ortho-doxy," or "right praise," which has to do with "the proper stance and bearing of human beings throughout their lives as pilgrims and children of God." This is a way of living by faith toward God in faithful praise and toward the neighbor in loving service and care. Boulton helpfully summarizes Luther's vision of human creatures before God as "*homo laudans*," or "human praising." This is the joy of faith that works through love and is lived unto God rather than the self (88–89). Luther states this in doxological terms: "man will praise, glorify and love Thee when he realizes the goodness of Thy mercy and does not, in his self-righteousness, praise himself. For those who claim to be righteous . . . do not praise Thee, but praise themselves" (88).

To be a human creature made and remade through God's work in and through the church is to have one's life ordered outwardly toward others. This outward turn is expressed in thanking and praising God freely out of an abundance of joy stirred by God's self-giving in Christ. Boulton refers to this as a "liturgical anthropology" that depicts human creatures as receiving their true selves in praising God and loving their neighbors. This is a way of life consisting of faith and love that takes the form or image of Christ, a living in and through Christ in all of life so as to be Christ for others, which is to be truly Christian (89–90).

Moreover, a way of being Christian that is "doxological" is able to shape both the content and form of preaching. It is in praising God that Christian language is tested and remade according to our participation in God's ongoing work. Framed both by Scripture and the worship of God, doxology is an embodied mode of speaking that is at once "bold and humble, ambitious and modest, free and compassionate . . . subject to none and subject to all" (91). As Brian Brock comments, "Doxology makes [God's] gifts visible as forms of

God's love in all their glorious particularity."[6] Doxology, then, is the point where we meet God, who offers himself in Christ as both the promise and form of a renewed humanity in the world.[7]

The remaking of the affections in offering thankful praise for the works of creation and redemption is important for Luther's understanding of how our minds, perceptions, actions, and words are renewed by the gospel.[8] Miikka E. Anttila comments on Luther's perception of theological beauty: "In the cross of Christ there is supreme beauty concealed beneath the most abominable ugliness. Yet there is no ugliness in God. The ugliness of the cross belongs to us, whereas the beauty is God's. God is most beautiful not only when compared to us. He proves to be most beautiful when he makes us beautiful, that is, gives his beauty to us. This is an aesthetic variation on the doctrine of justification."[9]

Love, good pleasure, and delight thus occupy an important place in Luther's interpretation of Christian believing, thinking, feeling, and speaking. The gospel is the church's source of genuine pleasure in God as it is happily celebrated, sung, prayed, and proclaimed. Moreover, the joy of proclaiming the gospel resonates deeply to evoke genuine delight in God, who creates and redeems.[10] As Mattes notes, "It is through Christ that we experience God as truthful, beautiful, and good."[11]

God is known and loved as favorable and pleasing in the Word, which Christ adorns with his beauty. At the same time, by faith in

---

6. Brian Brock, *Singing the Ethos of God: On the Place of Christian Ethics in Scripture* (Grand Rapids: Eerdmans, 2007), 166.

7. Brock, *Singing the Ethos of God*, 167.

8. Here I am indebted to Brock's discussion of Luther's reading of the Psalter, praising God, and the remaking of the affections. Cf. "Luther's Ethos of Consoling Doxology," in *Singing the Ethos of God*, 165–240. On Luther and the affections, see Oswald Bayer, *Theology the Lutheran Way*, ed. and trans. Jeffrey G. Silcock and Mark C. Mattes (Grand Rapids: Eerdmans, 2007), 9–13.

9. Miikka E. Anttila, "Music," in *Engaging Luther: A (New) Theological Assessment*, ed. Olli-Pekka Vainio (Eugene, OR: Cascade, 2010), 218.

10. Anttila, "Music," 215–17.

11. Mattes, *Martin Luther's Theology of Beauty*, 100.

the Word we take hold of our true form in Christ, who adorns us with his righteousness and love. As Mattes comments on Luther's theology of beauty, "Therefore, in the gospel, God can be acknowledged as beautiful based on the goodness of his gifts in creation and salvation."[12] Mattes's important work clarifies the importance of beauty and the aesthetic core of faith for Luther, which bears directly on discerning the beauty of preaching. His comments are worth sharing at length.

> The embodiment of the Word . . . is rich in significance for our work since it acknowledges that faith at its core is markedly aesthetic, awakening the senses, opening receptivity, kindling wonder, and evoking gratitude. . . . God's proper work is beautiful indeed. And that proper work of granting Jesus Christ as gift or sacrament to all who believe regenerates believers such that their senses are renewed and they experience the world more aware of the beauty God has worked into it. . . . God does not find sinners to be attractive. Instead, in the gospel, God makes these sinners to be attractive and beautiful for Jesus' sake . . . in the biblical view of the atonement, in the servant who has "no form or comeliness" and the cross that seems the very embodiment of impotence and foolishness, beauty is to be found.[13]

This "strange beauty" is perceived in the deformity of Christ, through whom God absorbs the ugliness of sin and shares his beauty with sinners. "God loves sinners not because they are beautiful, but they are beautiful because they are loved."[14] This happy exchange renews the heart and affections through the work of divine mercy, which restores human lives distorted and diminished by sin.[15] Moreover, faith in God, who humbly shares his beauty in the "ug-

12. Mattes, *Martin Luther's Theology of Beauty*, 14.
13. Mattes, *Martin Luther's Theology of Beauty*, 3–4.
14. Mattes, *Martin Luther's Theology of Beauty*, 110.
15. Mattes, *Martin Luther's Theology of Beauty*, 14.

liness" of Christ, is key to perceiving the goodness of created beauty. "Praising God and believing in him means that one delights in the fact that there is anything beautiful at all. . . . Faith opens the human mind to see and appreciate the goodness of God in everything. Thus, faith is a deeply aesthetic way to look at the world."[16] This leads us to consider the beauty of prophetic preaching as a form of praise to God, who "wishes to clothe sinners in his beauty, his righteousness. . . . It is the unique task of preaching to impart this beauty."[17]

Prophetic Beauty

Luther was perceived as a prophet by many in his time.[18] He was likened to a messenger from God in the manner of the Old Testament, so that the evangelical message of his preaching was seen as a significant contribution to something new emerging in the history of the church. He placed strong emphasis on the work of the Spirit, which is mediated externally by signs, symbols, sacraments, and language. He thus saw the external Word as a check on the tendency of human beings to confuse their feelings and opinions with the voice of God. Luther

---

16. Anttila, "Music," 219.

17. Mattes, *Martin Luther's Theology of Beauty*, 203–4; Ford and Hardy write, "To praise and know God is itself prophetic. It affirms the most comprehensive truth of history and the future. . . . Prophecy is discerning this God and God's ways, and following their practical consequences. . . . This God is in Godself glorious, a play of mutually communicated delight and love always lively and fresh. The prophetic point of this is simple: it is the message of a life of joy with the God of joy. 'The God of joy' is a name of God which rings strangely after a century whose history seems to mock it. *To rejoice in this God is a prophetic act which at once stings the habitual worldly wisdom fed on suspicion, bad news and equivocal or cynical judgements. It also stings the practical atheism of many 'believers.'"* Ford and Hardy, *Living in Praise*, 173–75 (emphasis added).

18. Here I am following the discussion in David C. Steinmetz, "The Domestication of Prophecy in the Early Reformation," in Steinmetz, *Taking the Long View: Christian Theology in Historical Perspective* (Oxford: Oxford University Press, 2011), 81–90. Hereafter, page references from this work will be given in parentheses in the text.

believed the word God speaks to address the human heart is the same word that was spoken by the prophets and apostles (81–82).

Unlike preachers who claimed they had received a "message" from God through the Spirit's inner voice, Luther listened for the voice of God mediated in Scripture, a commitment that occupied him as an interpreter, preacher, and teacher. Scripture contains images, narratives, and words that speak with power to change reality, the efficacy of the word of God, whose voice is heard in the voices of the biblical witness. Because God is a speaking God, the words of Scripture do more than describe reality; the words of Scripture are powerful to create and transform reality (83–84).

Faith in a speaking God led Luther to define pastoral ministry in light of the prophetic calling of proclaiming God's word. He was even agreeable to accepting the designation of prophet, so long as it was understood that prophet meant bearing a living Word mediated through the words of Scripture (85).

Luther's commitment to the external reality of the Word generated renewed attention to biblical study in the service of proclaiming Christ. In addition, the Reformation commitment to the preaching of the Word was also important for Luther's robust understanding of Christ as a prophet who was authorized by his baptism for the prophetic task. Moreover, this christological view of prophetic speech contributed to elevating the sermon to a central place in Protestant worship. As Steinmetz concludes, "The Protestant Reformation could be described as a prophetic movement in the late medieval Catholic church" (89–90).

Luther believed that the life of the church is generated by the Spirit, who is received in the preaching of the Word and celebration of the sacraments. God therefore communicates himself in revelatory signs through the Spirit's bonding with the "external Word" and the church's bodily acts of worship.[19] This enabled Luther to emphasize the decisive encounter between God and humanity in the assembly's

---

19. Bernd Wannenwetsch, *Political Worship: Ethics of Christian Citizens*, trans. Margaret Kohl (Oxford: Oxford University Press, 2004), 65–69.

prayer and praise. He extended this understanding to preaching, uniting homiletical theory and practice in faith that gladly receives the Word as the gift of God's self in Christ.[20]

Becoming a preacher of the Word, then, requires learning to pray, listen, and be led in the way of Jesus Christ. Luther acknowledged that false prophets seek to render their own opinions and judgments as more important than the Word. He was also aware of the temptation to use the Word as a means of gaining praise, profit, and honor. However, he viewed this strategy as only temporary in nature, since it emits a bad stench rather than the sweet aroma of the gospel. On the other hand, those who speak and live for the praise of God are adorned with the name of God and decorated with God's glory, so that Christ himself is embodied in the person of faith.[21] Commenting on Psalm 147, Luther asserts that Christian people can boast only because they have been given God's Word. "Who can completely express the greatness of this gift? For who can exhaust all the virtue and power of God's Word? The Holy Scriptures, sermons, and all Christian books do nothing but praise God's Word, as we also do daily in our reading, writing, preaching, singing, poetizing, and painting."[22] He offers wise counsel to preachers regarding the importance of attending to the radiant beauty of God's work in Christ: "Now, above all the works of God, these especially should be studied with pleasure. . . . Here one should contemplate, diligently regard, and consider what a glorious and beautiful work it is that Christ has delivered us from sin, death, and the devil. Here one should consider what our condition would be if these wonderful works had not been performed for us. . . . It is all so great and wonderful!"[23]

20. Wannenwetsch, *Political Worship*, 198–201.

21. Martin Luther, "Psalm 111," in *Selected Psalms II*, vol. 13 in *Luther's Works*, ed. Jaroslav Pelikan (St. Louis: Concordia, 1956), 387. See the discussion of Ps. 111 in Brock, *Singing the Ethos of God*, 229–32.

22. Martin Luther, "Psalm 147," in *Selected Psalms III*, vol. 14 of *Luther's Works*, ed. Jaroslav Pelikan (St. Louis: Concordia, 1958), 131.

23. Luther, "Psalm 111," 373.

Prophetic preaching is the work of the Spirit, who through the voice of preachers expounds the beauty of the Word in Scripture to renew the church in faith and love. According to Luther, it is the upright who see, admire, and praise the greatness, beauty, and excellence of God's works.[24] "[Christians] realize and behold this honor and adornment, as the Holy Spirit has given them and daily gives . . . many rich and beautiful gifts of true heavenly wisdom, understanding, and skill, together with every virtue."[25]

In "Preface to the Prophets," Luther addressed the subject of false worship, asserting that it is insufficient for preachers to say, "I am doing it to honor God; I intend the true God. Also, I want to worship the one God."[26] He notes that although all idolaters say and intend such things, merely thinking or intending is not what counts. If this were true, even those who martyred the apostles would have been God's servants because of their intentions. However, the worship of God and service to the neighbor are initiated by the Word, not pious notions and good intentions. "For such a God who would have us institute divine worship according to our own choice and conceit—without God's command and word—is nowhere to be found."[27]

Luther acknowledged that the way of the ungodly possesses an attractiveness that gives a certain authority to its counsel and judgment. He adds, however, that although God knows the ungodly, he does not approve. Although their way may flourish and appear to be eternal, it will perish in the end, since it possesses a false beauty that reflects the foolishness of the world. False beauty must be countered by the wisdom of the cross, through which Christ's beauty is seen with the eyes of faith. "It is hidden even to the righteous . . . for His

---

24. Luther, "Psalm 111," 367.

25. Luther, "Psalm 111," 370.

26. Martin Luther, "Preface to the Prophets 1545 (1532)," in *The Interpretation of Scripture*, vol. 6 of *The Annotated Luther*, ed. Euan K. Cameron (Minneapolis: Fortress, 2017), 319–33.

27. Luther, "Preface to the Prophets 1545 (1532)," 333.

right hand leads them in such a wonderful way." Faith, then, is a way of knowing that sees in the darkness to behold the invisible.[28]

In "The Freedom of a Christian," Luther writes of the *form* of faith that both conceals and reveals the beauty of Christ. "Christian individuals do not live in themselves but in Christ and the neighbor, or else they are not Christian. They live in Christ through faith, in the neighbor through love. Through faith they are caught up beyond themselves into God."[29] When Christians grasp the abundance of Christ and his goodness, faith overflows in love to bless and serve its neighbors. Proclaiming the Word of God in Christ is therefore rich in "life, truth, peace, righteousness, salvation, joy, liberty, wisdom, power, grace, glory and every available blessing" (491). Moreover, the promises of God in Christ are so "holy, true, righteous, free, peaceful and full of goodness" that the soul that clings to them with firm faith is united with them, shares in their power, and is "saturated and intoxicated by them." Like a heated iron that glows like fire because of the union of fire with it, the Word of God imparts its qualities to the soul (496–97).

Faith thus possesses a particular beauty displayed in the "saving and efficacious" use of the Word that communicates Christ and is communicated by Christ. Here Luther's insights are worthy of the consideration of preachers in our time.

I believe that it has become clear that it is not sufficient or even Christian if, as those who are the very best preachers today do, we only preach Christ's works, life, and words just as a kind of story or as historical exploits (which would be enough to know for an example of how to conduct our lives). . . . Moreover, some even preach Christ and recite stories about him for this purpose:

28. Martin Luther, "Psalm 1," in *Selected Psalms III*, 309.
29. Martin Luther, "The Freedom of a Christian," in *The Roots of Reform*, vol. 1 in *The Annotated Luther*, ed. Timothy J. Wengert (Minneapolis: Fortress, 2015), 530. Hereafter, page references from this work will be given in parentheses in the text.

to play on human emotions either to arouse sympathy for him or to incite anger against the Jews. . . . Preaching, however, ought to serve this goal: that faith in Christ is promoted. Then he is not simply "Christ" but "Christ for you and me," and what we say about him and call him affect us. This faith is born and preserved by preaching why Christ came, what he brought and gave, and what are the needs and the fruit that his reception entail. This kind of preaching occurs where Christian freedom, which we gain from him and which makes us Christians all kings and priests, is rightly taught. In it we are lords of all, and we trust whatever we might do is pleasing and acceptable in God's sight. (508)

Through faith that comes by hearing the word of Christ, we are freed to desire, love, and serve God without advantage or gain. Luther comments, "This is truly the Christian life; here truly 'faith is effective through love.' That is, with joy and love [faith] reveals itself in work of freest servitude, as one person, abundantly filled with the completeness and richness of his or her own faith, serves another freely and willingly" (521).

Christ is himself the form of faith, but he is also the form of God in the form of a servant. The works we do, and the words we speak, are a sharing of the gifts we receive in Christ without concern for the outcome. The Spirit draws the heart "curved in on itself" to see the neighbor in the light of Christ, who is the "form" of a servant, "living, working, suffering, and dying just like other humans." Because Christians are freed from the necessity of works, they are free to humble themselves by taking on the form of a servant, helping and doing everything for their neighbor as God has done unto them in Christ (521-22).

For Luther, the abundance of God's goodness received by faith in Christ provides the design of Christian believing, living, and speaking. Christians are freed from living and speaking by measure or calculation, from self-preservation, and from heroic plans and efforts. Need, scarcity, and deficiency no longer rule when Christ and his good things are proclaimed and received with an abundance of faith. The words and actions of Christians are therefore measured by the beauty of God's generous love, which is expressed in Christ and is pleasing to God (524–25). Luther makes a rather remarkable assertion about the nature of living faith: "[A Christian] lives in Christ through faith, in his [or her] neighbor in love. By faith [they] are caught up beyond [themselves] into God. By love [they] descend beneath themselves into the neighbor" (530).

Samuel Torvend has shown the clear connection Luther made between Christian worship, Christian freedom, and service in the world. Because preaching the Word and celebrating the sacraments create the Christian community, Christian people are primarily recipients of God's prior grace. "From this theological and Christological center, mediated sacramentally through human words and actions, there flowed words and actions that informed Christian presence in the economic, political, and social fabric of society."[30] Luther saw that serving the neighbor in love will inform and orient Christian thought, speech, and action without taking account of "gratitude or ingratitude, praise or blame, profit or loss . . . nor does it distinguish between friends and enemies. . . . Instead it expends itself in a free and happy manner" (524). In an earlier work, Luther had already stated this in theological terms.

The first part is clear because the love of God, which dwells in human beings, loves sinners, evil persons, fools, and weaklings in order to make them righteous, good, wise, and strong. Rather than seeking its own good, the love of God flows forth and bestows good. Therefore sinners are attractive because they are loved; they are not loved because they are attractive. . . . Thus Christ says: "For I came not to call the righteous, but sinners." This is the love of the cross, which turns in the direction where

30. Samuel Torvend, *Luther and the Hungry Poor: Gathered Fragments* (Minneapolis: Fortress, 2008), 128.

it does not find good it may enjoy, but where it may confer good upon the bad and needy person. "It is more blessed to give than to receive" says the Apostle. Hence Ps. 41:1 states, "Happy are those who consider the poor. . . ."[31]

According to Luther, the good things we receive from God are the measure of true freedom: "These good things flowed and flow into us in Christ, who put us on and acted for us, as if he himself were what we are. They now flow from us into those who have need of them. . . . For this is what Christ did for us. For this is true love and the genuine rule of the Christian life."[32] Joy and delight in the gospel flow from the faith of all who preach, sing, and celebrate the story of God's good news in Christ. In the "Preface to the New Testament," Luther provides a beautiful description of Christian freedom taking form in the church through preaching, believing, and rejoicing in the gospel.

> Thus this gospel of God or New Testament is a good story or report, sounded forth into all the world by the apostles, telling of a true David who strove with sin, death and the devil, and overcame them, and thereby received all those who were captive to sin, afflicted with death, and overpowered by the devil. Without any merit of their own he made them righteous, gave them life, and saved them, so that they were given peace and brought back to God. For this they sing, and thank and praise God, and are glad forever, if only they believe firmly and remain steadfast in faith.[33]

The beauty of preaching is God's gift in Christ through the "lovely means of worship"—the holy gifts of Word and sacrament.

31. Martin Luther, "Heidelberg Disputation," in *The Roots of Reform*, 104–5.
32. Luther, "The Freedom of a Christian," 530.
33. Martin Luther, "Preface to the New Testament 1546," in *The Interpretation of Scripture*, 418.

Good works and words flow from hearts set right by renewed love and desire for God's glory rather than their own. As Luther comments on the power of faith in the Word, "One thing and one thing only is necessary for the Christian life, righteousness and freedom, and this is the most holy word of God, the Gospel of Christ."[34] Faith, then, has an aesthetic sensibility that perceives the form of Christ adorning the Word with his beauty. Bernd Wannenwetsch summarizes nicely the remaking of the affections: "In the power of the Spirit, faith renews the heart, and the renewed heart is clothed with new affects, which, in turn, enable good works."[35]

Poetic Beauty

Luther possessed great love for the Psalms, which he prayed, studied, taught, preached, and lived by. His reading of the Psalms was doxological in purpose: as an act of prayer and praise for God's works of creation and salvation that transform our perception of God and God's will. "Where does one find finer words of joy than in the praise psalms and thanksgiving psalms? . . . There you see what fine and pleasant flowers of the heart spring up from all sorts of beautiful and happy thoughts toward God, because of God's blessings."[36] As Brock comments on Luther's way of reading, "Prayer and praise are human activities of faith and are simultaneously an effect of God's action on us and our action of preparing the way for God to speak to us."[37]

A good example of this is found in Luther's commentary on Psalm 51, which he read as emphasizing salvation as a gift of God's

34. Luther, "The Freedom of a Christian," 490.
35. Bernd Wennenwetsch, "Luther's Moral Theology," in *The Cambridge Companion to Martin Luther*, ed. Donald K. McKim (Cambridge: Cambridge University Press, 2003), 129.
36. Martin Luther, "Preface to the Psalter 1528 (1545)," in *The Interpretation of Scripture*, 209-10.
37. Brock, *Singing the Ethos of God*, 267.

justifying grace.[38] God's favor and salvation evoke human words of praise to God that take the form of confessing sin and surrendering to God's beautifying work. There is a paradox in this, as Luther comments, "Whoever is most beautiful in the sight of God is the most ugly [in her own sight], and vice versa, whoever is the ugliest is the most beautiful." Beauty, however, is not a natural endowment or achievement we possess and offer to God; rather, it is God who makes us attractive in our confession of sin, which we can only see with the illumination of God's holiness and glory. Such confession and praise are beautiful, a humble recognition of God's mercy that adorns Christian people and displays God's justifying work. "Therefore, the one who is most attractive to God in the sight of God is not the one who seems most humble to herself, but the one who sees herself as most filthy and depraved."[39] The strange beauty that is hidden under the ugliness of sin is made visible by the praise of God in Christ shining brightly from preaching that serves the gospel.

Luther was astonished by the abundance of faith and love he received from the Psalms. He saw the "precious" Psalms as authored by the Holy Spirit, "the greatest and best Poet."[40] He was moved by the Psalter as a "school and exercise for the disposition of the heart" that makes us happy and thankful, and forms in our hearts a "rich treasury of understanding and affection."[41] Commenting on Psalm 118:16–18, Luther defines faith in aesthetic and doxological terms, as singing the praise of God's works and glorifying God for the gift of life and salvation. "They could not praise God without first becoming God's people through his Word." For Luther, then, "singing" means not only making melody and shouting; singing includes every sermon or confession by which "God's work, counsel, grace, help, comfort,

---

38. Martin Luther, "Lectures on Psalm 51, 1513–1515," in *The Interpretation of Scripture*, 213–28.

39. Luther, "Lectures on Psalm 51," 221–22.

40. Martin Luther, "Preface to Psalm 111," in *Selected Psalms II*, 351.

41. Luther, "Psalm 1," 310.

victory, and salvation are proclaimed and glorified in the world."[42] As Brock notes, "All other Christian action takes place within this conversation, altering its shape and making it a response of appreciation for God's action."[43]

The gospel is a living voice that needs to be spoken and sung. For example, a hymn written by Luther for Pentecost (1524) invokes the Holy Spirit to fill the hearts, minds, and desires of Christian people with goodness, love, and praise to God.

> Come, Holy Ghost Lord and God,
> fill full with thine own good
> the faithful ones' heart, mind, desire;
> in them light of thy love the fire.
> O Lord, through thy light's flashes fast,
> into the faith thou gathered hast
> the folk from ev'ry land and tongue.
> This to thy praise, O our God, be sung
> Alleluia, alleluia.[44]

Music and musical metaphors are important for understanding how Luther heard, believed, and preached the gospel. The language of beauty pervades his works and points to an aesthetic dimension of reality that is perceived through faith in Christ. Music is the messenger from God to us and from us to God, as a bodily, external thing bearing spiritual reality. There is an intimate connection to a theology of the Word, which in its preaching and hearing affects the intellect and heart in grasping the whole person before God.[45] Mattes observes how music is not only doxological but also proclaims the beauty of the gospel.

---

42. Martin Luther, "Psalm 118," in *Selected Psalms III*, 80–81.
43. Brock, *Singing the Ethos of God*, 178–79.
44. Martin Luther, "Selected Hymns," in *Pastoral Writings*, vol. 4 in *The Annotated Luther*, ed. Mary Jane Haemig (Minneapolis: Fortress, 2016), 142.
45. Anttila, "Music," 221.

For Luther, music expresses beauty. Participating in music, we are vessels of beauty, which is, for him, in a sense synonymous with the gospel itself. Music is best seen when understood in relation to the doctrine of justification by grace alone through faith alone because claimed sinners, when liberated from sin and the concomitant accusations of the law, can do nothing other than express grateful joy with the voice and tongue. . . . [Music] is likewise a metaphor for new life in Christ. Living from the word of the gospel, Christians have clean hearts and spontaneously want to express love for God and for neighbor.[46]

Luther understood the Spirit's reference to singing as wherever in the Psalms or the whole of Scripture there is mention of hymns, songs, and psalms. As Psalm 118:14 proclaims,

> The Lord is my strength and my song;
> he has become my salvation.
> (English Standard Version)

God delights in being confessed and praised for his works and wonders. Living faith, then, cannot be silent. Faith freely speaks and sings. Faith gladly gives voice to what it believes and knows of God. Faith passionately glorifies and honors God on behalf of all humanity. Luther looks to Psalm 116:10, "I believed, therefore I have spoken."[47]

Luther's meditation on Psalm 118 points to a homiletical aesthetic in the mode of praise and thanksgiving, or a "beautiful song." He connects "strength," "song," and "salvation" to trust, confession, and deliverance. God speaks first, or, as Luther notes, "the Psalmist sings . . . he preaches, confesses, and declares what he believes about God. Faith cannot do otherwise; it always confesses what it believes (Rom. 10:10)." Faith thus participates in a song the saints sing in

46. Mattes, *Martin Luther's Theology of Beauty*, 221.
47. Luther, "Psalm 118," 81.

unison. "Thus Moses and the Children of Israel (Ex. 15:1); likewise Deborah (Judg. 5:1ff) and Hannah (I Sam. 2:1ff) and all the rest. It is a unanimous story, it is the same."[48]

Both the song and the singing are made possible by faith in the grace, words, and power given in Christ. Sermons become hymns of praise by preachers who have been forgiven and thus delivered from sorrow, errors, lies, deception, and darkness. Moreover, preachers whose primary desire is for God are glad recipients of grace, righteousness, truth, understanding, consolation, and wisdom. Luther sums this up nicely: "We do not live in ourselves but in Him, and He acts and speaks all things in us."[49]

Luther interpreted the life of the church as a beautiful melody of praise with Christ as the subject of its "sermon and song." True saints are happy in God, who "delivers them from sin and death, that is, from every evil of body and soul. That out of sheer joy they sing their song over and over again." Such singing is the "art of forgetting the self"—through which Christians discern the will of God in offering their praise to God.[50] In "Preface to the Psalter," Luther expresses his delight in its loveliness.

> The Psalter ought to be a dear and beloved book, if only because it promises Christ's death and resurrection, so clearly—and pictures Christ's kingdom and the condition and nature of all Christendom—that it might well be called a "little Bible." The Psalter puts everything that is in the entire Bible most beautifully and briefly; it is truly a fine enchiridion or handbook. In fact, it seems to be that the Holy Spirit wanted to take the trouble to compile a short Bible and example book of Christendom or of all saints, so that whoever could not read the whole Bible would have here almost an entire summary of it, comprised in one little book.[51]

48. Luther, "Psalm 118," 79.
49. Luther, "Psalm 118," 79.
50. Luther, "Psalm 118," 85.
51. Luther, "Preface to the Psalter," 208.

Luther read the Psalms as a book of prayer and praise that in-creases love and delight in God's Word. Although this way does not provide comprehensive understanding, it does affirm that "The Spirit reserves much for Himself, so that we may always remain His pupils. There is much He reveals, only to lure us on. That He gives only to stir us up. . . . Our life is one of beginning and growth, not one of consummation."[52]

Luther saw a difference between the Psalms and the other biblical books that teach precepts and provide examples for human action. He discovered in his reading of the Psalter a way by which precepts are obeyed and examples are followed in union with the prayer of Christ. By the teaching of the Spirit, obedience to the law is trans-posed into a beautiful offering of praise through participation in the prayer of Christ.[53]

Desire for the law is holy, just, and good, flowing from faith in Christ and expressed in love for the neighbor. Luther read the prom-ise of Psalm 1, "Blessed is the man," as Christ and his people together, as a mirror and goal of life. Love is a unitive force that works in all who hear the Word through faith, which delights in God's good-ness, sweetness, power, and holiness: "How wonderful is the Word of God. . . . It is the mode and nature of all who love to chatter, sing, thank, compose and frolic freely about what they love and to enjoy hearing about it."[54] The beauty of the Word, therefore, is received with delight in the mouths, hearts, and ears of its lovers. Luther amplifies this truth:

> It is good when these words please a person and suit her or his case, this person becomes sure that they are in the communion of saints, as that it has gone with all the saints as it goes with him or herself, since they all sing with this person one little song. . . .

52. Martin Luther, "Preface to Psalm 1," in *Selected Psalms III*, 284–85.
53. Luther, "Preface to Psalm 1," 286.
54. Luther, "Psalm 1," 207–8.

In a word, if you would see the holy Christian church painted in living color and shape and put into one little picture then take up the Psalter. There you have a fine, bright, pure mirror that will show you what Christendom is. Indeed you also will find yourself in it and the true [knowledge of the self], as well as find God in God's self and all creatures.[55]

The wisdom of Psalm 1 illumines the path of a preacher whose ascetic and aesthetic sensibilities are nurtured by attentive receptivity to the Word. An example of this can be seen in Luther's meditation on Psalm 1:2, which points to delighting in the law of the Lord. The transformation of our loves and desires requires and leads to delight that "must necessarily come from heaven." This desire comes from faith in God through Christ, which produces delight in speaking what is holy, just, and good in the law, rather than its promises and threats, an approach Luther viewed as "mercenary and false."[56]

Meditating on Scripture is a delightful activity to preachers. Citing Psalm 37:30, "The mouth of the righteous utters wisdom," Luther refers to Augustine's rendering of "utters wisdom" as "to chatter." He continues, "Chattering is an exercise of the birds," which means meditating on God's Word with one's whole being, love, and desire. This leads him to reflect on the joy of preaching. "Therefore, it is the office of a man whose proper duty is to converse on something to discourse about the Law of the Lord. . . . It is not possible to describe satisfactorily the strength and beauty of these words. For this meditation consists first in close attention to the words of the Law, and then in drawing together various parts of Scripture. And this is a pleasant hunt, a game rather like the play of stags in the forest where the Lord arouses the stags, and uncovers the forests (Ps. 29:9)" (296).

The way of happiness in God is the joy of meditating on the law.

---

55. Luther, "Preface to the Psalter," 210–11.
56. Luther, "Psalm 1," 295. Hereafter, page references from this work will be given in parentheses in the text.

This is a heavenly desire present in creation that binds the lover and beloved. This desire, moreover, makes a preacher one with the Word of God through the affections, or, as Luther advises, "It is necessary that he taste how good, sweet, pure, holy, and wonderful is the Word of God" (297).

Luther warns of false chatter that says too much, pretends too much, deliberates too much, and possesses too little love for what is spoken. "Blessed is the man whose tongue or hands or opinion or fascination is in the Law of the Lord. For it is through these that [persons] puff up and flatter themselves; as if they were already holy and righteous." This is false beauty. The beauty of God's Word is learned by love, through humble faith in Christ that desires the law be sent down from heaven. Such God-given desire is the consuming passion that shapes a preacher's manner of being, living, and speaking. "Wherever love goes, there the heart and the body follow" (297).

Preaching begins within the will of God: with holy desire for the Word that produces words that benefit others. Luther sees this as a work of love: "Note this well; it is the mode and nature of all who love to chatter, sing, thank, compose and frolic freely about what they love and to enjoy hearing about it." An apt description of preachers would be lovers of God's Word who listen, meditate, and speak. "He who is of God hears the words of God." But it is also possible for a preacher to "feed on the husks of swine," chattering endlessly about his or her opinions and ideas, and thereby pointing to false beauty consisting of power, wealth, and privilege ("Psalm 1," 297-98).

The truth of preaching and living is received in the worship of God. "For it is not by our own striving that we fulfill the Law of God or imitate Christ. But we are to pray and wish that we may fulfill it and imitate Him; when we do, we are to praise and give thanks." Hearing and delighting in the Word conform the church to Christ, since the Word is taught by the Spirit of the Father, who addresses the church through the Son. As Luther concludes, "For when I preach, it is my word which my tongue preaches, though I am only the ear and not the tongue" (303).

Luther's meditation on Psalm 111 is an expression of praise that springs from contemplating the greatness and wonder of God's works. He practiced contemplation as a way of reading Scripture that fills the heart with admiration, pleasure, and joy. As an "art of the Holy Spirit," it is heartfelt, profound, and genuine in its witness. In addition, contemplation bears fruit in speech that is upright and righteous, reflecting a wholeness of one's heart and life, and an integrity of one's language and love for God. Preaching therefore begins with contemplating "the glorious and beautiful work it is that Christ has delivered us from sin, death, and the devil."[57]

Luther adds that preachers are also called to speak in the darkness, despair, and bitterness of a world filled with sin and suffering. They will do so, however, by remembering the beauty of God's Name. "Here let anyone who has tongues and pens bring them. Let anyone who can sing and shout do so. Let us attempt to do justice in some measure to these words, 'The Lord is gracious and merciful.' I do not know if God anywhere in the Scriptures lets Himself be called by lovelier names. So anxiously does He want to impress on our heart with sweet words that we really ought to accept and honor His remembrance with joy and love, with thanks and praise."[58] Homiletical wisdom flows from a "listening heart," which is renewed by intelligent and affective love for the Word. Luther notes that this wisdom begins with the fear of God, while contempt of God will lead to folly. Preachers are "beautifully educated" in God's wisdom by faith that contemplates God's Word, and divine grace that generates this desire and brings it to fruition in words of love.[59] The form of this education is demonstrated beautifully by Luther's reading of the Magnificat.[60]

---

57. Luther, "Psalm 111," 373.

58. Luther, "Psalm 111," 373–74.

59. Luther, "Psalm 111," 385–86. See here the helpful discussion in Brock, *Singing the Ethos of God*, 187–91.

60. Martin Luther, "The Magnificat," in *Pastoral Writings*. Hereafter, page references from this work will be given in parentheses in the text.

Magnificat: The Beauty of Mary's Praise

Luther's reading of the Magnificat exemplifies the practice of "aesthetic identification" by which the poetic power of speech brings the world of Scripture vividly to life. Exercising an "intuitive apprehension" of Mary's story, Luther perceived great things revealed in simple form.[61] He marveled at her "sacred hymn of praise" as the fruit of the Holy Spirit's instruction and enlightenment, as expressing an understanding of God's word that is experienced, tested, and felt (316). God is the God of the humble to whom he gives grace, which is the source of love and praise of God. We praise God by first loving God, and we love God because God makes himself known in a lovable and intimate fashion. God is thus known through the works he reveals in us, and which we feel and experience. The measure of this experiential knowledge is that "he is a God who looks into the depths and helps only the poor, despised, afflicted, miserable, forsaken, and those who are nothing, in whom a hearty love for God is born" (318).

Mary's praise flows from a heart filled with gladness, "leaping and dancing for the great pleasure it has found in God." Because she received this knowledge and joy from the Holy Spirit, her example and words are instructive for Christian people called to know, love, and praise God (318–19). Mary did not exalt herself for having received God's pleasure and gifts but remained strong of heart, letting God work his will, and drawing from it good comfort, joy, and trust. Luther adds, "Thus we should do also; that would be to sing a right Magnificat" (327).

Luther was also drawn to the moderation or temperance of Mary's praise. "Standing in the midst of such exceedingly great good things, she does not fall upon them or seek her own enjoyment in them, but keeps her spirit pure in loving and praising the bare goodness of God,

61. For the terms "aesthetic identification" and "intuitive apprehension," see the excellent discussion of Luther in Richard Lischer, preface to *Faith and Freedom: An Invitation to the Writings of Martin Luther*, ed. John F. Thornton and Susan B. Varenne (New York: Vintage Books, 2002), xxxvi.

ready and willing to have God withdraw them from her and leave her spirit poor and naked and needy" (330).[62] Luther therefore delighted in the loveliness of Mary's praise for the goodness she perceived in God's mighty works. "After lauding her God and Savior with a bare and pure spirit, and after truly singing the praises of his goodness by not boasting of his gifts, the Mother of God addresses herself in the next place to the praise of his works and gifts. For, as we have seen, we must not fall upon the good gifts of God or boast of them, but make our way through them and reach to him, to cling to him alone, and highly esteem his goodness" (337).

Doxology, or "right praise," produces a homiletic aesthetic well suited for proclaiming God's beauty in gratitude for God's goodness. Luther describes Mary's song of praise, "My soul magnifies God, the Lord," in the following manner: "These words express the strong ardor and exuberant joy with which all her heart and life are inwardly exalted in the Spirit" (320).

This is a form of praise that will consume a preacher's whole being and life. Luther's paraphrase of Mary's words thus provides a striking way of seeing the vocation of preaching: "My life and all my senses soar in the love and praise of God and in lofty pleasures, so that I can no longer control myself; I am exalted, more than I exalt myself, to praise the Lord." He notes that such praise and gladness is not a human work but rather is a "joyful suffering and the work of God" and the experience of those who are so "saturated with the divine sweetness and Spirit; they cannot find words to utter what they feel" (320).

62. Romanus Cessario, OP, *The Virtues, or the Examined Life* (New York: Continuum, 2002): "Temperance is a moral virtue, along with prudence, justice, and courage. While prudence makes temperance possible as a way of seeing rightly to act well, temperance moderates the affections related to pleasure and desire for the appreciation of beauty. Temperance frees us from excessive self-love to speak and walk humbly before God, and to recognize the beauty of creation as God's gift. Temperance also requires discipline, an ascetic sensibility that is intimately connected to an aesthetic perception that characterizes the moral beauty of upright life and speech" (96).

Luther's reading of the Magnificat displays both ascetic and aesthetic sensibilities, those habits and tastes that are cultivated through prayerful attentiveness and humble receptivity to the Word. These are learned in the school of the Holy Spirit and must be experienced, tested, and felt deeply, since without the Spirit's instruction there are only "empty words and prattle." Despite Mary's insignificance, lowliness, and poverty, she experienced the great things God was working in her. Her wisdom and insight were gifts of the Spirit, as she confessed that "God is the kind of Lord who does nothing but exalt those of low degree and put down the mighty from their thrones, in short, break what is whole and make whole what is broken" (316–17).

Luther viewed Mary's wisdom or "taste" according to the words of the psalmist, "Oh, taste and see that the Lord is sweet; blessed is he who trusts in him." He notes that because taste comes before seeing, Mary experienced and felt this by trusting God with her whole heart. "Such a person will experience the work of God within herself and will thus attain to this sensible sweetness and through it to all knowledge and understanding" (320–21).

The doxological speech voiced by Mary evokes a variety of responses. Luther points to "false spirits"—those who cannot sing the Magnificat rightly because they are unable to gladly offer praise. There are those who sing and praise only when God does well to them, and those who sing praise to themselves because of God's gifts. There are those who delight more in salvation than the Savior, others who love the gift more than the Giver, and some who enjoy the creature more than the Creator. Mary, however, praised God "even and right in the way," clinging to God and God's goodness in faith rather than her pleasure and enjoyment: "'My spirit rejoices in God my Savior.' It is indeed a spirit that exults only in faith and rejoices not in the good things of God, whom she did not feel and who is her salvation, known by her in faith alone" (326, 330).

The beauty of prophetic preaching is displayed in giving glory to God—rather than ourselves or our plans, agendas, efforts, and status. Luther asserts, "For no one can boast of any good thing in the sight of God without sin and perdition. In his sight we ought to boast only of his pure grace and goodness, which he bestows upon us unworthy ones; so that not our love and praise but his alone may dwell in us and may preserve us" (331–32). Prophetic preaching is therefore characterized by a spirit of humility that is only seen and known by God. "For . . . no one could boast of possessing it except the very proudest person" (332).

False humility is ugly, clinging to high and lofty things, while the beauty of humble faith is found in esteeming, seeking, and associating with the lowly. In contemplating the pleasure of God's works instead of our own, the eyes of our hearts are illumined to see God's goodness in those who are poor and despised by the world.[63] Luther notes that true humility is not even aware of itself: "Here the water flows from the well; here it follows naturally and as a matter of course, so that they will cultivate humble conduct, humble words, conditions, faces, and clothing, and shun as far as possible great and lofty things" (334–35).

Luther identifies this paradox in Mary's humble faith: the exceeding riches of God are with her poverty, divine honor is with her lowliness, divine glory is with her despisedness, divine grace is with her smallness, divine goodness is with her lack of merit, divine grace is with her unworthiness. He concludes, "On this basis our love and affection toward God would grow and increase with all confidence" (344–45).

According to Luther, God is the beauty of Mary's art: the Giver of all good gifts who generously gives himself in his grace and favor. Knowing God and understanding God's will grant integrity and clarity to praise that springs from wonder and gratitude in pondering God's works. Mary's prayers, sighs, and the groaning of her heart thus gave way to speech "not nicely chosen or prescribed." By the Spirit's help, she brought forth words that "live and have hands and feet; in

---

63. "The fulfillment of Christian life remains conformity to Christ that is progressively achieved through a life of self-emptying love." Cessario, *The Virtues*, 195.

fact, the whole body and life with all its members strive and strain for utterance—that is indeed a worship of God in spirit and truth, and such words are pure fire, light, and life" (345–46).

Such praise of God is the beauty of preaching. Although self-anointed "prophets" may try to exalt their wisdom, opinions, and goodness, "[God] scatters the proud in the imagination of their hearts" (364). Mary, on the other hand, concludes her praise by returning to the beginning, to the "chief thing," which is the greatest of God's works—the incarnation of the Son of God (374).

Luther's meditation on the Magnificat demonstrates how praising God, preaching, and receiving the beauty of God's self in Christ are united by faith that comes by hearing the Word. For Luther, the beauty of the gospel is proclaimed by faith that engages both the intellect and the will. Moreover, faith also renews the affections to delight in the beauty hidden and revealed in Christ's suffering and death on a cross. Commenting on Romans 10, Luther rejoices in the beauty of preaching that is seen and heard in a preacher's devotion to the gospel for the good of hearers.

> How beautiful are the feet of those who preach the Gospel of peace. In the first place, they are called "beautiful" because of their purity, since they do not preach the Gospel for personal advantage or empty glory . . . but only out of obedience to God as for the salvation of hearers. . . . The term beautiful . . . has more the meaning of something desirable or hoped for, something favored or worthy of love and affection. . . . "His Word runs swiftly" (Ps. 147:15). Whatever runs has feet: the Word runs, therefore the Word has feet, which are its pronunciations and sounds.[64]

Luther invites us preachers to see the beauty of the gospel as a divine gift rather than a human achievement. Because of God's living

---

64. Martin Luther, *Lectures on Romans*, Library of Christian Classics 15, ed. and trans. Wilhelm Pauck (Philadelphia: Westminster Press, 1961), 298.

Word in Christ, we are the good things we hear in the gospel. As the church puts feet on the Word in the ministry of its preachers, so Christ beautifully adorns the Word as it is spoken in the words of preachers. By God's mercy, the words of preachers become a bodily announcement of Christ's "good things" that are received by faith as lovely, desirable, and beautiful, effecting grace and forgiveness of sin, curing sickness, and nurturing life and salvation.

– *conclusion* –

BEAUTY, NOW AND THEN

The beauty of preaching is a gift of the triune God, whom Augustine addressed in the language of prayer and praise: "Late have I loved you, Beauty, so ancient and so new." I have sought to show how a theological aesthetic is "fitting" to attune our perceptions and words to the incarnate beauty of Christ, who is the image and expression of God's glory in human form (Heb. 1; Col. 1). In Christ, the image of God that for Israel is humanity, and the glory of God that for Israel is God himself, come wondrously to coincide in the incarnate Word, the scriptural Word, and the proclaimed Word in the worshiping church. "Now to God who is able to strengthen you according to my gospel and the proclamation of Jesus Christ, according to the revelation of the mystery that was kept secret for long ages but is now disclosed, and through the prophetic writings is made known to all the Gentiles, according to the command of the eternal God, to bring about the obedience of faith—to the only wise God, through Jesus Christ, to whom be the glory forever! Amen" (Rom. 16:25-27).

There is a kinship between a preacher's theological, aesthetic, and ascetic sensibilities for preaching and the relation of beauty to goodness and to glory. These sensibilities are active in our capacities of judging, recognizing, and perceiving what is visible, as well as apprehending what is real or illusory.[1] Spiritual wisdom and moral

1. Charles Mathewes, *A Theology of Public Life* (Cambridge: Cambridge University Press, 2007), 285-96.

wisdom, which are necessary for maturing as a preacher, are as much a matter of love, imagination, and perception as cognitive knowing and technical skill.

We are drawn by desire and delight to what we "see" as beautiful. Truth embodied in beautiful form evokes the power of imagination and stirs the affections to perceive its reality. Mark McIntosh suggests that the Christian life requires training in aesthetic vision for speech that is true, good, and beautiful—possessing a "generated depth, freshness, and vibrancy." This also requires freedom from visions of controlled, managed, flattened truth that captivate our homiletical imaginations and desires. McIntosh identifies this freedom as "loving attention," an apprehending of the beauty of God's truth shining within the world. "This is in some ways the most difficult act of discernment, the recognition that the great truth we so long to grasp, to make appear as beauty, to display, is more likely to make itself felt in a new quality of our regard for others, or reverence for life, our courage and loving perseverance in the face of suffering and death."[2]

Aesthetic vision is conditioned in love, by love, and for love. But there is also an ascetic requirement for discerning the intelligible beauty that awakens and turns us to behold the splendor of God's self-sharing. "Once we realize that everything is sheer gift, we begin to notice the radiance and glory of the universe shining with the divine life that gives it being."[3]

This is the "evangelical beauty" the church proclaims, inviting the world to see what it truly is: creation known, loved, and delighted in by the Creator. Illumined by the wisdom of Christ's self-giving love, the church is freed to reimagine the world in "lifting up those existing things into the flowing of giving and receiving, praise and delight that is the life of God."[4] Speaking the truth of God, humanity, and the world in Christ is indeed a "beautiful thing." Such homiletical

2. Mark A. McIntosh, *Discernment and Truth: The Spirituality and Theology of Knowledge* (New York: Crossroad, 2004), 204–5.

3. McIntosh, *Discernment and Truth*, 245.

4. McIntosh, *Discernment and Truth*, 247.

beauty springs from attentive, receptive listening, through faith that comes by hearing and is manifested in love. "By lifting up all things in praise, the mind is able to translate them, so to speak, back into their native tongue, which is the language of pure giving and receiving. In so doing, believers receive these things as gifts, know the deepest truth of them, and delight God who created them to be enjoyed."[5]

The beauty of preaching becomes beauty in the world through a people whose blessed duty and desire are delighting in the God of triune love, the source and goal of all things. Preaching is an expression of doxological speech, through which the Spirit's love awakens the church to delight in God's gifts of creation and salvation in Christ. In our baptism we are united with Christ in his self-offering to the Father by the Spirit, who sanctifies our life and speech for the praise of God's glory.[6] Dietrich Bonhoeffer offers an elegant description of the beauty of the Word that becomes the church as a compelling witness to the gospel, offering itself as a sacrifice of praise to God.

> We need to keep this firmly in mind: the word of God as found in the Bible and as it sounds forth to us in the proclamation of the gospel, needs no decoration. It is its own decoration; its own glory; its own beauty. This is certainly true. But as is especially true of human beauty, the word of God cannot withdraw itself from the decoration of those who love it. As is true of decorating which is truly beautiful, the decoration of the word of God can only consist of making its own inner beauty shine forth all the more gloriously—nothing alien to it, nothing false, nothing artificial, no kitschy trinkets and no cosmetics, nothing that covers up in its own beauty but only what reveals and brings it to light. And those who love this word of God that has sounded forth for two

---

5. McIntosh, *Truth and Discernment*, 248.

6. Elizabeth Newman, *Untamed Hospitality: Welcoming God and Other Strangers* (Grand Rapids: Brazos, 2006), 60; Brian Brock, *Christian Ethics in a Technological Age* (Grand Rapids: Eerdmans, 2010), 239–45.

thousand years have not let themselves be talked out of contributing the most beautiful thing they could as its decoration. And their most beautiful work could be nothing else than something invisible, namely, an obedient heart, but from this obedient heart, there springs forth the visible work, the audible song of praise of God and Jesus Christ.[7]

Preaching for the Praise of God's Glory

The magnificent opening doxology of the epistle to the Ephesians communicates a vision of the church's participation in and witness to the saving beauty of God for the sake of the world. In giving praise to God, the whole of our humanity—the intellect and will, imagination and affections—is oriented to beholding and giving God glory. "Praise is the primary form of communication of the gospel, the sheer enjoyment and appreciation of it before God, 'even when there is no point at all.'"[8] The "foolish weakness" of the cross provides new criteria for discerning who God is and how God acts in the world through faith that comes by hearing. In the preaching of the Word, then, our vision is purified by the Spirit to perceive the astonishing love of God, who creates and blesses the church with the beauty of divine grace.[9]

Blessed be the God and Father of our Lord Jesus Christ, who has blessed us in Christ with every spiritual blessing in the heavenly places, just as he chose us in him before the foundation of the

7. Dietrich Bonhoeffer, *Reflections on the Bible: Human Word and Word of God*, ed. Manfred Weber, trans. M. Eugene Boring (Peabody, MA: Hendrickson, 2005), 57.

8. David F. Ford and Daniel W. Hardy, *Living in Praise: Worshiping and Knowing God* (Grand Rapids: Baker Academic, 2005), 188; I have benefited from this excellent book in formulating the previous two paragraphs.

9. L. Gregory Jones and Kevin R. Armstrong, *Resurrecting Excellence: Shaping Faithful Christian Ministry* (Grand Rapids: Eerdmans, 2006), 23.

world to be holy and blameless before him in love. He destined us for adoption as his children through Jesus Christ, according to the good pleasure of his will, to the praise of his glorious grace that he freely bestowed on us in the Beloved. In him we have redemption through his blood, the forgiveness of our trespasses, according to the riches of his grace that he lavished on us. With all wisdom and insight he has made known to us the mystery of his will, according to his good pleasure that he set forth in Christ, as a plan for the fullness of time, to gather up all things in him, things in heaven and things on earth. (Eph. 1:3-10)

The beauty of divine love shines nowhere more resplendently than in the re-creation of our human being and life in rightly ordered praise for God's gracious activity in the creation and redemption of all things. Called to a life of doxological gratitude, the church is drawn by the Spirit into the beauty of Christ, who by assuming our weakness and vulnerability manifests God's glory within an incomplete and needy world. Jean Daniélou sums this up beautifully: "We are the awed witnesses of something that has made us its beneficiaries; but others may also be its beneficiaries. We haven't the slightest monopoly on salvation, and it does not belong to us to the slightest degree. Salvation is an absolutely gratuitous gift for which we can only give thanks, but which is offered just as much to others. That is why there is not arrogance or pretension for a Christian in bearing witness to Jesus Christ."[10]

This is the "strange, fragile" glory of God, who saves and sanctifies through the "utterly un-glorious" cross of Christ, in whom human life and speech are completed by the Spirit.[11] As Bryan Stone writes,

10. Jean Daniélou, *Prayer: The Mission of the Church*, trans. David Louis Schindler Jr. (Grand Rapids: Eerdmans, 1996), 101.

11. On the doxological nature of Christian theology and life, see Eugene H. Peterson, *Practice Resurrection: A Conversation on Growing Up in Christ* (Grand Rapids: Eerdmans, 2010); Don E. Saliers, *Worship as Theology: Foretaste of Glory Divine* (Nashville: Abingdon, 1994); Hans Urs von Balthasar, *The Glory of the*

"Christian beauty is fixed to Christ and is therefore cruciform." He elaborates on this important point: "Christ's purpose for the church is to call forth from it beauty, to present it to himself 'in splendor, without a spot or wrinkle or anything of the kind—yes, so that she might be holy and without blemish' (Eph. 5:27)."[12] Preaching compels us to reflect on the question of how, as preachers enraptured by the beauty of the Word, we come to name God, the world, and the church's identity and being in relation to God and the world. Irenaeus of Lyons (d. 207) states this beautifully: "The glory of God is a living [human being]; and the life of [humanity] consists in beholding God. For if the manifestation of God which is by means of creation, affords life to all living in the earth, much more does that revelation of the Father which comes through the Word, give life to those who see God."[13] Irenaeus states that it is the good pleasure of the Spirit to prepare humanity to see God and receive God's glory, which is to know and enjoy God's goodness in Christ.[14] The end of preaching is that the church will become the gospel it proclaims through the power of the Spirit, who adorns its life with the beauty of Christ.

> In Christ we have also obtained an inheritance, having been destined according to the purpose of him who accomplishes all things according to his counsel and will, so that we, who were the first to set our hope on Christ, might live for the praise of his glory. In him you also, when you had heard the word of truth, the gospel of your salvation, and had believed in him, were marked

---

Lord: A Theological Aesthetics, vol. 7, Theology: The New Covenant, ed. John Riches, trans. Brian McNeil, CRV (San Francisco: Ignatius, 1989).

12. Bryan Stone, Evangelism after Christendom: The Theology and Practice of Christian Witness (Grand Rapids: Brazos, 2007), 290, 237; see also Steven R. Guthrie, Creator Spirit: The Holy Spirit and the Art of Becoming Human (Grand Rapids: Brazos, 2011), 197–215.

13. Irenaeus of Lyons, Against Heresies, ed. Alexander Roberts and James Donaldson, rev. ed. of the English translation, Ante-Nicene Fathers, vol. 1 (Louisville: Ex Fontibus, 2010), 461–62.

14. Irenaeus of Lyons, Against Heresies, 460.

with the seal of the promised Holy Spirit; this is the pledge of our inheritance toward redemption as God's own people, to the praise of his glory. (Eph. 1:11–14)

The joy of preaching is found in proclaiming the story of God's saving beauty displayed in Christ through the Spirit's grace. Steven Guthrie comments on the association of beauty with Christ and the Spirit. "The beauty of the new creation is the beauty of Jesus Christ because Jesus is the *eschatos*. He is the new creation, the pioneer of the resurrection from the dead that God intends for all creation. And the eschatological work of the Spirit can be characterized as 'beautifying' because his work is to remake us in the likeness of the altogether beautiful humanity of Christ."[15]

The desires of our hearts are moved and move themselves most freely by what we love, enjoy, and adore, rather than by pronouncements of what we need to know and do.[16] Our habits as preachers—how we think, feel, act, and speak as whole persons—point ourselves and listeners either toward or away from the glory radiating from the resurrection life of the crucified Jesus, who triumphed over the darkness of death.[17]

I pray that the God of our Lord Jesus Christ, the Father of glory, may give you a spirit of wisdom and revelation as you come to know him, so that, with the eyes of your heart enlightened, you

15. Guthrie, *Creator Spirit*, 198.

16. See here the extended argument in James K. A. Smith, *Desiring the Kingdom: Worship, Worldview, and Cultural Formation*, Cultural Liturgies 1 (Grand Rapids: Baker Academic, 2009).

17. Bruce Benson writes, "In preaching, one attempts to be like an icon, drawing the listener to God. In idols, we see ourselves; conversely, icons draw our attention toward God: they act as windows through which we gaze. The complication of preaching is that the one preaching is always pointing toward God, and yet human language is always inadequate in depicting God. Thus, we point toward that which exceeds our grasp. And yet we are called to speak." Bruce Ellis Benson, *Liturgy as a Way of Life: Embodying the Arts in Christian Worship* (Grand Rapids: Baker Academic, 2013), 148–49.

may know what is the hope to which he has called you, what are
the riches of his glorious inheritance among the saints, and what
is the immeasurable greatness of his power for us who believe,
according to the working of his great power. God put this power
to work in Christ when he raised him from the dead and seated
him at his right hand in the heavenly places, far above all rule
and authority and power and dominion, and above every name
that is named, not only in this age but also in the age to come.
(Eph. 1:17–21)

A Homiletical Aesthetic

A homiletical aesthetic directs our delight to the beauty of the Word
we confess, proclaim, and gladly obey. The interpretation of Scripture
in preaching is itself a form of praise that directs our gaze to the
reality of "God with us" in Christ. David Ford and Daniel Hardy
comment on reading Scripture doxologically: "The fact of praise of
God is a particularly good way of getting to the heart of the Bible
because in praise there was the supreme attempt to acknowledge
to God what was most fundamental for the community: God and
God's activity. . . . Praise was the time of ultimate directness, of
most active recognition of the presence and character of God."[18] In
preaching as a "means of grace," the Spirit delights in stirring the
church to give glory to the Father through the Son for all that is
worthy of praise. Saint Paul states this beautifully in his letter to the
Philippians. "Finally, beloved, whatever is true, whatever is honorable,
whatever is just, whatever is pure, whatever is pleasing, whatever
is commendable, if there is any excellence and if there is anything
worthy of praise, think about these things" (Phil. 4:8).

The closing exhortation of the epistle to the Philippians summarizes earlier themes in the letter that address the church's unity in

18. Ford and Hardy, *Living in Praise*, 31.

Christ, or having "the mind" of Christ that both ennobles and humbles. Paul writes of the peace of God that guards thoughts and hearts in Christ as his followers share his mind, and he is attentive to the pattern of his life as loving obedience to the Father. "It meditates on truth, goodness, and beauty, with the emphasis on those things which embrace truth and goodness in the delight of beauty, and which help us to develop our capacity to appreciate, to honor and to praise."[19]

The epistle identifies admirable qualities and habits of thinking, feeling, acting, and speaking particular to the Christian community. "It describes the activity of the mind that lives by praise. Rejoicing in the Lord and appreciating his glory is the only safe context for full and free intellectual and emotional life."[20] Paul viewed the preaching of the gospel as public truth, as truth for all nations and people, so that his final notes of encouragement embrace what is intrinsically beneficial to others. "Moral excellence in Christ works to expose and stand as an alternative to false or merely apparent excellence in the surrounding world. Learning how to discern what is truly excellent in God's eyes as opposed to what merely appears excellent according to common convention is a crucial task in creating Christian discourse."[21]

Paul encourages "anything of moral excellence or praise," since virtue and example matter for the life of faith that is called forth and exemplified by Christ.[22] This includes truth, God's truth in Christ, which describes the world as it truly is or is meant to be; nobility, a life of integrity, worthy of honor; justice, being righteous before God and in relation to others; purity, pointing to moral uprightness; pleasantness, an aesthetic perception of what is beautiful in creation and human lives; admirability, a life well spoken of but also well sounding, attractive, or beautiful in speech.[23]

19. Ford and Hardy, *Living in Praise*, 39.

20. Ford and Hardy, *Living in Praise*, 39.

21. Stephen E. Fowl, *Philippians*, Two Horizons New Testament Commentary (Grand Rapids: Eerdmans, 2005), 188.

22. Marcus Bockmuehl, *The Epistle to the Philippians*, Black's NT Commentaries (London: A&C Black, 1998), 249.

23. Fowl, *Philippians*, 185–88. "Rather than translating his exhortations into a

The apostle offers practical wisdom for preachers called to discern the mind of Christ in the circumstances of everyday life. His words encourage us to perceive faithful ways of living that exceed common convention, cultural norms and expectations, and are congruent with the glorious, self-emptying love of Christ.[24] There is a particular grace and beauty in this, as the language of the created world is taken up by preachers, transformed and filled with the wisdom and goodness of Christ to denote what is truly noble, excellent, lovely, upright, wholesome, attractive, and worthy of our attention and admiration.[25] "Learning to attend to God's beauty and to see and hear through God-inspired eyes and ears calls forth the strongest patterns of feeling, thinking, and acting. . . . It is an excellence that is shaped by God's excellence, nurtured by the new life in Christ to which we are called in the power of the Holy Spirit."[26]

The doxological speech of the earlier parts of the letter directs attention to the eschatological vision through which Christian people are able to perceive what is "true, good and beautiful in persons, things, and actions which appear to be favorable and those that really are."[27] The beauty of Christian wisdom is thus displayed by citizens of heaven, who share God's continuing love for the world as God's good creation.[28] The goods of the world are to be so "used" and interpreted in light of the cross, made "fitting" to a way of speaking and living shaped by Christ's cruciform obedient love. Paul's concern is not only for the truth of the gospel but also for the beauty of its expression in human patterns of worship and service practiced by Christian communities.[29] Jones and Armstrong comment,

---

'public' language of pagan virtue, Paul has throughout the epistle been providing the Philippians with the resources they need to deploy that language within the context of a Christ-focused, cruciform common life" (187).

24. Jones and Armstrong, *Resurrecting Excellence*, 18–19.
25. Fowl, *Philippians*, 188.
26. Jones and Armstrong, *Resurrecting Excellence*, 21.
27. Fowl, *Philippians*, 185.
28. Fowl, *Philippians*, 186.
29. Fowl, *Philippians*, 187–88.

Beautiful ministry both calls forth and demands the very best we can provide; it calls for excellence in all that we are and do. Philippians is marked by both abundant grace and a sense of the stakes involved in faithfully following Christ in the power of the Holy Spirit: the high calling from God to live our lives in a manner worthy of the gospel, the encouragement to be ambitious for the gospel, the injunction to let the pattern of our feeling, thinking, and acting be the same as was displayed in Christ Jesus, and the challenge to develop analogical means of patterning our lives in Christ in the particular situation in which we find ourselves.[30]

Paul concludes on a practical note: such things are seen, heard, and received from others. Moral excellence and beautiful speech are handed down in traditions of thinking, feeling, and speaking that are virtuous, compelling, and praiseworthy.[31] Wisdom is learned through practice, by which the Spirit creates the beauty of communion that is God's peace. The beauty of the gospel is perceived by appreciating all that is good, truthful, and beneficial, as seen by the radiant light of Christ's self-giving love.[32] Proclaiming the gospel makes known the glory of God in the lowliness of the Son, perceived in the form of Christ. Jones and Armstrong suggest that pastoral ministry in this manner requires the virtue of courage, which is shared by "people who have cultivated the wisdom and skill to have eyes to see and ears to hear the beauty of God, the beauty of this world, and the beauty of a congregation's life together. Such wisdom and skill are learned and lived in the friendships and practices of the Christian life—because the beauty we are called to see and hear is not culturally defined but rather shaped by the Triune God's abundant, gracious, loving engagement with us and the world."[33]

30. Jones and Armstrong, *Resurrecting Excellence*, 20.
31. Jones and Armstrong, *Resurrecting Excellence*, 21–22.
32. Jones and Armstrong, *Resurrecting Excellence*, 16–19.
33. Jones and Armstrong, *Resurrecting Excellence*, 8.

The Blessed Uselessness of Preaching

Preaching nurtures our imagination to "see" God's glory, which inspires us to take up a doxological way of living. The assumption is theological: that the heart of the church is worship, and the fundamental desire for doxology is inspired by the eschatological vision of God and creation reconciled as narrated by the whole of Scripture.[34] As Geoffrey Wainwright comments, "Worship is the most eschatological activity of the church."[35]

When an eschatological vision is distorted by demand for what is immediately useful or efficient, the doxological character of Christian life and speech is distorted and diminished. The church's worship, including preaching, is no longer "congruent with the beauty of holiness, incarnate in human history, yet transcendent in glory beyond all created things."[36] As doxological speech, preaching finds its true home in the eschatological activity of worship: "It is . . . the beauty of holiness, regarded eschatologically, that is at the heart of authentic liturgical participation. Every song, every word, every prayer, every act of washing, eating, and drinking together, is eschatological—that is, God intends it to point toward completion in the future."[37]

There is much about the current "time of the world" that is antidoxological: forms of language and life that negate true worship and oppose and corrupt the vocation of giving glory to God as the goal of all human activity. As Don Saliers notes, "The glory of God is reflected in the lives of those who follow in trust and wonderment at the glory. . . . [But] without gratitude, personal and communal,

---

34. See here David H. Kelsey, *Eccentric Existence: A Theological Anthropology* (Louisville: Westminster John Knox, 2009), 1:441–604.

35. Geoffrey Wainwright, *Worship with One Accord: Where Liturgy and Ecumenism Embrace* (Oxford: Oxford University Press, 1997), 31.

36. Saliers, *Worship as Theology*, 215. Josef Pieper writes, "'We praise you, we glorify you, we give you thanks for your glory'. . . How can that ever be understood in the categories of rational usefulness and efficiency?" Josef Pieper, *Leisure: The Basis of Culture*, trans. Gerald Malsbary (South Bend, IN: St. Augustine's, 1998), 68.

37. Saliers, *Worship as Theology*, 210–11.

we cannot see."[38] The center of our vision is Christ, the One through whom all things were made and in whom all things are being united for the praise of God's glory.[39] Preaching from the First Epistle of John, Augustine points to the eschatological longing of the church to see Christ in his fullness.

> The whole life of the good Christian is a holy longing. What you long for, as yet you do not see; but longing makes in you the room that shall be filled, when that which you are to see shall come. When you would fill a purse, knowing how large a present it is to hold, you stretch wide its cloth or leather; knowing how much you are to put in it, and seeing that the purse is small, you extend it to make room in it. So, brethren, let us long, because we are to be filled. . . . Let us stretch ourselves out towards him, that when he comes he may fill us full. For "we shall be like him; because we shall see him as he is."[40]

One of our primary challenges and joys as preachers will be recovering this vision. This entails a capacity to "see" that God is not distant or removed from the world but is providentially at work in history and creation, since God has come to be with us out of the depths of God's self-giving love in Christ.[41] As preachers, our imaginations must be rightly formed to delight in the "sacramental beauty"

---

38. Saliers, *Worship as Theology*, 46.

39. Bernd Wannenwetsch writes, "No higher end can be imputed to the worshipping community; the act of worship puts this beyond doubt, since in the act of worship the Eschaton, itself, breaks into time. There is nothing higher than God's dwelling with his people (Rev. 21) and it cannot be cashed in for some political good like liberation or welfare. The liberation experienced in worship is already political in and of itself—the blessing of being 'members of God's household and fellow-citizens with the saints' (Eph. 2:19)." *Political Worship: Ethics for Christian Citizens*, trans. Margaret Kohl (Oxford: Oxford University Press, 2004), 25.

40. Augustine, "Ten Homilies on the First Epistle General of St. John," in *Augustine: Later Works*, trans. John Burnaby, Library of Christian Classics 8 (Philadelphia: Westminster, 1965), 290.

41. Mathewes, *A Theology of Public Life*, 315.

of God displayed in creation, Israel, the incarnation, Holy Scripture, and the holiness of the church.

Seeing God, the church, and the world rightly requires the discipline of love, a way of being and living centered in praise. God's love cleanses and transforms the "thoughts of our hearts" to perceive history and the world truly for what they are: the gift and creation of a good God who are their source and end. Moreover, this disciplined way bears fruit in an aesthetic of love. We see our lives, the whole of time and history, not as that which the church must control, but as that which we may know in love and serve as a sign and expression, or "word," of God's abundant goodness and delight.[42] Fr. Corbon thus claims, "If our gaze is to liberate the beauty hidden in all things, it must first be bathed with light in [God] whose gaze sends beauty streaming out. If our words are to express the symphony of the Word, they must first be immersed in the silence and harmony of the Word. If our hands are to fashion the icon of creation, we must allow ourselves to be fashioned by him who unites our flesh to the splendor of the Father."[43]

When preaching is ordered by worship, as an offering to the Father with the Son through the gift of the Spirit, it participates in the song of praise that is creation's calling and consummation in God. Our exegesis and preaching are shaped by following the way of disciplined love that so purifies our vision to see the world truly, to act rightly, and to speak eloquently of the pilgrimage of faith, hope, and love narrated by Scripture's witness to Christ.[44] Mathewes comments that the reading of Scripture and preaching are "an attempt to exhibit and to invite others more fully to enter into the ongoing communal activity of exploring the world as framed and illuminated by the Scriptures. God is not very interested in our modern preoccupation with 'religious' and 'spiritual' concerns. God's object of love and de-

---

42. See here the excellent discussion of the church and its pilgrimage in Mathewes, *A Theology of Public Life*, 287–310.

43. Cited in Saliers, *Worship as Theology*, 200.

44. Mathewes, *A Theology of Public Life*, 308–21.

light is the world, this dying old world, which yearns for and awaits its glorious renewal in the doxological joy which is our true endless end, the song of God's love."[45]

We may welcome this as an invitation to rediscover deeper roots, especially for the practice of preaching. William Dyrness notes that this will entail a renewed "theology of desire," that we long to be drawn out and beyond ourselves by something or someone that is perceived as gracious, glorious, and disruptive of our ordinary ways, and thus capable of awakening our imaginations and eliciting our love and desire.[46] This is not a turn more deeply into the self but rather a kind of joy, pleasure, and delight that is both true and good, a vulnerable receptivity to God's self-sharing in wonder and gratitude, "the poetics of everyday life."[47]

Our deepest need as human creatures is to be awakened to the astonishing power of divine love that illumines the "eyes" of our hearts to perceive the truth, beauty, and goodness of God's works. Attentiveness to the "otherness" of God does not take us out of the world but rather situates the church as a social reality that occupies a social space and historical path that represents, incompletely, God's Trinitarian purposes for creation. "The church should be in the business of reflecting, visibly and concretely, the 'desire of the nations,' not just because that answers to contemporary longings, but because that best represents this Triune God."[48]

At the end of the *City of God*, Augustine affirms this hope, pointing to the splendor of God's eternal glory that illumines our worship and work during the present time of the world. "There we shall be still and see, see and love, love and praise. Behold what will be, in the end to which there will be no end!"[49]

---

45. Mathewes, *A Theology of Public Life*, 100.
46. William A. Dyrness, *Poetic Theology: God and the Poetics of Everyday Life* (Grand Rapids: Eerdmans, 2013), 11–21.
47. Dyrness, *Poetic Theology*, 25.
48. Dyrness, *Poetic Theology*, 243.
49. Cited in E. L. Mascall, *Grace and Glory* (New York: Morehouse Barlow,

A Homiletical Aesthetic for a Pilgrim People

I want to return to Augustine, who will help us to see how preaching, as a "beautiful thing," springs from reading Scripture guided by the rule of love for God and neighbor. He saw that right ordering of the passions by the love of God is taught in Scripture, which contains "the syllabus of instruction for Christians."[50] As a form of theological and pastoral wisdom, preaching addresses the human need to delight in the truth of God as the source and goal of human goodness, loveliness, and happiness. Augustine comments on the importance of delight in moving the emotions and affections in preaching.

> Just as he (the listener) is delighted if you speak agreeably, so in the same way he is moved if he loves what you promise him, fears what you threaten him with, hates what you find fault with, embraces what you commend to him, deplores what you strongly insist is deplorable; if he rejoices over what you declare to be a matter of gladness, feels intense pity for those whom your words present to his very eyes as objects of pity, shuns those who in terrifying tones you proclaim are to be avoided; and anything else that can be done by eloquence in the grand manner to move the

---

1961), 87. Mascall comments on this time of the world and the church's disposition. "But treat it as the creation of God, as truly good because it is God's handiwork and yet not the highest good because it is not God himself, live in this world as one who knows that the world is God's and yet as one who knows that his [or her] true home is not here but in eternity, and the world itself will yield to you joys and splendors of whose very existence the mere worldling is utterly ignorant. Then you will see the world's transience and fragility, its finitude and powerlessness to satisfy, not as signs that life is a bad joke with man as the helpless victim, but as pale and splintered reflections of the splendor and beauty of the eternal God—that 'beauty ever old and ever new'—in whom alone man can find lasting peace and joy" (83).

50. Augustine, *The City of God*, ed. David Knowles, trans. Henry Bettenson (New York: Pelican, 1972), 9.5.

spirits of the listeners, not to know what is to be done, but to do what they already know is to be done.[51]

Carol Harrison writes of Augustine's understanding of the "use" of Scripture in preaching, "There is no divorce between style and substance, words and meaning, signs and signification in a Christian context, because the former are sacraments of the latter. In this sense, too, then, the former cannot be taken as ends in themselves . . . but are to be so 'used' so that their truth can ultimately be enjoyed."[52]

As the gift of "divine eloquence," the voice of Scripture is living and active: "For Scripture is concerned for man, and it uses such language to terrify the proud, to arouse the careless, to exercise the inquirer, and to nourish the intelligent; and it would not have this effect if it did not first bend down and, as we may say, descend to the level of those on the ground."[53] "Augustine was convinced that God spoke (and speaks) in and through Scripture. . . . Augustine's Christian faith affirmed both the 'speaking' God as well as the usefulness of material means, such as human languages and written texts for human comprehension of the 'speaking God.'"[54]

Augustine's approach to Scripture demonstrates an intimate relation of knowledge, love, and enjoyment in the work of preachers seeking to proclaim God's will in Christ and the church as his body.[55]

51. Augustine, *Teaching Christianity (De doctrina Christiana)*, vol. I/11 in *The Works of Saint Augustine: A Translation for the 21st Century* (Hyde Park, NY: New City Press, 1996), 4.12.27.

52. Carol Harrison, "The Rhetoric of Scripture and Preaching: Classical Decadence or Christian Aesthetic?," in *Augustine and His Critics: Essays in Honor of Gerald Bonner*, ed. Robert Dodaro and George Lawless (London: Routledge, 2000), 226-27.

53. Augustine, *City of God* 11.4.

54. Tarmo Toom, "Augustine on Scripture," in *T&T Clark Companion to Augustine and Modern Theology*, ed. C. C. Pecknold and Tarmo Toom (London: Bloomsbury T&T Clark, 2012), 77; see also the insightful essays in Pamela Bright, ed. and trans., *Augustine and the Bible*, Bible through the Ages 2 (Notre Dame: University of Notre Dame Press, 1986).

55. Mathewes, *A Theology of Public Life*, 314.

Robert Wilken's discussion of early Christian thought is helpful in understanding Augustine's reading and use of Scripture in preaching. "Christians reasoned from the history of Israel and Jesus Christ, from the experience of Christian worship, and from the Holy Scriptures . . . from history, from ritual, and from texts. Christian thinking [and thus speaking] is anchored in the church's life, sustained by such devotional practices as the daily recitation of the Psalms, and nurtured by the liturgy, in particularly the regular celebration of the Eucharist."[56]

The gospel is not a principle, idea, concept, or life lesson but rather "a narrative about a person and things that had actually happened in space and time."[57] The knowledge of God begins with God's drawing near to human beings in Jesus Christ. Wilken points to the importance of the metaphor of "seeing," which was favored by early Christian thinkers. Thus, "Blessed are the pure in heart, for they will see God" (Matt. 5:8) was a favored place in Scripture for Augustine.

The knowledge of God is a gift of divine revelation received by looking to the image of the invisible God incarnate in Christ. Beauty, moreover, is a corollary of seeing God's self-disclosure; words such as "glory," "splendor," "light," "image," and "face" are associated with the delight of the eye. The eye's delight, pleasure, and enjoyment is to behold beauty. "God's revelation can be seen from the perspective of its ineffable beauty as well as its truth and goodness. . . . In the Bible God is the actor and revelation in a drama in which God acts and man responds. . . . Without love, there can be no knowledge of God."[58] Unlike much contemporary use of the Bible in preaching, for early Christian preachers, "the biblical narrative was not reduced to a set of ideas or a body of principles; no conceptual scheme was allowed to displace the evangelical history."[59]

56. Robert L. Wilken, *The Spirit of Early Christian Thought: Seeking the Face of God* (New Haven: Yale University Press, 2003), xvii–xviii.

57. Wilken, *The Spirit of Early Christian Thought*, 15.

58. Wilken, *The Spirit of Early Christian Thought*, 20.

59. Wilken, *The Spirit of Early Christian Thought*, 24.

The activity of reading Scripture and preaching constitutes our participation in a conversation initiated by the triune God that enables a perception, albeit partial, of the "reasonableness and beauty of the idea that, in becoming man, God acted humbly."[60] As Augustine writes in the *Confessions*, this conversation requires practice "in the Lord's style of language."[61] Learning the Lord's style of language requires an intellectual form of humility that is necessary for cultivating beautiful homiletical expressions of the Word, which is Christ himself. Christ is the beauty of Scripture that illumines and informs the thoughts and words of preachers according to the truth and goodness of its subject—Christ and a people transfigured by his love.[62] Wilken writes, "Through exegesis, Christian interpreters discovered the words and images of the Scriptures; the signs given by God, what they celebrated in the church's liturgy, heard in its preaching, learned in its catechesis, confessed in its creeds."[63]

Scripture is read, proclaimed, and heard in a participatory way by which the church encounters the being, truth, beauty, and goodness of God.[64] "[Augustine] insists that figures of speech in the scriptures constitute necessary features of God's revelation of justice to the human mind. . . . He argues the same faith and humility with which Christians approach the incarnation as mystery is required in interpreting scriptural sacraments [biblical examples imparted by divine grace] and mysteries, as they reveal true understanding of virtue."[65] Exegesis and preaching centered on Christ address both

60. Robert Dodaro, *Christ and the Just Society in the Thought of Augustine* (Cambridge: Cambridge University Press, 2004), 74.

61. Cited in Wilken, *The Spirit of Early Christian Thought*, 71.

62. Here I have benefited from Markus Bockmuehl, *Seeing the Word: Refocusing New Testament Study* (Grand Rapids: Baker Academic, 2006). "So also the meaning of a sacred text is understood not primarily by intellectual genius or once-and-for-all dissection, but by the interplay of divine gift with human welcome and delight" (91).

63. Wilken, *The Spirit of Early Christian Thought*, 74.

64. Dodaro, *Christ and the Just Society*, 72.

65. Dodaro, *Christ and the Just Society*, 116–19.

the content and form of faith, providing instruction and guidance for "how to live as a church, the body of Christ, on its way through the world."[66]

Proclaiming the Way of Love

Writing in *De doctrina Christiana* (*Teaching Christianity*), Augustine refers to the apostle Paul's statement that "knowledge puffs up, love builds up" to highlight the importance of a humble heart that submits to the gentle yoke of Christ to read Scripture wisely. Drawing from Ephesians 3:17-19, he interprets the breadth, length, height, and depth of God's love that includes the deliverance of Israel from Egypt and the death and resurrection of Christ. Remembering the narrative of God's mighty acts nourishes a way of life that consists of knowing, imitating, and being transformed by the cruciform love of Christ. "This sign of the cross encompasses the whole of Christian activity; doing good works in Christ and persevering in adhering to him; hoping for heavenly things, not profaning the sacraments. Purified by this kind of activity, we shall have the capacity to know also the love of Christ which surpasses all knowledge, in which he through whom all things were made is equal to the Father, so that we may be filled with all the fullness of God."[67]

Augustine was keenly aware of the temptation to use God, the self, others, and things as means of satisfying desires kindled by self-love. True desire, however, is human love reoriented to knowing the God of love, who alone satisfies human longing. He writes,

> Thus all your thoughts and your whole life and all your intelligence should be focused on him from whom you have the very things you devote to him.

---

66. Mathewes, *A Theology of Public Life*, 101.
67. Augustine, *Teaching Christianity* 2.41.62.

Now when he said *with your whole heart, your whole soul, your whole mind*, he did not leave out any part of life, which could be left vacant, so to speak, and leave room for wanting to enjoy something else. . . . And if God is to be loved more than any human being, we all ought to love God more than ourselves.[68]

At the heart of Christian preaching is the truthful acknowledgement of God's extravagant self-giving, which "is meant to allow us . . . to recognize and inhabit our lives as gifts from a loving God whose central expectation of us in response to the gift of our life is that we join in the 'work' of delightfully loving and enjoying creation *as* Creation, as a gift of sheer gratuity."[69] As the Mediator, Christ is God's eloquent speech, who in his self-humiliation became the road traversed by humanity set free from the exile of sin and death to follow the humble way of love.[70] Augustine offers the following lovely description: "Furthermore, we are still on the way, a way, however, not from place to place, but one traveled by the affections. And it was being blocked, as by a barricade of thorn bushes, by the malice of our past sins. So what greater generosity and compassion could he show, after deliberately making himself the pavement under our feet along which we could return home, than to forgive us all our sins once we had turned back to him, and by being crucified to root out the ban blocking our return that had been so firmly fixed in place."[71]

On the journey traveled by the affections, the heart is freed from excessive attachments to both the self and created things, and thus re-turned to the way of Christ, who both manifests and mediates the beauty of divine love.[72] As John Cavadini notes, "This

68. Augustine, *Teaching Christianity* 1.20.

69. Mathewes, *A Theology of Public Life*, 293.

70. John Cavadini, "The Sweetness of the Word: Salvation and Rhetoric in Augustine's *De Doctrina Christiana*," in *De Doctrina Christiana: A Classic of Western Culture*, ed. Duane W. H. Arnold and Pamela Bright (Notre Dame: University of Notre Dame Press, 1995), 164.

71. Augustine, *Teaching Christianity* 1.17.16.

72. Cavadini, "The Sweetness of the Word," 170.

way has been formed for us by the beauty of God's speech, Christ, who becomes the content and form of our affections in faith, hope, and love."[73]

Preaching must be attractive and persuasive in order to disentangle our affections from attachment to false loves, desires, and delights. Sermons must be capable of delighting with the sweetness and joy of Christ, who evokes desire for God and the things of God. Paradoxically, God's joy is expressed in the "foolish wisdom" of preaching, the "weak power" of Christ, who by humbling himself has become both the goal and way of faith.[74] Faith that comes by hearing exceeds merely knowing that which is true and obeying that which is good. Faith thus loves and delights in the beauty of the true and good revealed in Christ, moving and binding the will to God, a reordering of the desires and affections of the heart to God. Williams comments, "For Augustine, the problem of life in the two cities is, like every other question presented to the theologian [and preacher], inextricably linked with the fundamental issue of what it is to be a creature animated by desire, whose characteristic marks are lack and hunger, who is made to be this kind of creature by a central and unforgettable absence, by lack and hunger."[75]

Human freedom is restored by delighting in and obeying what God commands but does not impose, a healing of the affections and realigning of human loves with our natural longings and desires for God.[76] Such healing is the work of the Spirit, illumining the eyes of the heart to perceive that glad obedience to God's commands is the satisfaction of human life as it was created to be. "Augustine is really interested in how the Body of Christ lives: not because he is interested in 'church' more than 'the state' or because he has any

73. Cavadini, "The Sweetness of the Word," 169.
74. Cavadini, "The Sweetness of the Word," 166–67.
75. Rowan Williams, *On Augustine* (London: Bloomsbury, 2016), 126.
76. On the conversion of the imagination and affective reading, see Smith, *Desiring the Kingdom*, 194–97.

notion of schism between private and public virtue, but because he would argue that only a theology of reconciliation with God's act and a participation in that act can deliver real justice."[77]

Focusing on the affections, Augustine preached to engage and reorient the deep emotions of desire, fear, joy, and grief as instruments of Christ's justice, which is the delight of being reconciled to God and worshiping God in the whole of life.[78] Preaching true justice will attend to the proper formation of the heart, of desire and delight in the knowledge and love of God mediated by the humble obedience of Christ.[79] Williams describes this as the "pedagogy of the Church's preaching and liturgy," by which he means "the significance of Christ as the source of justice, because he is the embodiment of truth, of true relation to the Father, and of self-forgetting compassion and humble acceptance of the constraints of fleshly life [that] all come together in the vision of fully reconciled social existence."[80] The beauty of creation and created things, the words and actions of human creatures, are therefore to be taken seriously as ways in which God is deeply involved and already in communication with them. While the things of creation are not ultimately satisfying in themselves, when seen in light of the story of Scripture and faith of the church, "They are places where, because of God's continuing presence in Creation and God's redemptive work in Christ and by the Spirit, God is also active, nurturing, calling, and drawing persons—and indeed all of creation—toward the perfection God intends for them."[81]

77. Williams, *On Augustine*, 128–29.

78. Augustine, *City of God* 14.10.

79. See the discussion of desire in Wilken, *The Spirit of Early Christian Thought*, 299–311. "It is not possible to live a mature Christian life without the affections. Even the saints are moved to action by feelings and attitudes and emotions. . . . The movements of the soul are the springs of activity that move the will to the good. . . . The Christian intellectual tradition is an exercise in thinking about God who is known and seeking the One who is loved" (304–5, 311).

80. Williams, *On Augustine*, 129.

81. Dyrness, *Poetic Theology*, 5–6.

The mark of "true" religion, and therefore true justice, is rightly distinguishing the Creator from the creature, a discernment that begins with remembering the words and works of the one true God. Augustine describes the blessings bestowed by God on the whole creation as an elegant demonstration of God's great love. This is a special privilege, however, of those who believe and seek God as the goal of this human pilgrimage.[82]

Proclaiming the truth of Scripture thus aims to inspire love for God, who purifies the heart to apprehend the Word in a manner more characteristic of a poet or artist than a philosopher.[83] The Word expressed in Christ is thus invested with eloquence and wisdom, conveying to the ear and eye a beauty possessing a splendor and graceful style able to kindle and elicit love of love itself.[84] Scripture and preaching are united in love that "shows the beauty of God anew so as to convert the affections of . . . hearers on their way in pilgrimage to the heavenly city."[85] Augustine writes,

> That He might give it [the soul] what He commands, and may, by inspiring into it the sweetness of His grace through His Holy Spirit, cause the soul to delight more in what He teaches it, than it delights in what opposes His instruction. In this manner it is that the great abundance of His sweetness—that is the law of faith—His love which is in our hearts, and diffused, is perfected in them that hope in Him, that good may be wrought by the soul, healed not by the fear of punishment, but by the love of justice.[86]

82. Augustine, *City of God* 7.31.

83. Carol Harrison, *Augustine: Christian Truth and Fractured Humanity* (Oxford: Oxford University Press, 2000), 65, 66–67; see the excellent description of Augustine's practice in William Harmless, SJ, *Augustine and the Catechumenate* (Collegeville, MN: Liturgical Press, 1995), chap. 9.

84. Michael Hanby, *Augustine and Modernity* (London: Routledge, 2003), 61–62.

85. Jason Byassee, *Praise Seeking Understanding: Reading the Psalms with Augustine* (Grand Rapids: Eerdmans, 2007), 152.

86. Cited in Hanby, *Augustine and Modernity*, 81.

Augustine's homiletical wisdom directs our attention to the Word of God, which is known by the intellect, delighted in by the affections, and desired by the will. "Lacking concepts in the mind and words on the tongue we cannot speak what we do not know, but if we do not love the God to whom the words lead, we do not understand."[87]

A Sacramental Beauty

Averil Cameron shows how Christian discourse made its way through the wider and larger social world of late antiquity less by revolutionary novelty and more by working through the familiar, by appealing from the known to the unknown.[88] "As Christ was the Word, so Christianity was its discourse and discourses" (31–32). This was in large part because Christian discourse was not useful merely for persuasion as an end in itself but rather was figural, that it signified. "Metaphor is the heart of Christian language" (58). Cameron adds, "Augustine was committed to the view that *language, and especially the language of the Scriptures, signified reality*" (45; emphasis added).

Cameron calls attention to the figural and demonstrative side of Christian discourse, and its performative and declarative quality, its "habits of the heart" (28, 50–51). Homiletical performance or demonstration was a "showing forth" more than making an argument, the

87. Wilken, *The Spirit of Early Christian Thought*, 311; On Augustine's "rhetoric of delight," I am indebted to the work of Mark Clavier, *On Consumer Culture, Identity, the Church, and the Rhetorics of Delight* (London: Bloomsbury/T&T Clark, 2019): "What Augustine's theology of delight does is create a contest between godly or spiritual delights and worldly or illicit ones. . . . Augustine believed that all of humanity has been conquered by sinful delights—fallen humanity delights in whatever the devil wills and, ultimately, in its own ruin. . . . We're like an audience completely enamoured with an eloquent demagogue. What's needed is a great orator, someone more eloquent than the devil, someone who can overwhelm sinful delights with true delight. That orator is God and the Holy Spirit his eloquence" (72).

88. Averil Cameron, *Christianity and the Rhetoric of Empire: The Development of Christian Discourse* (Berkeley: University of California Press, 1991). Hereafter, page references from this work will be given in parentheses in the text.

expression of Christian truth in "word pictures" (53–54). Preaching drew from a rich array of biblical figures, metaphors, narratives, and images to communicate by analogy; from human words to the divine Word, to "express the inexpressible" (58–59). Cameron comments, "As for Christians, they had learned the practice of preaching the faith from the Jews . . . and themselves engaged in preaching against the background of public orational displays, rapt audiences, spoken discourse, and popular acclamation. Christian sermons, it may be argued, had a different message but their form, expression, and delivery linked them as much with the rhetorical practice of the wider society, as with Jewish custom" (84).

Christian preaching was able to move across barriers of class not open to classical Roman writers (111–12). Christian preachers accommodated their speech to familiar forms of discourse in a manner that gave them access to audiences, laying claim to past history in a way that captivated the imagination with a particular attractiveness and desirability. Images were used to tell stories of holy people, scriptural examples that spoke through their figural quality (121–58). "Preaching therefore became for most Christians the medium through which they heard and were regularly reminded of the interpretation of Scriptures, the relation of the Old Testament to Jesus, and of both to the overall divine providence" (79).

This amounted to a wholesale taking over and reinterpretation on the intellectual, moral, and emotional levels (120–25). Cameron views Augustine as exemplifying a homiletical beauty, noting the wholeness of his capacity with language to reach all levels of people and society. The beauty of Augustine's preaching is in the expressiveness of its appeal by means of concrete language, making it possible for all sorts of listeners to absorb the message of the gospel; an emphasis on metaphors, images, paradox, and story (67–69). He did so by preaching within the church's worship, with an insistence on mystery that appealed to the imagination through the affections, speaking the language of desire and delight (15–21). The aim was to draw human hearts to the knowledge and love of God, and to generate a perception of, and participation in, what is true and good of human life in relation to God and neighbor (45–51). Here Mark Clavier's summary of Augustine's vision of preaching is worth quoting in full.

> The Christian orator, thererefore, is a prayer who teaches, delights, and persuades. He or she shares in God's great oratory, participating in his rhetorical performance that contests the destructive rhetoric of the devil and draws men and women to their freedom in Christ. One might think of this role as a rhetorical sacrament since it embodies sensibly God's eloquent wisdom. It's through the orator's mind and voice that God delivers his wisdom and eloquence; it's through the orator's prayer and love that people encounter the spiritual delight that reshapes their identity and grants them a freedom that comes only through love of God and neighbor. Throughout is God's grace, empowering, encouraging, sustaining, and transforming both speaker and hearer—and, Augustine is keen to add, drawing everyone together into every greater delight.[89]

A good example is provided by an exposition of Psalm 44 (45), in which Augustine offers an eloquent expression of God's beauty displayed in the union of Christ and the church.[90] Harrison notes, "It is the faith, hope, and love inspired by the revelation of God's beauty on earth which purifies, heals, and reforms [humanity] in order see God's supreme beauty."[91] Augustine's imaginative use of Scripture's words, images, and figures invites listeners to direct their gaze to the splendor of God's justice in Christ, the "Word made flesh."

89. Clavier, *On Consumer Culture*, 136.
90. Augustine's exposition of Ps. 44 is found in Augustine, *Expositions of the Psalms*, vol. 2 (Pss. 33–50), vol. III/16 in *The Works of Saint Augustine: A Translation for the 21st Century* (Hyde Park, NY: New City Press, 2000), 289–309.
91. Carol Harrison, *Beauty and Revelation in the Thought of Saint Augustine* (Oxford: Clarendon, 1992), 241.

This leads Augustine to reflect on preaching in light of the Word. He notes that just as we speak a word from our innermost heart, so God brings forth a Word from his heart, a speaking that is eternal. God has therefore spoken through the prophets, the apostles, and the saints. However, God has spoken once through his Word, in whom are all the words of God. "Let anyone who understands about this Word listen to the Speaker, and contemplate both the Father and his everlasting Word, in whom are present all things that will come to be in the future, as are present still all those that have passed away."[92]

Christ thus comes with the sweetness of grace on his lips. He has made us gratuitously, and when we had come to ruin in sin, he sought, found, and called us back. This too is all of grace. He is therefore fair and lovely before all humanity, the source of its joy. "My heart overflows with a good word." The psalmist delights in God's beauty and praises him with thanksgiving, the great pleasure of offering to God our good works and good words.[93]

Augustine's reading of the psalm "figures" the church as a people anointed by the scent of Christ, which diffuses a sweet aroma.[94] The saints are Christ's garments, the whole church that he makes fitting and beautiful for himself, free from spot or wrinkle. Here Augustine's use of imagery draws from Paul's words in 2 Corinthians 2:15, "We are a sweet fragrance, both for those who are on the way to salvation, and for those who are perishing." According to Augustine, Paul was glorious in his preaching. He was loved by all who loved Christ in him, and he was loved for his running after Christ's beautiful perfume, which is the beauty of divine grace. Augustine refers to "the bride, who says in the Song of Songs, 'let us run toward the fragrance of your ointments' [Song 1:3]." God justifies the ungodly and gives

---

92. Augustine, *Expositions of the Psalms*, 2:286.

93. Augustine, *Expositions of the Psalms*, 2:285–87.

94. See books 2 and 3 of *De doctrina Christiana* for Augustine's presentation of figural interpretation. A good introduction to Augustine's interpretive wisdom in preaching is James A. Andrews, *Hermeneutics and the Church: In Dialogue with Augustine* (Notre Dame: University of Notre Dame Press, 2012).

new birth as a beautiful creature: "by him you are adorned, by him redeemed, by him healed. Whatever you have that can please him, you have as his gift."[95]

The beauty of God's children radiates from within, as inner beauty, the beauty of conscience. "He who sees you loves you within, he fashions your inner beauty." Reward is found not in the praise of others but in the loveliness of one's heart, desire, and intent. While the beauty is within, in the heart and desire, the teaching is spoken and demonstrated outwardly and publicly. Augustine sees the church as a living temple built with stones that are God's faithful, bound together by the charity of those who live there. The beauty of Christ indwells a people who live by faith, are joined through love, and whose hope is in God. "To this city will the peoples confess in praise forever, this city to which the psalm sings, 'Glorious things are spoken of you, city of God' (Ps. 86 [87]:4)." Then the glory of God will be seen clearly and completely: "For then will the hearts of all be transparent and manifest as they shine with charity made perfect."[96]

Augustine perceived a kind of sacramental beauty associated with the use of Scripture in preaching by a "reading" of creation and history as eloquently ordered by God's wisdom. This sacramental beauty is available in God's temporal revelation in creation, the incarnation, Holy Scripture, and the life of the church on pilgrimage through time. "The whole temporal dispensation was made by divine providence for our salvation. We should use it, not with an abiding but with a tran-

---

95. Augustine, *Expositions of the Psalms*, 2:299–300. Mathewes comments, "When we understand God's purposes for us, we can see the world anew, and see it as not ultimately what we think of it as 'world' at all, but as part of God's ongoing gratuitous gift of Creation, in and through which (but not from which) we have our being. . . . We must come to see our world as the old world, waiting to be transformed into the new, and ourselves—the aged and withered, the tired and cynical—as those who are always being reborn as little children, infants in God's graceful tutelage." Mathewes, *A Theology of Public Life*, 314–15.

96. Augustine, *Expositions of the Psalms*, 2:306–8.

sitory love and delight so that we love those things by which we are carried along for the sake of that toward which we are carried."[97]

The whole creation is a "mirror" through which we might see the Creator, who is our true and final end. It is a sacrament that conceals but also reveals God as its true source and reality. This entails a reordering of our affections through which the Spirit enlarges our capacity to perceive the incarnate beauty of God and God's works in the vulnerable flesh of Christ.[98] This occurs as the church looks away from itself in prayer and praise to behold the Word by whom the creation was formed, who impressed the image of God in humanity, and who as the incarnate Lord reforms and restores the beauty of human creatures as a participation in the justice of Christ.[99] In a homily from 1 John 4, Augustine offers this elegant depiction of God's saving work in Christ, which transforms our deformity by drawing us into the beauty of God's Trinitarian life.

What manner of love is this, that transforms the lover into beauty! God is ever beautiful, never ugly, never changing. He that is ever beautiful, he first loved us—and loved none that were

97. Harrison, *Augustine*, 98; Harrison, *Beauty and Revelation in the Thought of St. Augustine*, 266–68.

98. Here the wisdom of poet Wendell Berry is fitting: "It all turns on the affections. . . . The word 'affection,' and the terms that cluster around it—love, care, sympathy, mercy, forbearance, respect, reverence—have histories and meanings that raise the issue of worth. We should, as our culture has warned us over and over, give our affections to things that are true, just, and beautiful. When we give ourselves to things that are destructive, we are wrong." Wendell Berry, *It All Turns on Affection: The Jefferson Lecture and Other Essays* (Berkeley, CA: Counterpoint, 2012), 15.

99. Harrison, *Augustine*, 77–78, 96–97; see also the excellent discussion of Augustine's idea of reform in the *City of God* in Gerhart B. Ladner, *The Idea of Reform: Its Impact on Christian Thought and Action in the Age of the Fathers* (Eugene, OR: Wipf & Stock, 2004), 239–83. "Correction, reformation of the human person is for Augustine the sole remedy against the evils of history. This means that even in the Church only the saint truly *is* and also that the Church exists truly only in its saints; this is, perhaps, the deepest meaning of the Augustinian City of God, which is the society of the angels and the elect" (179).

not ugly and misshapen. Yet the end of this love was not to leave us ugly, but to transform us, creating beauty in the place of deformity. And how shall we win this beauty, but through loving him who is ever beautiful? Beauty grows in you with the growth of love; for charity itself is the soul's beauty. "We are to love, because he first loved us."[100]

Christian preaching consists of such abundance and excess, a delightful overflow of praise that springs from reading Scripture with our loves and fears transformed by the Spirit according to the wisdom of Christ's death and glorious resurrection.[101]

This is a way of preaching that entails both ascetic and aesthetic sensibilities, cultivated in awed, vulnerable receptivity to the Word encountered in Scripture's narratives, figures, metaphors, images, and words. Most importantly, this is a way of preaching that possesses potency to purify and transform the thoughts of our hearts to see, name, and inhabit the world more truly as the Father's self-gift—rather than as we will it to be.[102] *This is the beauty of preaching.*

Almighty God, unto whom all hearts are open, all desires known, and from whom no secrets are hid: Cleanse the thoughts of our hearts by the inspiration of thy Holy Spirit, that we may perfectly love thee, and worthily magnify thy holy Name: through Christ our Lord. Amen.

—The Holy Eucharist: Rite One,
from *The Book of Common Prayer*

100. Augustine, "Ten Homilies on the First Epistle General of St. John," in *Later Works*, 336.

101. See here the discussion "The Cruciform Beauty of Christ" in Stephen John Wright, *Dogmatic Aesthetics: A Theology of Beauty in Dialogue with Robert W. Jenson* (Minneapolis: Fortress, 2014), 101–42.

102. Here I recommend that preachers see the excellent introduction to the Augustinian insight that we are what we love, and that we become what we adore. James K. A. Smith, *You Are What You Love: The Spiritual Power of Habit* (Grand Rapids: Brazos, 2016).

BIBLIOGRAPHY

Abraham, William J. "Wesley as Preacher." In *The Cambridge Companion to John Wesley*, edited by Randy L. Maddox and Jason E. Vickers. Cambridge: Cambridge University Press, 2010.

Alison, James. *Raising Abel: The Recovery of Eschatological Imagination*. New York: Crossroad Herder, 1996.

Andrews, James A. *Hermeneutics and the Church: In Dialogue with Augustine*. Notre Dame: University of Notre Dame Press, 2012.

Anttila, Miikka E. "Music." In *Engaging Luther: A (New) Theological Assessment*, edited by Olli-Pekka Vainio. Eugene, OR: Cascade, 2010.

Auerbach, Erich. *Literary Language and Its Public in Late Antiquity and in the Middle Ages*. Translated by Ralph Manheim. New York: Bollingen, 1965.

Augustine. *Augustine: Later Works*. Translated by John Burnaby. Library of Christian Classics 8. Philadelphia: Westminster, 1965.

———. *The City of God*. Edited by David Knowles. Translated by Henry Bettenson. New York: Pelican, 1972.

———. *Confessions*. Vol. I/1 in *The Works of Saint Augustine: A Translation for the 21st Century*. Hyde Park, NY: New City Press, 1997.

———. *Essential Sermons*. Vol. III/25 in *The Works of Saint Augustine: A Translation for the 21st Century*, edited by Boniface Ramsey, translated by Edmund P. Hill, OP, introduction and notes by Daniel E. Doyle, OSA. Hyde Park, NY: New City Press, 2007.

————. *Expositions of the Psalms*, vol. 2 (Psalms 33–50). Vol. III/16 in *The Works of Saint Augustine: A Translation for the 21st Century*. Hyde Park, NY: New City Press, 2000.

————. *Expositions of the Psalms*, vol. 5 (Psalms 99–120). Vol. III/19 in *The Works of Saint Augustine: A Translation for the 21st Century*. Hyde Park, NY: New City Press, 2003.

————. *Instructing Beginners in Faith*. The Augustine Series, vol. 5. Hyde Park, NY: New City Press, 2006.

————. *Sermons on the Liturgical Seasons*. Vol. III/6 in *The Works of Saint Augustine: A Translation for the 21st Century*. New Rochelle, NY: New City Press, 1993.

————. *The Spirit and the Letter*. In *Augustine: Later Works*. Translated by John Burnaby. Library of Christian Classics 8. Philadelphia: Westminster, 1965.

————. *Teaching Christianity*. Vol. I/11 in *The Works of Saint Augustine: A Translation for the 21st Century*. Hyde Park, NY: New City Press, 1996.

————. "Ten Homilies on the First Epistle General of St. John." In *Augustine: Later Works*. Translated by John Burnaby. Library of Christian Classics 8. Philadelphia: Westminster, 1965.

Auski, Peter. *Christian Plain Style: The Evolution of a Spiritual Ideal*. Montreal: McGill-Queen's University Press, 1995.

Ayres, Lewis. *Augustine and the Trinity*. Cambridge: Cambridge University Press, 2010.

Balthasar, Hans Urs von. *The Glory of the Lord: A Theological Aesthetics*. San Francisco: Ignatius, 1981–1989.

Barclay, John M. G. *Paul and the Gift*. Grand Rapids: Eerdmans, 2015.

Barth, Karl. *Church Dogmatics* II. *The Doctrine of God*. Edinburgh: T&T Clark, 1957.

————. *Evangelical Theology: An Introduction*. Grand Rapids: Eerdmans, 1985.

Bayer, Oswald. *Theology the Lutheran Way*. Edited and translated by Jeffrey G. Silcock and Mark C. Mattes. Grand Rapids: Eerdmans, 2007.

Beitler, James E., III. *Seasoned Speech: Rhetoric in the Life of the Church.* Downers Grove, IL: IVP Academic, 2019.

Bell, Daniel M., Jr. *The Economy of Desire: Christianity and Capitalism in a Postmodern World.* Grand Rapids: Baker Academic, 2012.

Benson, Bruce Ellis. *Liturgy as a Way of Life: Embodying the Arts in Christian Worship.* Grand Rapids: Baker Academic, 2013.

Bernard of Clairvaux. *The Song of Songs: Interpreted by Early Christian and Medieval Commentators.* Edited and translated by Richard Norris Jr. Grand Rapids: Eerdmans, 2003.

Berry, Wendell. *It All Turns on Affection: The Jefferson Lectures and Other Essays.* Berkeley, CA: Counterpoint, 2012.

Bockmuehl, Marcus. *The Epistle to the Philippians.* Black's New Testament Commentary. London: A&C Black, 1998.

———. *Seeing the Word: Refocusing New Testament Study.* Grand Rapids: Baker Academic, 2006.

Bonhoeffer, Dietrich. *Reflections on the Bible: Human Word and Word of God.* Edited by Manfred Weber. Translated by M. Eugene Boring. Peabody, MA: Hendrickson, 2005.

Boulton, Matthew Myer. "Angels of Light: Luther's Liturgical Attack on Christendom." In *Luther Refracted: The Reformer's Ecumenical Legacy,* edited by Piotr J. Maylysz and Derek R. Nelson. Minneapolis: Fortress, 2015.

Bright, Pamela, ed. and trans. *Augustine and the Bible.* Bible through the Ages 2. Notre Dame: University of Notre Dame Press, 1986.

Brock, Brian. *Christian Ethics in a Technological Age.* Grand Rapids: Eerdmans, 2010.

———. *Singing the Ethos of God: On the Place of Christian Ethics in Scripture.* Grand Rapids: Eerdmans, 2007.

Brown, Peter. *Augustine of Hippo: A Biography.* Berkeley: University of California Press, 2000.

———. *Through the Eye of a Needle: Wealth, the Fall of Rome, and the Making of Christianity in the West, 350–550 AD.* Princeton: Princeton University Press, 2012.

Brown, William P. *Sacred Sense: Discovering the Wonder of God's Word and World*. Grand Rapids: Eerdmans, 2015.

Brueggemann, Walter. *Cadences of Home: Preaching among Exiles*. Louisville: Westminster John Knox, 1997.

———. *Finally Comes the Poet: Daring Speech for Proclamation*. Minneapolis: Augsburg, 1989.

———. *Israel's Praise: Doxology against Idolatry and Ideology*. Philadelphia: Fortress, 1988.

———. *The Practices of Prophetic Imagination: Preaching an Emancipating Word*. Minneapolis: Fortress, 2012.

Brunner, Peter. *Worship in the Name of Jesus*. Translated by M. H. Bertram. St. Louis: Concordia, 1968.

Buechner, Frederick. *A Room Called Remember: Uncollected Pieces*. San Francisco: Harper & Row, 1992.

Burns, J. Patout. "Delighting the Spirit: Augustine's Practice of Figurative Interpretation." In *De Doctrina Christiana: A Classic of Western Culture*, edited by Duane W. H. Arnold and Pamela Bright, 182–94. Notre Dame: University of Notre Dame Press, 1995.

Burton, Vicki Tolar. *Spiritual Literacy in John Wesley's Methodism: Reading, Writing, and Speaking to Believe*. Waco, TX: Baylor University Press, 2008.

Byassee, Jason. *Praise Seeking Understanding: Reading the Psalms with Augustine*. Grand Rapids: Eerdmans, 2007.

Cameron, Averil. *Christianity and the Rhetoric of Empire: The Development of Christian Discourse*. Berkeley: University of California Press, 1991.

Campbell, Charles L., and Johan H. Cilliers. *Preaching Fools: The Gospel as a Rhetoric of Folly*. Waco, TX: Baylor University Press, 2012.

Campbell, Ted A. "The Image of Christ in the Poor: On the Medieval Roots of the Wesleys' Ministry with the Poor." In *The Poor and the People Called Methodists, 1729–1999*, edited by Richard P. Heitzenrater. Nashville: Abingdon, 2002.

Carron, Julian. *Disarming Beauty: Essays on Faith, Truth, and Freedom*. Notre Dame: University of Notre Dame Press, 2017.

Casarella, Peter J. "The Expression and Form of the Word: Trinitarian Hermeneutics and the Sacramentality of Language in Hans Urs von Balthasar's Theology." In *Glory, Grace, and Culture*, edited by Ed Block Jr., 37–68. Mahwah, NJ: Paulist, 2005.

Cavadini, John. "The Anatomy of Wonder: An Augustinian Taxonomy." *Augustinian Studies* 42, no. 2 (2011): 153–72.

———. "The Sweetness of the Word: Salvation and Rhetoric in Augustine's De Doctrina Christiana." In *De Doctrina Christiana: A Classic of Western Culture*, edited by Duane W. H. Arnold and Pamela Bright, 164–81. Notre Dame: University of Notre Dame Press, 1995.

Cessario, Romanus, OP. *The Virtues, or the Examined Life*. New York: Continuum, 2002.

Charry, Ellen T. *By the Renewing of Your Minds: The Pastoral Function of Christian Doctrine*. Oxford: Oxford University Press, 1997.

Clapp, Rodney. *Border Crossings: Christian Trespasses on Popular Culture and Public Affairs*. Grand Rapids: Brazos, 2000.

Clavier, Mark. *On Consumer Culture, Identity, the Church, and the Rhetorics of Delight*. London: T&T Clark, 2019.

Conybeare, Catherine. "Reading the *Confessions*." In *A Companion to Augustine*, edited by Mark Vessey, 99–110. Oxford: Wiley-Blackwell, 2015.

Corbon, Jean, OP. *The Wellspring of Worship*. Translated by Matthew J. O'Connell. San Francisco: Ignatius, 1988.

Currie, Thomas W., III. "The Splendid Embarrassment: Theology's Home and the Practice of Ministry." In *The Power to Comprehend with All the Saints: The Formation and Practice of a Pastor-Theologian*, edited by Wallace M. Alston Jr. and Cynthia A. Jarvis, 272–80. Grand Rapids: Eerdmans, 2009.

Daniélou, Jean. *Prayer: The Mission of the Church*. Translated by David Louis Schindler Jr. Grand Rapids: Eerdmans, 1996.

Danker, Ryan Nicholas. *Wesley and the Anglicans: Political Division in Early Evangelicalism*. Downers Grove, IL: IVP Academic, 2016.

Davies, Horton. *Worship and Theology in England.* Vol. 2, *From Watts to Wesley to Martineau, 1690–1900.* Grand Rapids: Eerdmans, 1996.

Davies, Oliver. *A Theology of Compassion: Metaphysics of Difference and the Renewal of Tradition.* Grand Rapids: Eerdmans, 2003.

Davis, Ellen F. *Biblical Prophecy: Perspectives on Christian Theology, Discipleship, and Ministry.* Louisville: Westminster John Knox, 2014.

Davis, Ellen F., with Austin McIver Dennis. *Preaching the Luminous Word: Biblical Sermons and Homiletical Essays.* Grand Rapids: Eerdmans, 2016.

Day, Dorothy. *Dorothy Day: Selected Writings.* Edited by Robert Ellsberg. Maryknoll, NY: Orbis, 2011.

DeYoung, Rebecca Konyndyk. *Vainglory: The Forgotten Vice.* Grand Rapids: Eerdmans, 2014.

Dodaro, Robert. *Christ and the Just Society in the Thought of Augustine.* Cambridge: Cambridge University Press, 2004.

Dyrness, William A. *Poetic Theology: God and the Poetics of Everyday Life.* Grand Rapids: Eerdmans, 2013.

Ellingsen, Mark. *The Richness of Augustine: His Contextual and Pastoral Theology.* Louisville: Westminster John Knox, 2005.

Episcopal Church. *The Book of Common Prayer and Administration of the Sacraments and Other Rites and Ceremonies of the Church: Together with the Psalter or Psalms of David, according to the Use of the Episcopal Church.* Mountain View, CA: Wiretap, 1979.

Erasmus, Desiderius. *The Correspondence of Erasmus: Letters 298 to 445, 1514 to 1516.* Vol. 3 of *The Collected Works of Erasmus.* Translated by James M. Estes et al. Edited by Douglas F. S. Thomson. Toronto: University of Toronto Press, 1976.

Fodor, Jim. "Reading the Scriptures: Rehearsing Identity, Practicing Character." In *The Blackwell Companion to Christian Ethics*, edited by Stanley Hauerwas and Samuel Wells, 141–55. Oxford: Blackwell, 2006.

Ford, David F., and Daniel W. Hardy. *Living in Praise: Worshiping and Knowing God.* Grand Rapids: Baker Academic, 2005.

Forte, Bruno. *The Portal of Beauty: Towards a Theology of Aesthetics.* Translated by David Glenday and Paul McPartlan. Grand Rapids: Eerdmans, 2008.

Fowl, Stephen E. *Philippians.* Two Horizons New Testament Commentary. Grand Rapids: Eerdmans, 2005.

Francis (pope). *The Joy of the Gospel (Evangelii Gaudium): Apostolic Exhortation.* Vatican City: Libreria Editrice Vaticana, 2013.

Frei, Hans W. *The Eclipse of Biblical Narrative: A Study in Eighteenth and Nineteenth Century Hermeneutics.* New Haven: Yale University Press, 1974.

Greer, Rowan A. *Broken Lights and Mended Lives: Theology and Common Life in the Early Church.* University Park: Pennsylvania State University Press, 1986.

Grieb, A. Katherine. *The Story of Romans: A Narrative Defense of God's Righteousness.* Louisville: Westminster John Knox, 2002.

Griffiths, Paul J. *Intellectual Appetite: A Theological Grammar.* Washington, DC: Catholic University of America Press, 2009.

Gruchy, John W. de. *Christianity, Art, and Transformation: Theological Aesthetics in the Struggle for Justice.* Cambridge: Cambridge University Press, 2008.

Guthrie, Steven R. *Creator Spirit: The Holy Spirit and the Art of Becoming Human.* Grand Rapids: Brazos, 2011.

Hadot, Pierre. *Philosophy as a Way of Life.* Edited by Arnold I. Davidson. Translated by Michael Chase. Oxford: Blackwell, 1995.

Hanby, Michael. *Augustine and Modernity.* New York: Routledge, 2003.

Hanson, Paul D. *Isaiah 40–66.* Interpretation: A Bible Commentary for Teaching and Preaching. Louisville: John Knox, 1995.

Hardy, Daniel W., and David F. Ford. *Praising and Knowing God.* Philadelphia: Westminster, 1985.

Harmless, William, SJ. *Augustine and the Catechumenate.* Collegeville, MN: Liturgical Press, 1996.

———. "A Love Supreme: Augustine's 'Jazz' of Theology." *Augustinian Studies* 43, no. 1–2 (2012): 149–77.

Harrison, Carol. *Augustine: Christian Truth and Fractured Humanity.* Oxford: Oxford University Press, 2000.

———. *Beauty and Revelation in the Thought of Saint Augustine.* Oxford: Clarendon, 1992.

———. "The Rhetoric of Scripture and Preaching: Classical Decadence or Christian Aesthetic?" In *Augustine and His Critics: Essays in Honor of Gerald Bonner*, edited by Robert Dodaro and George Lawless, 214–30. London: Routledge, 2000.

Hart, David Bentley. *The Beauty of the Infinite: The Aesthetics of Christian Truth.* Grand Rapids: Eerdmans, 2003.

Hauerwas, Stanley. *Christian Existence Today: Essays on Church, World, and Living in Between.* Durham, NC: Labyrinth, 1988.

———. *Matthew.* Brazos Theological Commentary on the Bible. Grand Rapids: Brazos, 2006.

———. *Performing the Faith: Bonhoeffer and the Practice of Nonviolence.* Grand Rapids: Brazos, 2004.

———. *Without Apology: Sermons for Christ's Church.* New York: Seabury, 2013.

Hauerwas, Stanley, and Samuel Wells. "The Gift of the Church." In *The Blackwell Companion to Christian Ethics*, edited by Stanley Hauerwas and Samuel Wells, 13–27. Oxford: Blackwell, 2006.

Hays, Richard B. *The Conversion of the Imagination: Paul as Interpreter of Israel's Scripture.* Grand Rapids: Eerdmans, 2005.

———. *Echoes of Scripture in the Gospels.* Waco, TX: Baylor University Press, 2016.

———. *Echoes of Scripture in the Letters of Paul.* New Haven: Yale University Press, 1989.

Healy, Nicholas M. *Church, World, and the Christian Life: Practical-Prophetic Life.* Cambridge: Cambridge University Press, 2000.

Heitzenrater, Richard P., ed. *The Poor and the People Called Methodists, 1729–1999.* Nashville: Abingdon, 2002.

Hempton, David. *Methodism: Empire of the Spirit.* New Haven: Yale University Press, 2005.

Heschel, Abraham J. *The Prophets.* New York: Harper & Row, 1962.

Hildebrandt, Franz, and Oliver A. Beckerlegge, eds. *A Collection of*

Hymns for the Use of the People Called Methodists. Nashville: Abingdon, 1983.

Howell, James C. *The Beauty of the Word: The Challenge and Wonder of Preaching.* Louisville: Westminster John Knox, 2011.

Irenaeus. *Against Heresies.* Edited by Alexander Roberts and James Donaldson. Louisville: Ex Fontibus, 2010.

Jacobsen, David Schnasa. "How the World Lost Its Story." In *The New Religious Humanists,* edited by Gregory Wolfe, 135–49. New York: Free Press, 1997.

————. Introduction to *Homiletical Theology: Preaching as Doing Theology,* edited by David Schnasa Jacobsen, 3–22. Promise of Homiletical Theology 1. Eugene, OR: Cascade, 2015.

Jennings, Willie James. *Acts.* Belief: A Theological Commentary on the Bible. Louisville: Westminster John Knox, 2017.

Jenson, Robert W. *Song of Songs.* Interpretation: A Bible Commentary for Teaching and Preaching. Louisville: Westminster John Knox, 2005.

Johnson, Luke Timothy. *Prophetic Jesus, Prophetic Church: The Challenge of Luke-Acts to Contemporary Christians.* Grand Rapids: Eerdmans, 2011.

Jones, L. Gregory, and Kevin R. Armstrong. *Resurrecting Excellence: Shaping Faithful Christian Ministry.* Grand Rapids: Eerdmans, 2006.

Jones, Scott J. *John Wesley's Conception and Use of Scripture.* Nashville: Kingswood Books, 1995.

Kärkkäinen, Veli-Matti. *Christ and Reconciliation.* A Constructive Christian Theology for the Pluralistic World, vol. 1. Grand Rapids: Eerdmans, 2013.

Kaufman, Peter Iver. *Augustine's Leaders.* Eugene, OR: Cascade, 2017.

————. *Incorrectly Political: Augustine and Thomas More.* Notre Dame: University of Notre Dame Press, 2007.

Kayama, Shinji. "Augustine and Preaching: A Christian Moral Pedagogy." In *The Authority of the Gospel: Explorations in Moral and Political Theology in Honor of Oliver O'Donovan,* edited by Robert Son and Brent Waters, 86–103. Grand Rapids: Eerdmans, 2015.

Kelsey, David H. *Eccentric Existence: A Theological Anthropology.* 2 vols. Louisville: Westminster John Knox, 2009.

Kimbrough, S. T. "Perfection Revisited." In *The Poor and the People Called Methodists, 1729–1999*, edited by Richard P. Heitzenrater. Nashville: Abingdon, 2002.

Kimbrough, S. T., and Carlton R. Young, eds. *Help Us to Help Each Other: Hymns for Life and Ministry with the Poor.* Drew, NJ: Charles Wesley Society, 2010.

King, John N. *English Reformation Literature: The Tudor Origins of the Protestant Tradition.* Princeton: Princeton Unversity Press, 1982.

King, Jonathan. *The Beauty of the Lord: Theology as Aesthetics.* Bellingham, WA: Lexham, 2018.

Kreider, Alan, and Eleanor Kreider. *Worship and Mission after Christendom.* Scottdale, PA: Herald, 2011.

LaCugna, Catherine Mowry. *God for Us: The Trinity and Christian Life.* San Francisco: HarperSanFrancisco, 1991.

Ladner, Gerhart B. *The Idea of Reform: Its Impact on Christian Thought and Action in the Age of the Fathers.* Eugene, OR: Wipf & Stock, 2004.

Langford, Thomas A. *Practical Divinity: Theology in the Wesleyan Tradition.* Vol. 1. Rev. ed. Nashville: Abingdon, 1998.

Lash, Nicholas. *The Beginning and End of Religion.* Cambridge: Cambridge University Press, 1996.

———. *Holiness, Speech, and Silence: Reflections on the Question of God.* Aldershot, UK: Ashgate, 2004.

Lathrop, Gordon W. *The Four Gospels on Sunday: The New Testament and the Reform of Christian Worship.* Minneapolis: Fortress, 2012.

Levering, Matthew. *The Theology of Augustine: An Introductory Guide to His Most Important Works.* Grand Rapids: Baker Academic, 2013.

Lischer, Richard. *The End of Words: The Language of Reconciliation in a Culture of Violence.* Grand Rapids: Eerdmans, 2005.

———. Preface to *Faith and Freedom: An Invitation to the Writings of Martin Luther.* Edited by John F. Thornton and Susan B. Varenne. New York: Vintage Books, 2002.

Lohfink, Gerhard. *Does God Need the Church? Toward a Theology of the*

People of God. Translated by Linda M. Maloney. Collegeville, MN: Liturgical Press, 1999.

———. *Is This All There Is? On Resurrection and Eternal Life*. Translated by Linda M. Maloney. Collegeville, MN: Liturgical Press, 2017.

———. *Jesus of Nazareth: What He Wanted, Who He Was*. Translated by Linda M. Maloney. Collegeville, MN: Liturgical Press, 2012.

Long, D. Stephen. *The Goodness of God: Theology, the Church, and Social Order*. Grand Rapids: Brazos, 2001.

———. *John Wesley's Moral Theology: The Quest for God and Goodness*. Nashville: Abingdon, 2005.

Loughlin, Gerard. "The Basis and Authority of Doctrine." In *The Cambridge Companion to Christian Doctrine*, edited by Colin E. Gunton, 41–64. Cambridge: Cambridge University Press, 1997.

Loyer, Kenneth M. *God's Love through the Spirit: The Holy Spirit in Thomas Aquinas and John Wesley*. Washington, DC: Catholic University Press of America, 2014.

Luther, Martin. "The Freedom of a Christian." In *The Roots of Reform*, vol. 1 of *The Annotated Luther*, edited by Timothy J. Wengert. Minneapolis: Fortress, 2015.

———. "Heidelberg Disputation." In *The Roots of Reform*, vol. 1 of *The Annotated Luther*, edited by Timothy J. Wengert. Minneapolis: Fortress, 2015.

———. *Lectures on Isaiah* (40–66). Vol. 17 of *Luther's Works*. Edited by Jaroslav Pelikan. St. Louis: Concordia, 1972.

———. "Lectures on Psalm 51, 1513–1515." In *The Interpretation of Scripture*, vol. 6 of *The Annotated Luther*, edited by Euan K. Cameron. Minneapolis: Fortress, 2017.

———. *Lectures on Romans*. Library of Christian Classics 15. Edited and translated by Wilhelm Pauck. Philadelphia: Westminster, 1961.

———. "The Magnificat." In *Pastoral Writings*, vol. 4 of *The Annotated Luther*, edited by Mary Jane Haemig. Minneapolis: Fortress, 2016.

———. "Preface to the New Testament 1546." In *The Interpretation of Scripture*, vol. 6 of *The Annotated Luther*, edited by Euan K. Cameron. Minneapolis: Fortress, 2017.

———. "Preface to the Prophets 1545 (1532)." In *The Interpretation of Scripture*, vol. 6 of *The Annotated Luther*, edited by Euan K. Cameron. Minneapolis: Fortress, 2017.

———. "Preface to the Psalter 1528 (1545)." In *The Interpretation of Scripture*, vol. 6 of *The Annotated Luther*, edited by Euan K. Cameron. Minneapolis: Fortress, 2017.

———. "Selected Hymns." In *Pastoral Writings*, vol. 4 of *The Annotated Luther*, edited by Mary Jane Haemig. Minneapolis: Fortress, 2016.

———. *Selected Psalms II*. Vol. 13 of *Luther's Works*. Edited by Jaroslav Pelikan. St. Louis: Concordia, 1956.

———. *Selected Psalms III*. Vol. 14 of *Luther's Works*. Edited by Jaroslav Pelikan. St. Louis: Concordia, 1958.

MacIntyre, Alasdair. *After Virtue*. Notre Dame: University of Notre Dame Press, 1981.

Maddox, Randy. *Responsible Grace: John Wesley's Practical Theology*. Nashville: Kingswood Books, 1994.

———. "'Visiting the Poor': John Wesley, the Poor, and the Sanctification of Believers." In *The Poor and the People Called Methodists, 1729–1999*, edited by Richard P. Heitzenrater. Nashville: Abingdon, 2002.

Mallard, William. *Language and Love: Introducing Augustine's Religious Thought through the Confessions Story*. University Park: Pennsylvania State University Press, 1994.

Mannion, M. Francis. *Masterworks of God: Essays in Liturgical Theory and Practice*. Chicago: Hillenbrand Books, 2004.

Mascall, E. L. *Grace and Glory*. New York: Morehouse Barlow, 1961.

Mathewes, Charles. *The Republic of Grace: Augustinian Thoughts for Dark Times*. Grand Rapids: Eerdmans, 2010.

———. *A Theology of Public Life*. Cambridge: Cambridge University Press, 2007.

Mattes, Mark C. *Martin Luther's Theology of Beauty: A Reappraisal*. Grand Rapids: Baker Academic, 2017.

McGill, Arthur C. *Suffering: A Test of Theological Method*. Foreword by Paul Ramsey and William F. May. Philadelphia: Westminster, 1982.

McIntosh, Mark A. *Discernment and Truth: The Spirituality and Theology of Knowledge*. New York: Crossroad, 2004.

———. *Divine Teaching: An Introduction to Christian Theology*. Oxford: Blackwell, 2008.

———. "Faith, Reason, and the Mind of Christ." In *Reason and the Reasons of Faith*, edited by Paul J. Griffiths and Reinhard Hütter. London: T&T Clark, 2005.

———. *Mystical Theology: The Integrity of Spirituality in Theology*. Oxford: Blackwell, 1998.

Minear, Paul S. *The Kingdom and the Power: An Exposition of the New Testament Gospel*. Louisville: Westminster John Knox, 2004.

Mitman, F. Russell. *Worship in the Shape of Scripture*. Cleveland: Pilgrim, 2001.

Moltmann, Jürgen. *The Way of Jesus Christ: Christology in Messianic Dimensions*. Translated by Margaret Kohl. Minneapolis: Fortress, 2003.

Muller, Hildegund. "Preacher: Augustine and His Congregation." In *A Companion to Augustine*, edited by Mark Vessey, with the assistance of Shelley Reid, 297–309. Oxford: Blackwell, 2012.

Murphy, Debra Dean. *Happiness, Health, and Beauty: The Christian Life in Everyday Terms*. With Questions for Consideration by Andrew Kinsey. Eugene, OR: Cascade, 2015.

———. *Teaching That Transforms: Worship as the Heart of Christian Education*. Grand Rapids: Brazos, 2004.

Newbigin, Lesslie. *Foolishness to the Greeks: The Gospel and Western Culture*. Grand Rapids: Eerdmans, 1986.

Newman, Elizabeth. *Untamed Hospitality: Welcoming God and Other Strangers*. Grand Rapids: Brazos, 2006.

Nicholas, Marc. *Jean Danielou's Doxological Humanism: Trinitarian Contemplation and Humanity's True Vocation*. Eugene, OR: Pickwick, 2012.

Nichols, Aidan. *The Art of God Incarnate: Theology and Image in Christian Tradition*. London: Darton, Longman & Todd, 1980.

———. "Balthasar's Aims in the 'Theological Aesthetics.'" In *Glory, Grace, and Culture: The Works of Hans Urs von Balthasar*, edited by Ed Block Jr., 107–26. Mahwah, NJ: Paulist, 2005.

———. *Redeeming Beauty: Soundings in Sacral Aesthetics*. Aldershot, UK: Ashgate, 2007.

———. *The Word Has Been Abroad: A Guide through Balthasar's Aesthetics*. Washington, DC: Catholic University of America Press, 1998.

Niebuhr, H. Richard. *The Meaning of Revelation*. New York: Macmillan, 1960.

Oakes, Edward T., SJ. "The Apologetics of Beauty." In *The Beauty of God: Theology and the Arts*, edited by Daniel J. Treier, Mark Husbands, and Roger Lundin. Downers Grove, IL: IVP Academic, 2007.

O'Daly, Gerard J. P. *Augustine's City of God: A Reader's Guide*. Oxford: Oxford University Press, 1999.

O'Donovan, Oliver. *Self, World, and Time: Ethics as Theology, Volume 1; An Induction*. Grand Rapids: Eerdmans, 2013.

Old, Hughes Oliphant. *Moderation, Pietism, and Awakening*. Vol. 5 in *The Reading and Preaching of the Scriptures in the Worship of the Christian Church*. Grand Rapids: Eerdmans, 2004.

Outler, Albert C. *Evangelism and Theology in the Wesleyan Spirit*. Nashville: Discipleship Resources, 2004.

Owens, L. Roger. *The Shape of Participation: A Theology of Church Practices*. Eugene, OR: Cascade, 2010.

Pasquarello, Michael, III. *Christian Preaching: A Trinitarian Theology of Proclamation*. Grand Rapids: Baker Academic, 2007; reprint, Eugene, OR: Wipf & Stock, 2011.

———. *Dietrich: Bonhoeffer and a Theology of the Preaching Life*. Waco, TX: Baylor University Press, 2017.

Peterson, Eugene H. *Eat This Book: A Conversation in the Art of Spiritual Reading*. Grand Rapids: Eerdmans, 2006.

———. *The Jesus Way: A Conversation on the Ways That Jesus Is the Way.* Grand Rapids: Eerdmans, 2007.

———. *Practice Resurrection: A Conversation on Growing Up in Christ.* Grand Rapids: Eerdmans, 2010.

———. *Under the Unpredictable Plant: An Exploration in Vocational Holiness.* Grand Rapids: Eerdmans/Gracewing, 1992.

Pieper, Josef. *Leisure: The Basis of Culture.* Translated by Gerald Malsbary. South Bend, IN: St. Augustine's, 1998.

Pinckaers, Servais, OP. *The Sources of Christian Ethics.* Translated by Sr. Mary Thomas Noble, OP. Washington, DC: Catholic University Press of America, 1995.

Purves, Andrew. *Reconstructing Pastoral Theology: A Christological Foundation.* Louisville: Westminster John Knox, 2005.

Rashkover, Randi, and C. C. Pecknold, eds. *Liturgy, Time, and the Politics of Redemption.* Grand Rapids: Eerdmans, 2006.

Rist, John M. *What Is Truth? From the Academy to the Vatican.* Cambridge: Cambridge University Press, 2008.

Robinson, Anthony B., and Robert W. Wall. *Called to Be Church: The Book of Acts for a New Day.* Grand Rapids: Eerdmans, 2006.

Rowe, C. Kavin. *World Upside Down: Reading Acts in the Graeco-Roman Age.* Oxford: Oxford University Press, 2009.

Saliers, Don E. *Worship as Theology: Foretaste of Glory Divine.* Nashville: Abingdon, 1994.

———. *Worship Come to Its Senses.* Nashville: Abingdon, 1996.

Sanlon, Peter T. *Augustine's Theology of Preaching.* Minneapolis: Fortress, 2014.

Schindler, David L. "The Significance of Hans Urs von Balthasar in the Contemporary Situation." In *Glory, Grace, and Culture,* edited by Ed Block Jr., 16–36. Mahwah, NJ: Paulist, 2005.

Second Clement. In *The Apostolic Fathers,* edited by Michael W. Holmes, translated by J. B. Lightfoot and J. R. Harmer, 132–65. 2nd ed. Grand Rapids: Baker Books, 1989.

Sherry, Patrick. *Spirit and Beauty: An Introduction to Theological Beauty.* London: SCM, 2002.

Sherwin, Michael S. *By Knowledge and by Love: Charity and Morality in the Moral Theology of St. Thomas Aquinas.* Washington, DC: Catholic University of America Press, 2005.

Short, L. Faye, and Kathryn D. Kiser. *Reclaiming the Wesleyan Social Witness: Offering Christ.* Franklin, TN: Providence House Publishers, 2008.

Shuger, Debora K. *Sacred Rhetoric: The Christian Grand Style in the English Renaissance.* Princeton: Princeton University Press, 1988.

Skinner, Matthew L. *Intrusive God, Disruptive Gospel: Encountering the Divine in the Book of Acts.* Grand Rapids: Brazos, 2015.

Smart, J. D. *History and Theology in Second Isaiah.* Philadelphia: Westminster, 1965.

Smith, Christian, and Melinda Lundquist Denton. *Soul Searching: The Religious and Spiritual Lives of American Teenagers.* Oxford: Oxford University Press, 2005.

Smith, James K. A. *Desiring the Kingdom: Worship, Worldview, and Cultural Formation.* Cultural Liturgies 1. Grand Rapids: Baker Academic, 2009.

————. *You Are What You Love: The Spiritual Power of Habit.* Grand Rapids: Brazos, 2016.

Spinks, Bryan D. *The Worship Mall: Contemporary Responses to Contemporary Culture.* New York: Church Publishing, 2010.

Steinmetz, David C. *Taking the Long View: Christian Theology in Historical Perspective.* Oxford: Oxford University Press, 2011.

Stone, Bryan. *Evangelism after Christendom: The Theology and Practice of Christian Witness.* Grand Rapids: Brazos, 2007.

Studer, Basil. *Trinity and Incarnation: The Faith of the Early Church.* Edited by Andrew Louth. Translated by Matthias Westerhoff. Collegeville, MN: Liturgical Press, 1993.

Toom, Tarmo. "Augustine on Scripture." In *T&T Clark Companion to Augustine and Modern Theology,* edited by C. C. Pecknold and Tarmo Toom, 75–90. London: Bloomsbury T&T Clark, 2012.

Torrell, Jean-Pierre, OP. *Saint Thomas Aquinas: Spiritual Master.* Vol. 2.

Translated by Robert Royal. Washington, DC: Catholic University of America Press, 2003.

Torvend, Samuel. *Luther and the Hungry Poor: Gathered Fragments*. Minneapolis: Fortress, 2008.

Tran, Jonathan. *Foucault and Theology*. London: T&T Clark, 2011.

Tucker, Karen B. Westerfield. "Wesley's Emphasis on Worship and the Means of Grace." In *The Cambridge Companion to John Wesley*, edited by Randy L. Maddox and Jason E. Vickers. Cambridge: Cambridge University Press, 2010.

Vickers, Jason E. *Invocation and Assent: The Making and Remaking of Trinitarian Theology*. Grand Rapids: Eerdmans, 2008.

———. *Minding the Good Ground: A Theology of Church Renewal*. Grand Rapids: Baker Academic, 2011.

———. *Wesley: A Guide for the Perplexed*. London: T&T Clark, 2009.

Volf, Miroslav, and Matthew Croasmun. *For the Life of the World: Theology That Makes a Difference*. Grand Rapids: Brazos, 2019.

Wainwright, Geoffrey. *Doxology: The Praise of God in Worship, Doctrine, and Life*. Oxford: Oxford University Press, 1980.

———. *For Our Salvation: Two Approaches to the Work of Christ*. Grand Rapids: Eerdmans/SPCK, 1997.

———. "The Trinitarian Hermeneutic of John Wesley." In *Reading the Bible in Wesleyan Ways: Some Constructive Proposals*, edited by Barry L. Callen and Richard P. Thompson. Kansas City, MO: Beacon Hill, 2004.

———. "Trinitarian Theology and Wesleyan Holiness." In *Orthodox and Wesleyan Spirituality*, edited by S. T. Kimbrough Jr. Crestwood, NY: St. Vladimir's Seminary Press, 2002.

———. *Worship with One Accord: Where Liturgy and Ecumenism Embrace*. Oxford: Oxford University Press, 1997.

Wall, Robert W. "Toward a Wesleyan Hermeneutic of Scripture." In *Reading the Bible in Wesleyan Ways: Some Constructive Proposals*, edited by Barry L. Callen and Richard P. Thompson. Kansas City, MO: Beacon Hill, 2004.

———. "Wesley as Biblical Interpreter." In *The Cambridge Companion to*

John Wesley, edited by Randy L. Maddox and Jason E. Vickers. Cambridge: Cambridge University Press, 2010.

Wannenwetsch, Bernd. "Luther's Moral Theology." In *The Cambridge Companion to Martin Luther*, edited by Donald K. McKim. Cambridge: Cambridge University Press, 2003.

———. *Political Worship: Ethics for Christian Citizens*. Translated by Margaret Kohl. Oxford: Oxford University Press, 2004.

Ward, Graham. "The Beauty of God." In *Theological Perspectives on God and Beauty*, edited by John Milbank, Graham Ward, and Edith Wyschogrod, 35–65. Harrisburg, PA: Trinity Press International, 2003.

Weaver, Rebecca Harden. "Reading the Signs: Guidance for the Pilgrim Community." *Interpretation* 58, no. 1 (2004): 28–41.

Webster, John. *The Culture of Theology*. Edited by Ivor J. Davidson and Alden C. McCray. Grand Rapids: Baker Academic, 2019.

Welker, Michael. *God the Spirit*. Translated by John F. Hoffmeyer. Minneapolis: Fortress, 1994.

Wells, Samuel. *God's Companions: Reimagining Christian Ethics*. Malden, MA: Blackwell, 2006.

———. *Improvisation: The Drama of Christian Ethics*. Grand Rapids: Brazos, 2004.

Wesley, Charles. "Ambitious, covetous, vain." In *Help Us to Help Each Other: Hymns for Life and Ministry with the Poor*, edited by S. T. Kimbrough Jr., and Carlton R. Young. Madison, NJ: Charles Wesley Society, 2010.

———. "Love Divine, All Loves Excelling." In *The United Methodist Hymnal: Book of United Methodist Worship*. Nashville: United Methodist Publishing House, 2002.

Wesley, John. *The Works of John Wesley*. 3rd ed. Grand Rapids: Baker Books, 1978.

———. *The Works of John Wesley*. Bicentennial ed. Edited by Albert C. Outler. Nashville: Abingdon, 1984.

Wilder, Amos Niven. *Theopoetic: Theology and the Religious Imagination*. Philadelphia: Fortress, 1976.

Wilken, Robert Louis. "Augustine's City of God Today." In *The Two Cities of God: The Church's Responsibility for the Earthly City*, edited by Carl E. Braaten and Robert W. Jenson, 28–41. Grand Rapids: Eerdmans, 1997.

———. *The Spirit of Early Christian Thought: Seeking the Face of God*. New Haven: Yale University Press, 2003.

Williams, A. N. "Contemplation." In *Knowing the Triune God: The Work of the Spirit in the Practices of the Church*, edited by James J. Buckley and David S. Yeago, 121–47. Grand Rapids: Eerdmans, 2001.

Williams, Rowan. *Christ on Trial: How the Gospel Unsettles Our Judgement*. Grand Rapids: Zondervan, 2000.

———. *The Edge of Words: God and the Habits of Language*. London: Bloomsbury, 2014.

———. *On Augustine*. London: Bloomsbury, 2016.

———. *On Christian Theology*. Oxford: Blackwell, 2000.

———. "Theology in the Face of Christ." In *Glory Descending: Michael Ramsey and His Writings*, edited by Douglas Dales, John Habgood, Geoffrey Rowell, and Rowan Williams, 176–87. Grand Rapids: Eerdmans, 2005.

———. *Why Study the Past? The Quest for the Historical Church*. Grand Rapids: Eerdmans, 2005.

Willimon, William H. *Acts: A Biblical Commentary for Teaching and Preaching*. Atlanta: John Knox, 1988.

———. *Preaching Master Class: Lessons from Will Willimon's Five-Minute Preaching Workshop*. Edited by Noel Snyder. Eugene, OR: Cascade, 2010.

Wilson, Kenneth. *Methodist Theology*. London: T&T Clark, 2011.

Wilson, Paul Scott. *Preaching as Poetry: Beauty, Goodness, and Truth in Every Sermon*. Nashville: Abingdon, 2014.

Wirzba, Norman. *Living the Sabbath: Discovering the Rhythms of Rest and Delight*. Grand Rapids: Brazos, 2008.

Witherington, Ben, III. *Women in the Earliest Churches*. Cambridge: Cambridge University Press, 1988.

Wolfe, Gregory. *The Operation of Grace: Further Essays on Art, Faith, and Mystery.* Eugene, OR: Cascade, 2015.

Wright, Stephen John. *Dogmatic Aesthetics: A Theology of Beauty in Dialogue with Robert W. Jenson.* Minneapolis: Fortress, 2014.

Young, Frances M. *God's Presence: A Contemporary Recapitulation of Early Christianity.* Cambridge: Cambridge University Press, 2013.

INDEX OF NAMES AND SUBJECTS

INDEX OF SCRIPTURE REFERENCES